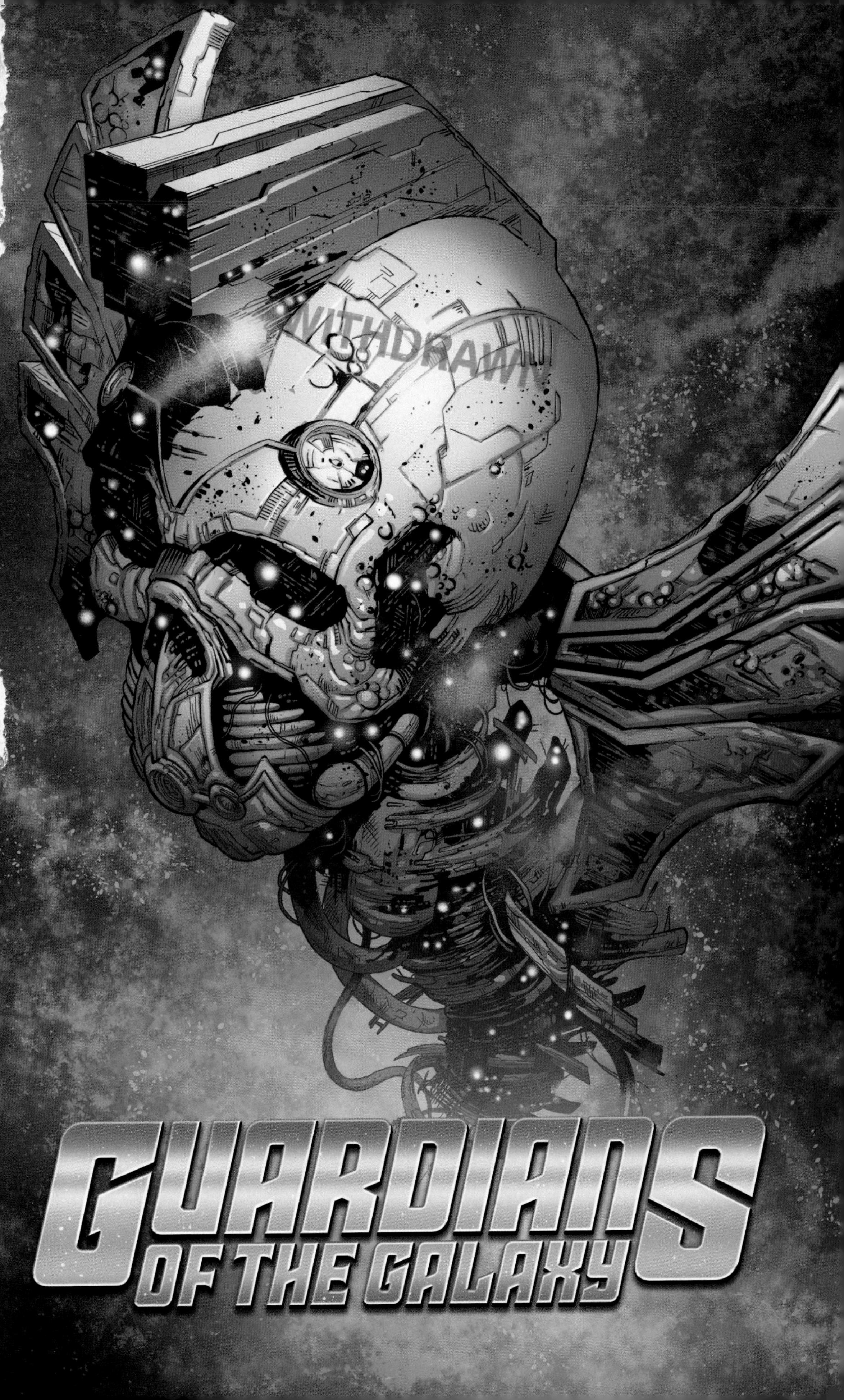
GUARDIANS
OF THE GALAXY

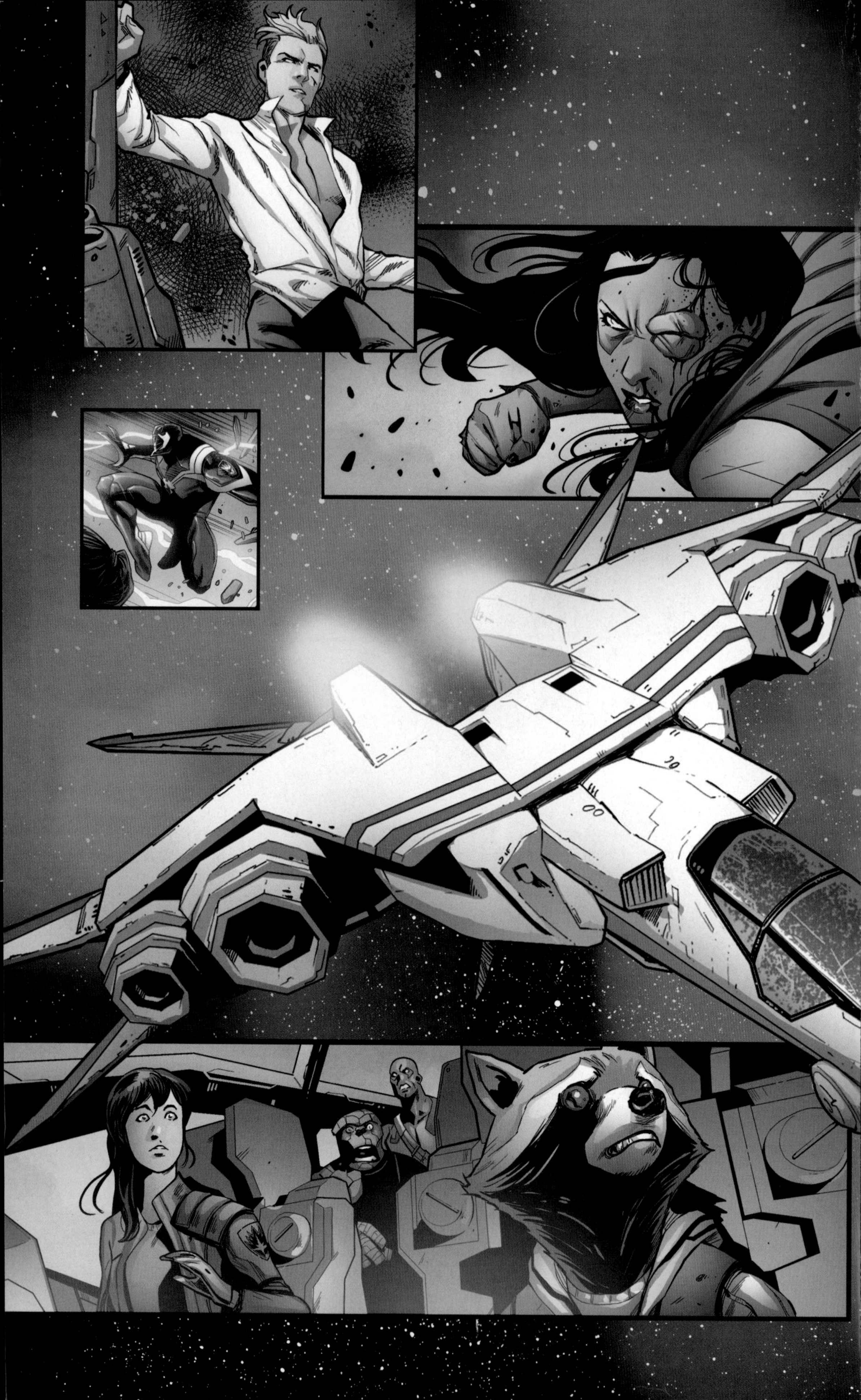

GUARDIANS OF THE GALAXY

EMPEROR QUILL

BRIAN MICHAEL BENDIS
WRITER

VALERIO SCHITI
ARTIST

RICHARD ISANOVE
COLOR ARTIST

VC'S CORY PETIT
LETTERER

ARTHUR ADAMS COVER ARTIST

DAVE STEWART (#1), JASON KEITH (#2, #4-5) & PETER STEIGERWALD (#3)
COVER COLORISTS

KATHLEEN WISNESKI
ASSISTANT EDITOR

JAKE THOMAS
ASSOCIATE EDITOR

NICK LOWE
EDITOR

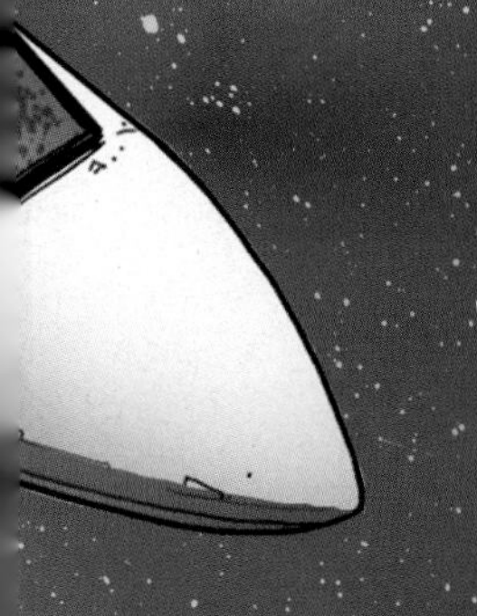

COLLECTION EDITOR: *JENNIFER GRÜNWALD*
ASSOCIATE EDITOR: *SARAH BRUNSTAD*
ASSOCIATE MANAGING EDITOR: *ALEX STARBUCK*
EDITOR, SPECIAL PROJECTS: *MARK D. BEAZLEY*
VP, PRODUCTION & SPECIAL PROJECTS: *JEFF YOUNGQUIST*
SVP PRINT, SALES & MARKETING: *DAVID GABRIEL*
BOOK DESIGNER: *JAY BOWEN*

EDITOR IN CHIEF: *AXEL ALONSO*
CHIEF CREATIVE OFFICER: *JOE QUESADA*
PUBLISHER: *DAN BUCKLEY*
EXECUTIVE PRODUCER: *ALAN FINE*

GUARDIANS OF THE GALAXY: NEW GUARD VOL. 1 — EMPEROR QUILL. Contains material originally published in magazine form as GUARDIANS OF THE GALAXY #1-5. First printing 2016. ISBN# 978-0-7851-9518-4. Published by MARVEL WORLDWIDE, INC., a subsidiary of MARVEL ENTERTAINMENT, LLC. OFFICE OF PUBLICATION: 135 West 50th Street, New York, NY 10020. **Printed in the U.S.A.** ALAN FINE, President, Marvel Entertainment; DAN BUCKLEY, President, TV, Publishing & Brand Management; JOE QUESADA, Chief Creative Officer; TOM BREVOORT, SVP of Publishing; DAVID BOGART, SVP of Business Affairs & Operations, Publishing & Partnership; C.B. CEBULSKI, VP of Brand Management & Development, Asia; DAVID GABRIEL, SVP of Sales & Marketing, Publishing; JEFF YOUNGQUIST, VP of Production & Special Projects; DAN CARR, Executive Director of Publishing Technology; ALEX MORALES, Director of Publishing Operations; SUSAN CRESPI, Production Manager; STAN LEE, Chairman Emeritus. For information regarding advertising in Marvel Comics or on Marvel.com, please contact Vit DeBellis, Integrated Sales Manager, at vdebellis@marvel.com. For Marvel subscription inquiries, please call 888-511-5480. **Manufactured between 2/12/2016 and 3/28/2016 by R.R. DONNELLEY, INC., SALEM, VA, USA.**

10 9 8 7 6 5 4 3 2 1

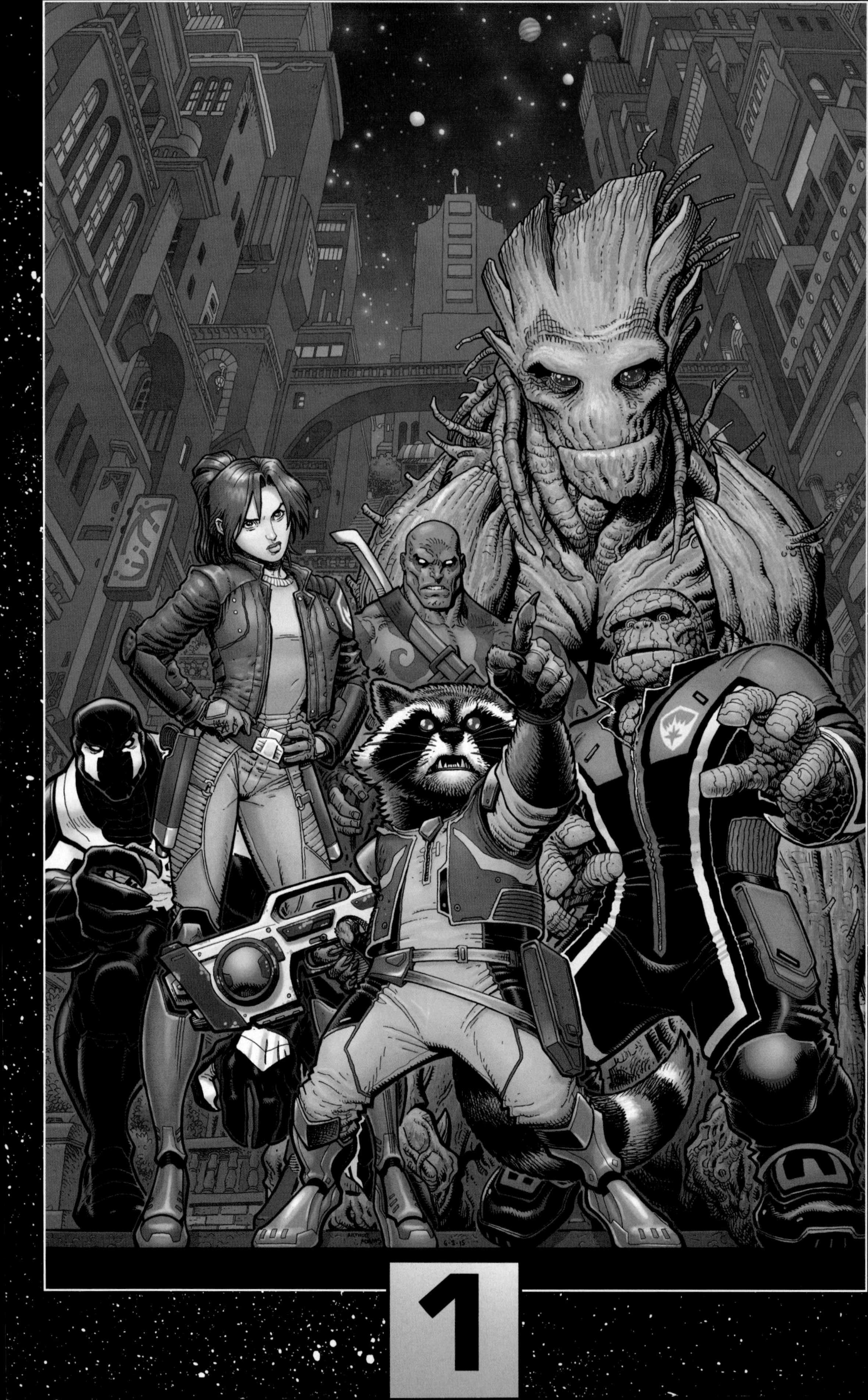

1

The entire galaxy is a mess. Warring empires and cosmic terrorists plague every corner. Someone has to rise above it all and fight for those who have no one to fight for them. Against their natures, a group of misanthropes and misfits came together to serve a higher cause. **Drax the Destroyer**, **Gamora**, the most dangerous woman in the universe, **Rocket Raccoon**, **Groot**, and **Flash Thompson**, a.k.a. **Venom** all joined together under the leadership of **Peter Quill, Star-Lord** to be the saviors of the spaceways, the conservators of the cosmos, the…

GUARDIANS OF THE GALAXY

But things have changed.

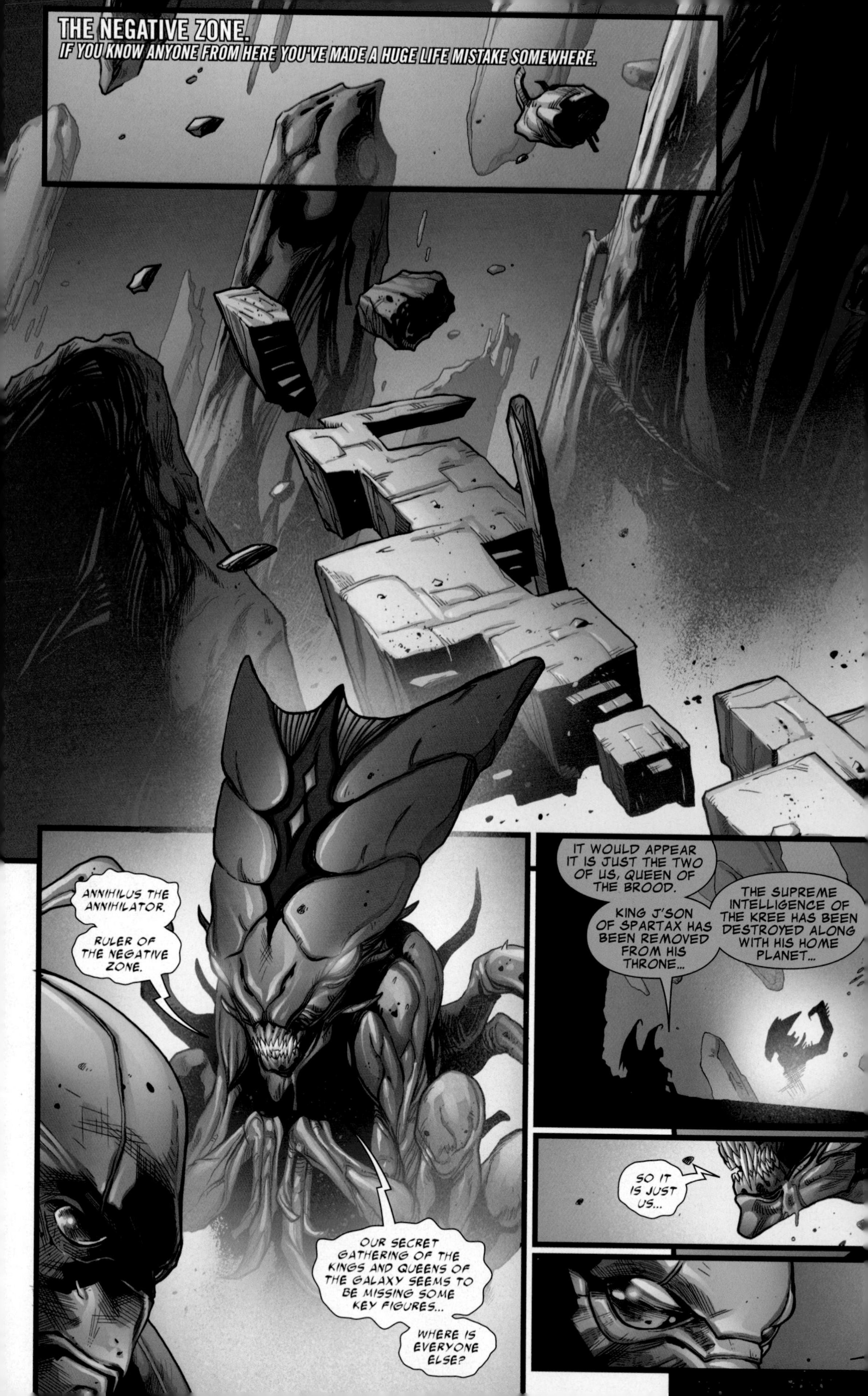
THE NEGATIVE ZONE.
IF YOU KNOW ANYONE FROM HERE YOU'VE MADE A HUGE LIFE MISTAKE SOMEWHERE.
ANNIHILUS THE ANNIHILATOR.
RULER OF THE NEGATIVE ZONE.
OUR SECRET GATHERING OF THE KINGS AND QUEENS OF THE GALAXY SEEMS TO BE MISSING SOME KEY FIGURES...
WHERE IS EVERYONE ELSE?
IT WOULD APPEAR IT IS JUST THE TWO OF US, QUEEN OF THE BROOD.
KING J'SON OF SPARTAX HAS BEEN REMOVED FROM HIS THRONE...
THE SUPREME INTELLIGENCE OF THE KREE HAS BEEN DESTROYED ALONG WITH HIS HOME PLANET...
SO IT IS JUST US...

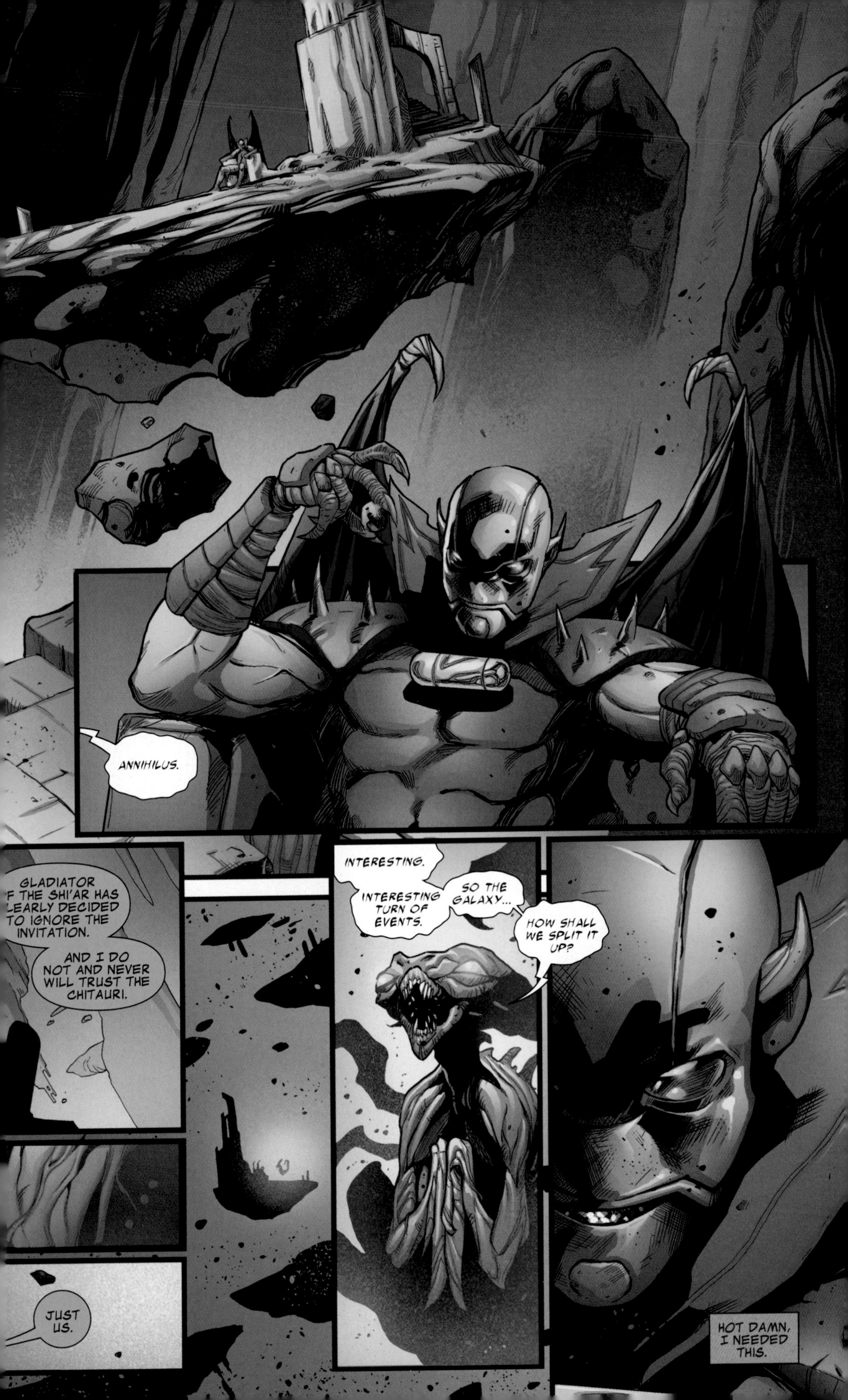
ANNIHILUS.
GLADIATOR
F THE SHI'AR HAS
LEARLY DECIDED
TO IGNORE THE
INVITATION.
AND I DO
NOT AND NEVER
WILL TRUST THE
CHITAURI.
JUST
US.
INTERESTING.
INTERESTING
TURN OF
EVENTS.
SO THE
GALAXY...
HOW SHALL
WE SPLIT IT
UP?
HOT DAMN,
I NEEDED
THIS.

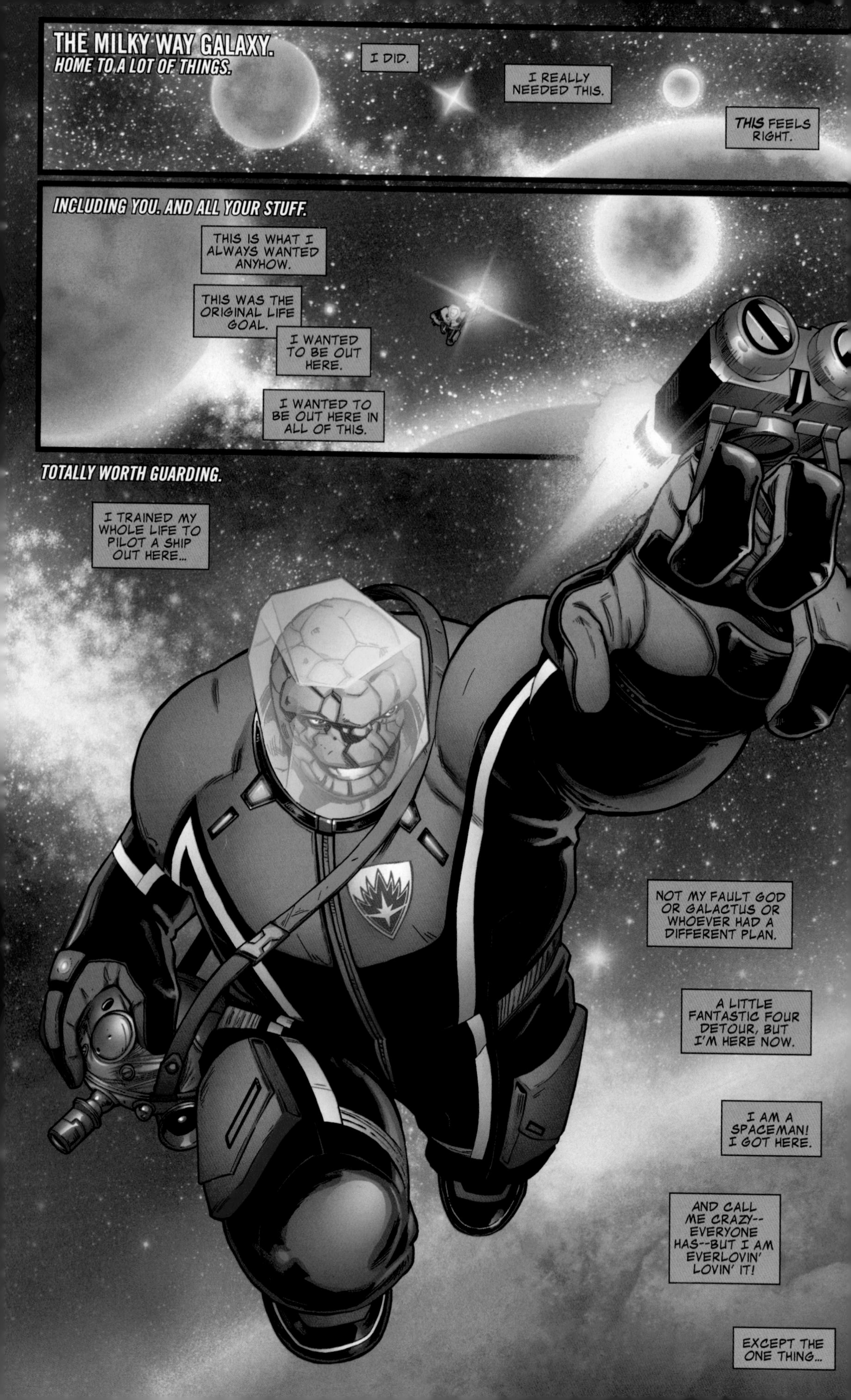
THE MILKY WAY GALAXY.
HOME TO A LOT OF THINGS.
I DID.
I REALLY NEEDED THIS.
THIS FEELS RIGHT.
INCLUDING YOU. AND ALL YOUR STUFF.
THIS IS WHAT I ALWAYS WANTED ANYHOW.
THIS WAS THE ORIGINAL LIFE GOAL.
I WANTED TO BE OUT HERE.
I WANTED TO BE OUT HERE IN ALL OF THIS.
TOTALLY WORTH GUARDING.
I TRAINED MY WHOLE LIFE TO PILOT A SHIP OUT HERE...
NOT MY FAULT GOD OR GALACTUS OR WHOEVER HAD A DIFFERENT PLAN.
A LITTLE FANTASTIC FOUR DETOUR, BUT I'M HERE NOW.
I AM A SPACEMAN! I GOT HERE.
AND CALL ME CRAZY--EVERYONE HAS--BUT I AM EVERLOVIN' LOVIN' IT!
EXCEPT THE ONE THING...

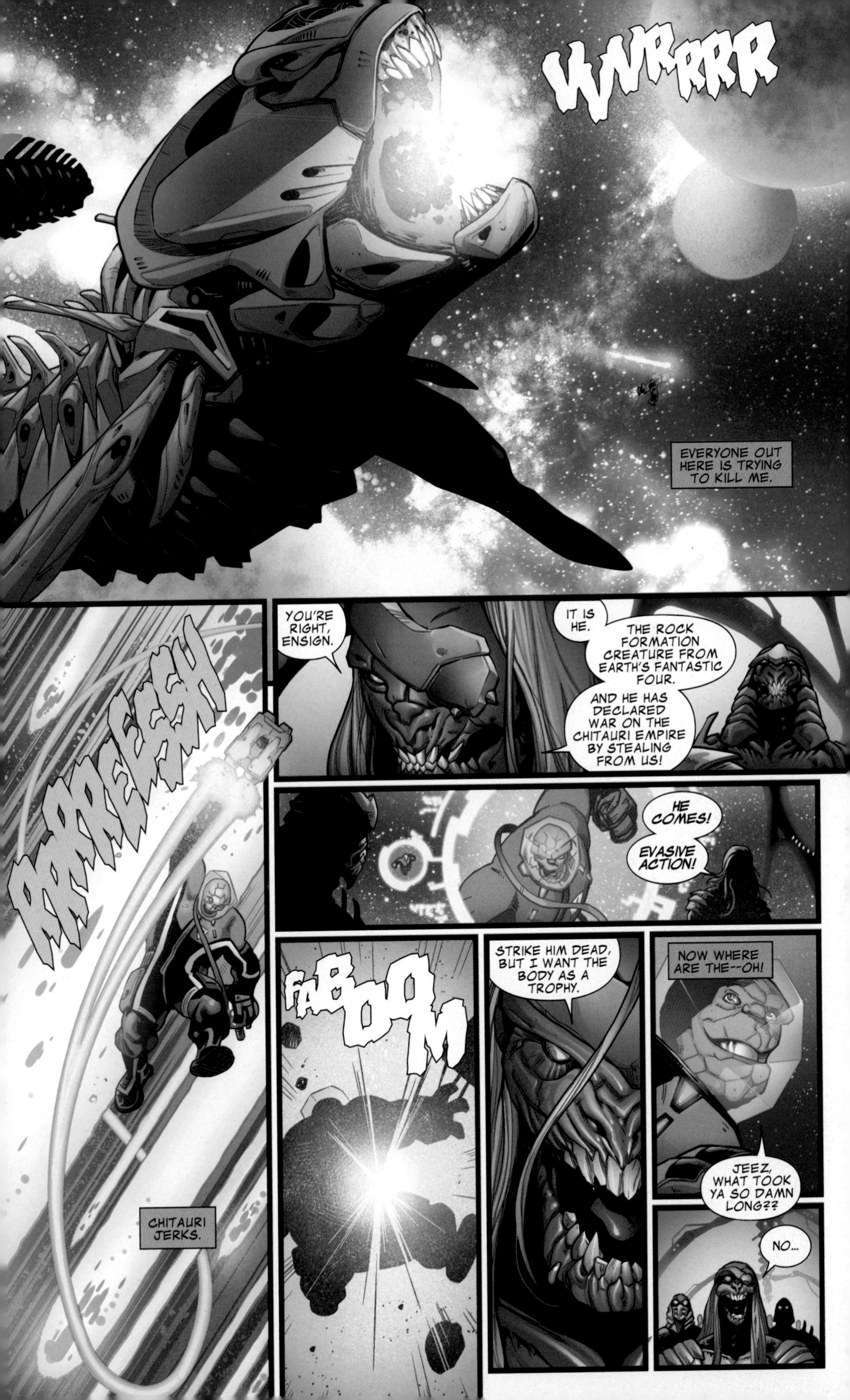

KWRRRR
EVERYONE OUT HERE IS TRYING TO KILL ME.
RRRREESH
CHITAURI JERKS.
YOU'RE RIGHT, ENSIGN.
IT IS HE.
THE ROCK FORMATION CREATURE FROM EARTH'S FANTASTIC FOUR.
AND HE HAS DECLARED WAR ON THE CHITAURI EMPIRE BY STEALING FROM US!
HE COMES!
EVASIVE ACTION!
FABOOM
STRIKE HIM DEAD, BUT I WANT THE BODY AS A TROPHY.
NOW WHERE ARE THE--OH!
JEEZ, WHAT TOOK YA SO DAMN LONG??
NO...

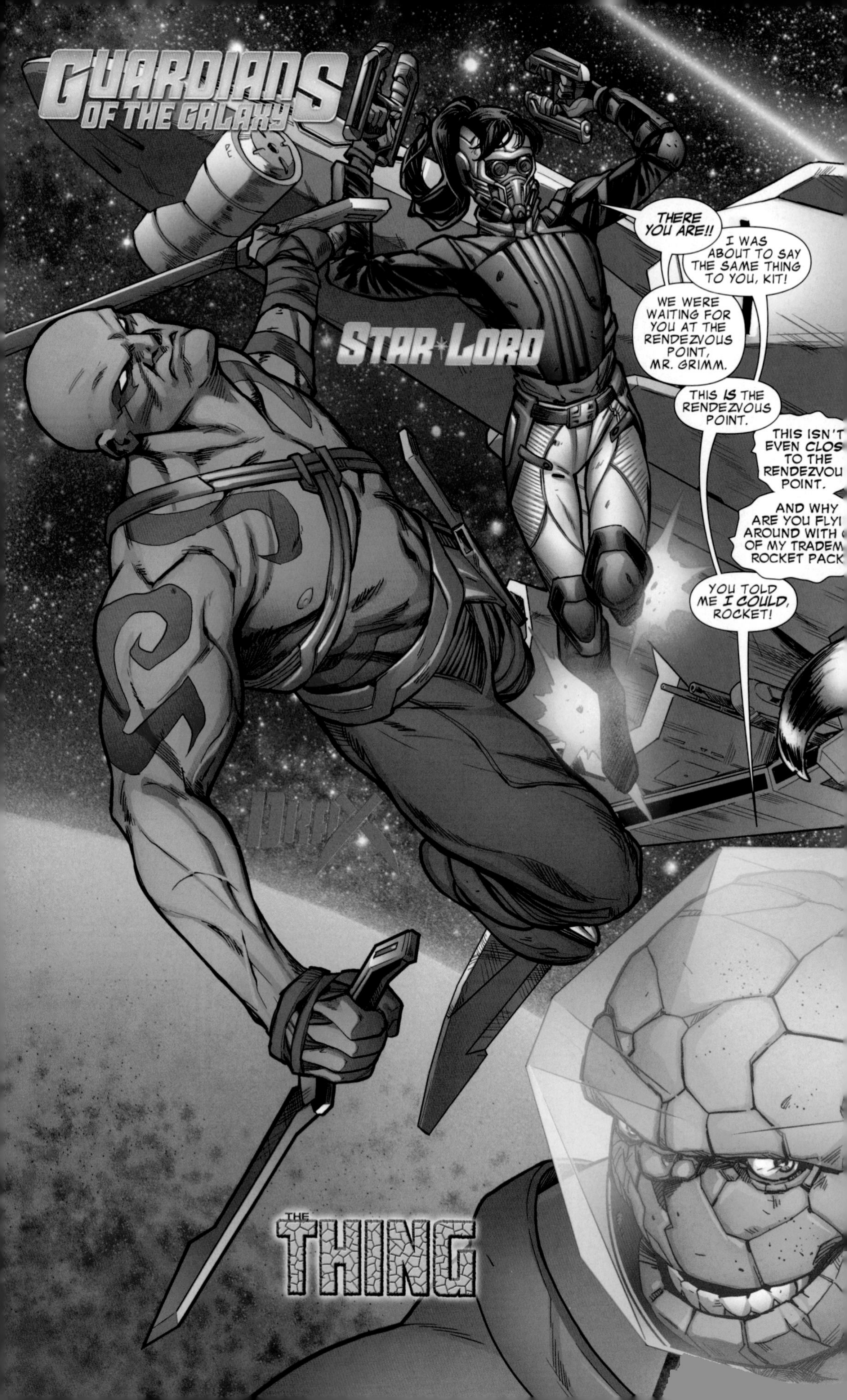
GUARDIANS OF THE GALAXY
STAR-LORD
THERE YOU ARE!!
I WAS ABOUT TO SAY THE SAME THING TO YOU, KIT!
WE WERE WAITING FOR YOU AT THE RENDEZVOUS POINT, MR. GRIMM.
THIS IS THE RENDEZVOUS POINT.
THIS ISN'T EVEN CLOS TO THE RENDEZVOU POINT.
AND WHY ARE YOU FLYI AROUND WITH OF MY TRADEM ROCKET PACK
YOU TOLD ME I COULD, ROCKET!
DRAX
THE THING

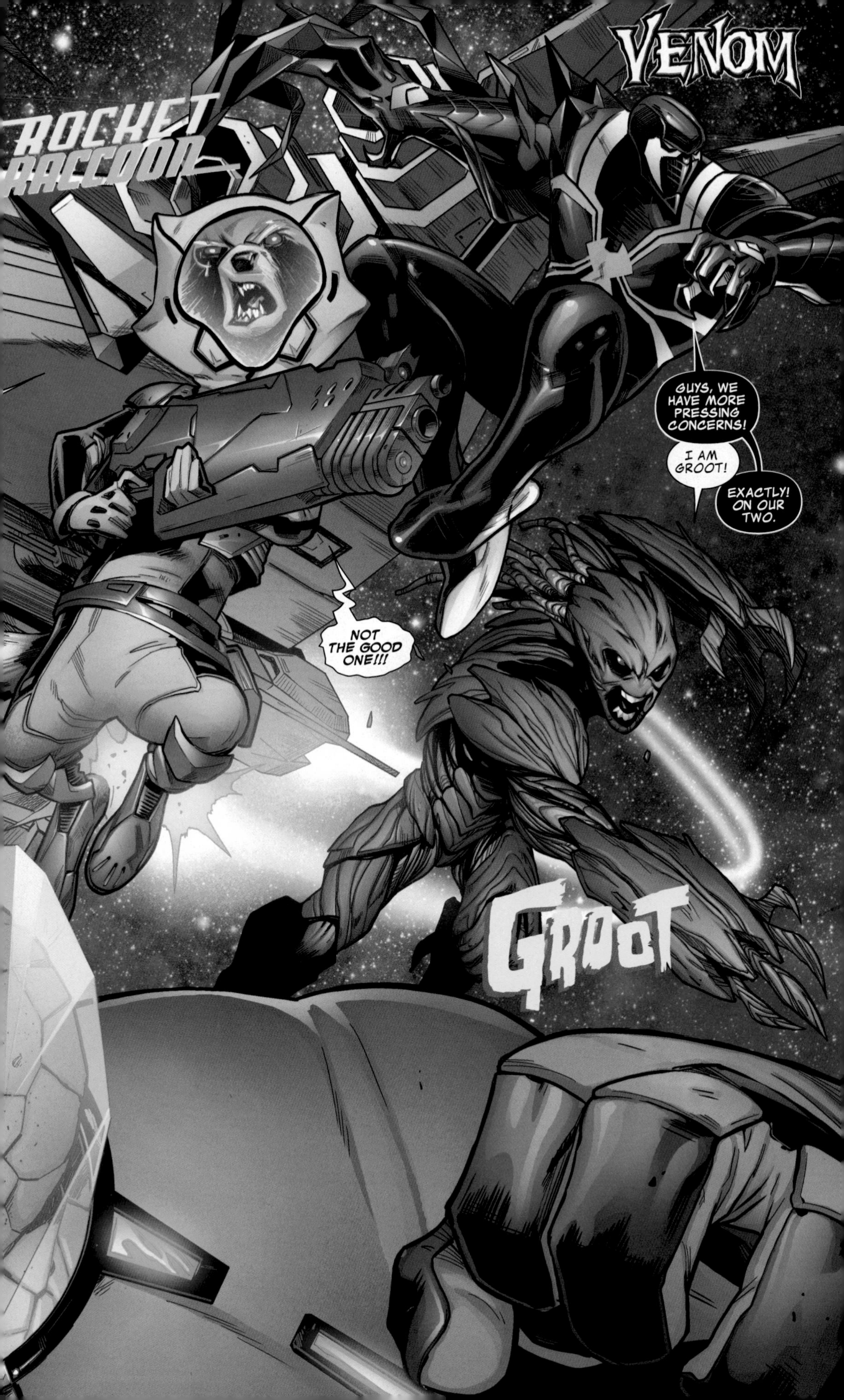
VENOM
ROCKET RACCOON
GUYS, WE HAVE MORE PRESSING CONCERNS!
I AM GROOT!
EXACTLY! ON OUR TWO.
NOT THE GOOD ONE!!!
GROOT

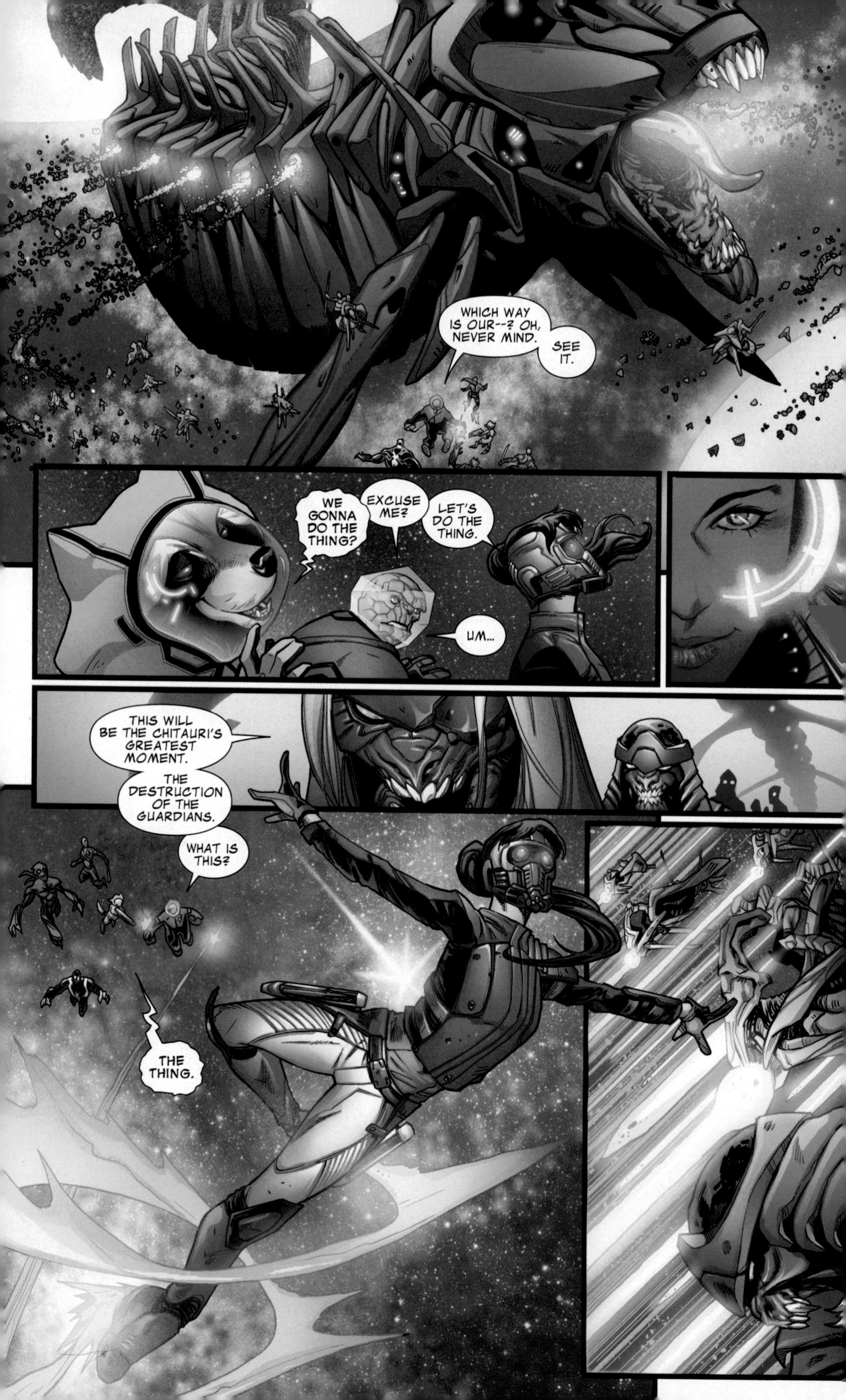

WHICH WAY IS OUR--? OH, NEVER MIND.
SEE IT.
WE GONNA DO THE THING?
EXCUSE ME?
LET'S DO THE THING.
UM...
THIS WILL BE THE CHITAURI'S GREATEST MOMENT.
THE DESTRUCTION OF THE GUARDIANS.
WHAT IS THIS?
THE THING.

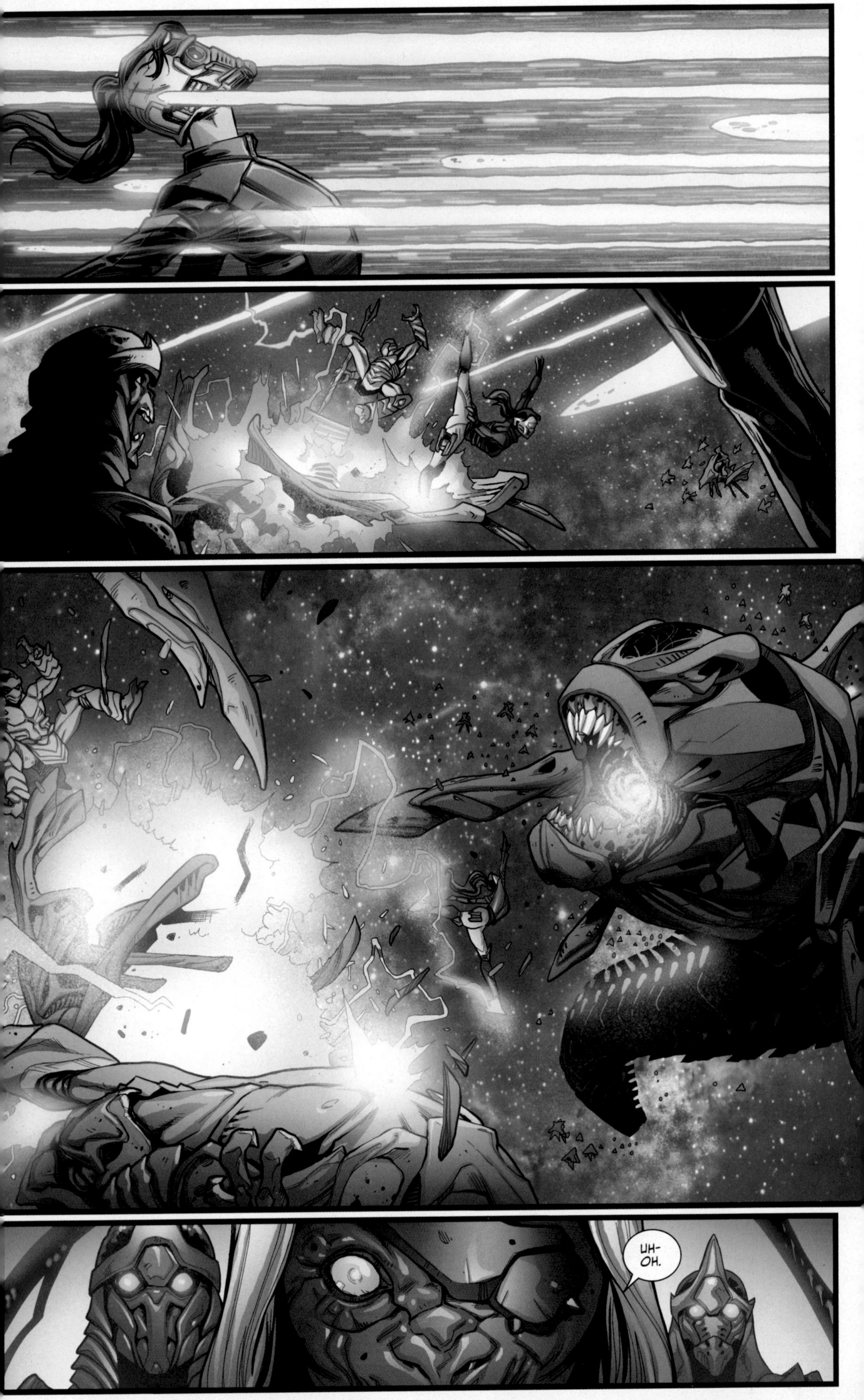
UH-
OH.

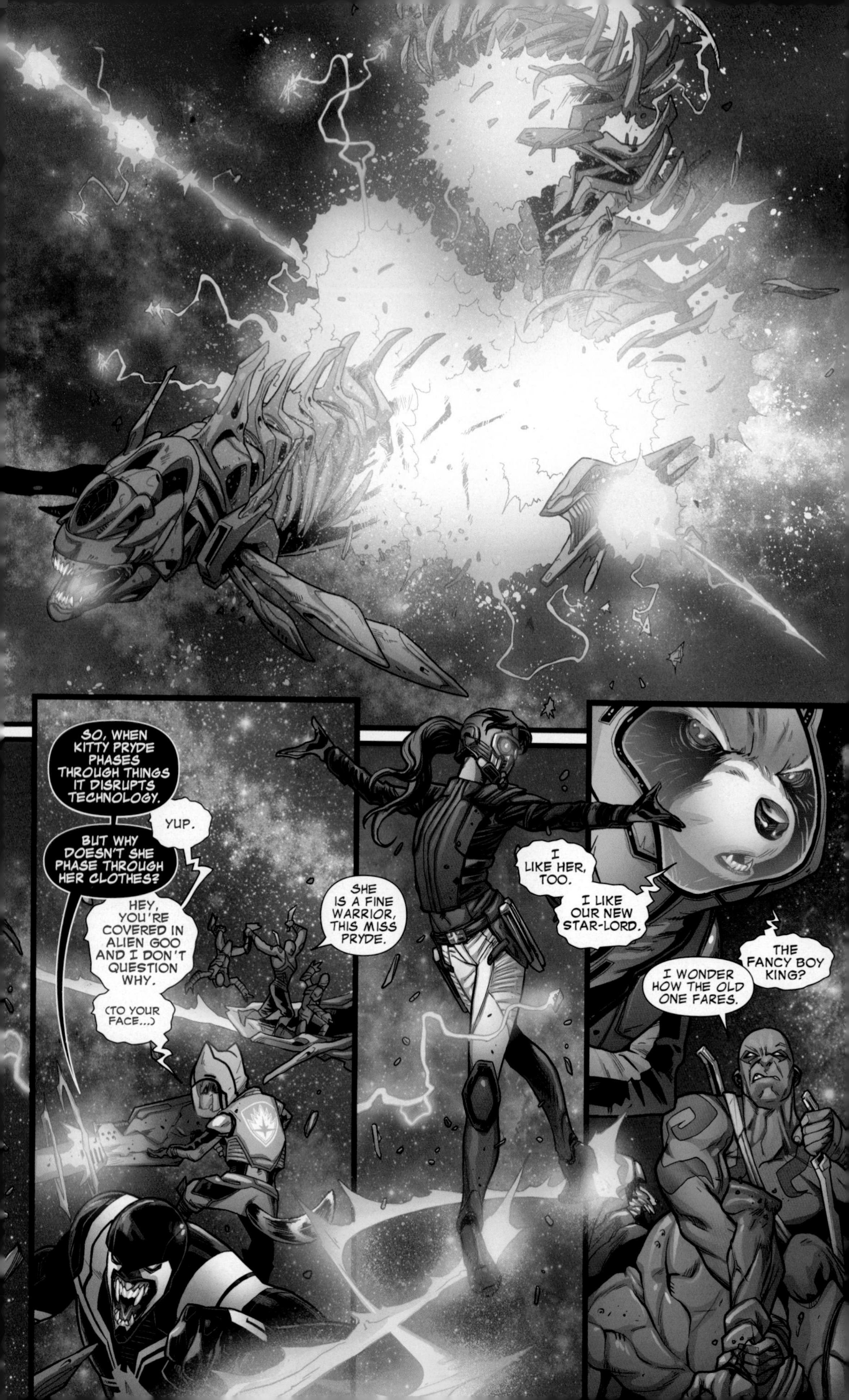
SO, WHEN KITTY PRYDE PHASES THROUGH THINGS IT DISRUPTS TECHNOLOGY.
YUP.
BUT WHY DOESN'T SHE PHASE THROUGH HER CLOTHES?
HEY, YOU'RE COVERED IN ALIEN GOO AND I DON'T QUESTION WHY.
(TO YOUR FACE...)
SHE IS A FINE WARRIOR, THIS MISS PRYDE.
I LIKE HER, TOO.
I LIKE OUR NEW STAR-LORD.
I WONDER HOW THE OLD ONE FARES.
THE FANCY BOY KING?

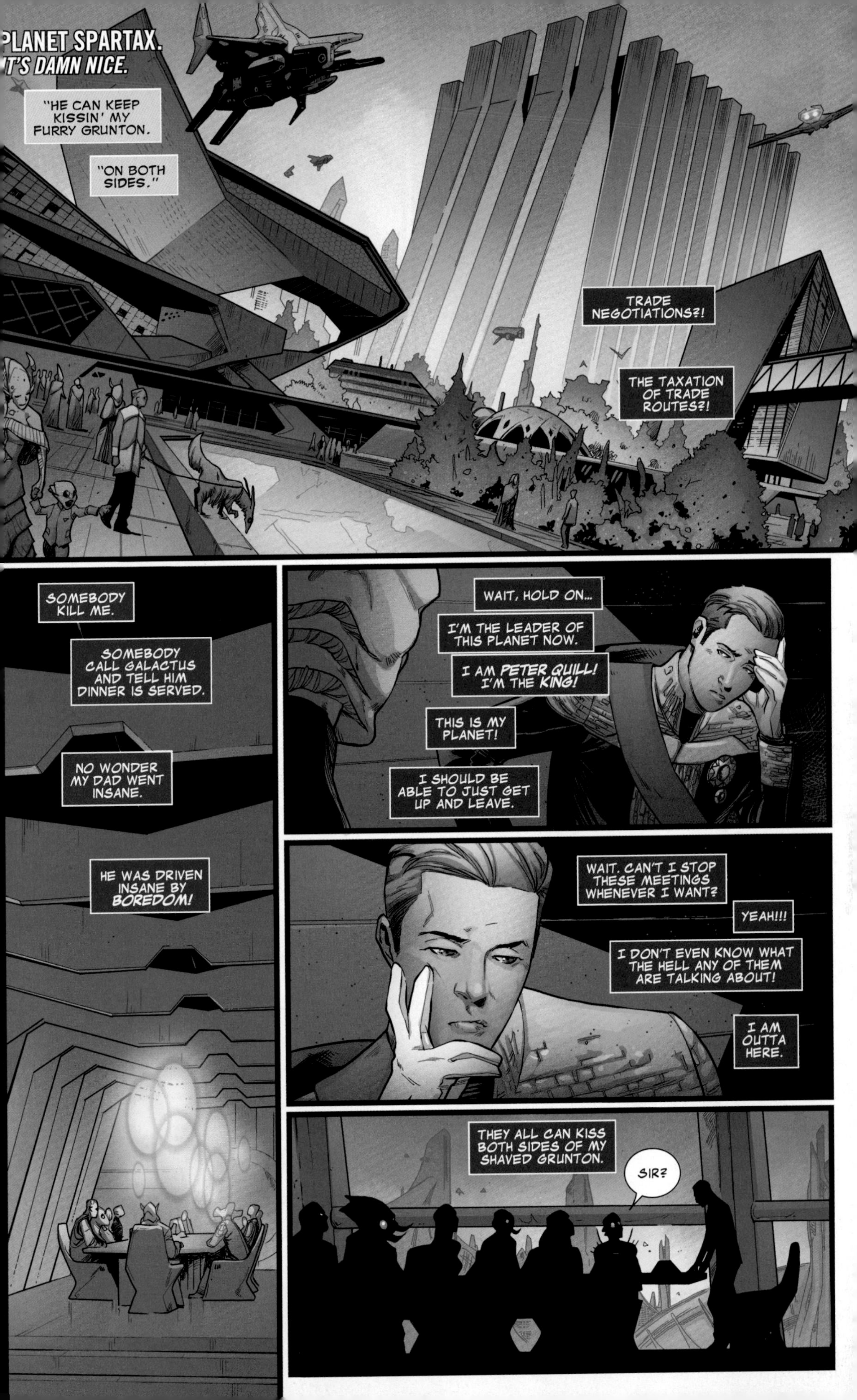
PLANET SPARTAX.
IT'S DAMN NICE.
"HE CAN KEEP KISSIN' MY FURRY GRUNTON.
"ON BOTH SIDES."
TRADE NEGOTIATIONS?!
THE TAXATION OF TRADE ROUTES?!
SOMEBODY KILL ME.
SOMEBODY CALL GALACTUS AND TELL HIM DINNER IS SERVED.
NO WONDER MY DAD WENT INSANE.
HE WAS DRIVEN INSANE BY BOREDOM!
WAIT, HOLD ON...
I'M THE LEADER OF THIS PLANET NOW.
I AM PETER QUILL! I'M THE KING!
THIS IS MY PLANET!
I SHOULD BE ABLE TO JUST GET UP AND LEAVE.
WAIT. CAN'T I STOP THESE MEETINGS WHENEVER I WANT?
YEAH!!!
I DON'T EVEN KNOW WHAT THE HELL ANY OF THEM ARE TALKING ABOUT!
I AM OUTTA HERE.
THEY ALL CAN KISS BOTH SIDES OF MY SHAVED GRUNTON.
SIR?

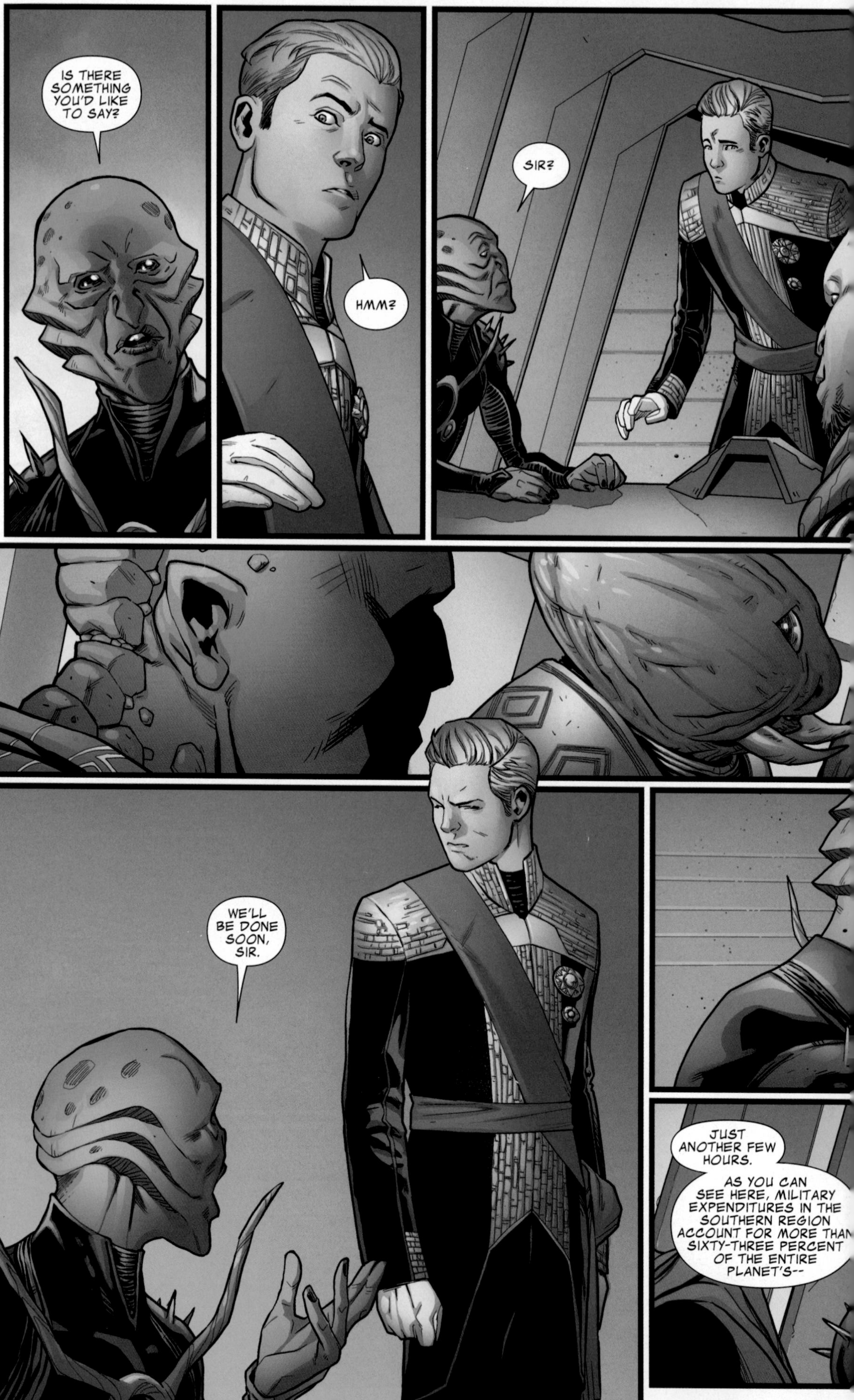
IS THERE SOMETHING YOU'D LIKE TO SAY?
HMM?
SIR?
WE'LL BE DONE SOON, SIR.
JUST ANOTHER FEW HOURS.
AS YOU CAN SEE HERE, MILITARY EXPENDITURES IN THE SOUTHERN REGION ACCOUNT FOR MORE THAN SIXTY-THREE PERCENT OF THE ENTIRE PLANET'S--

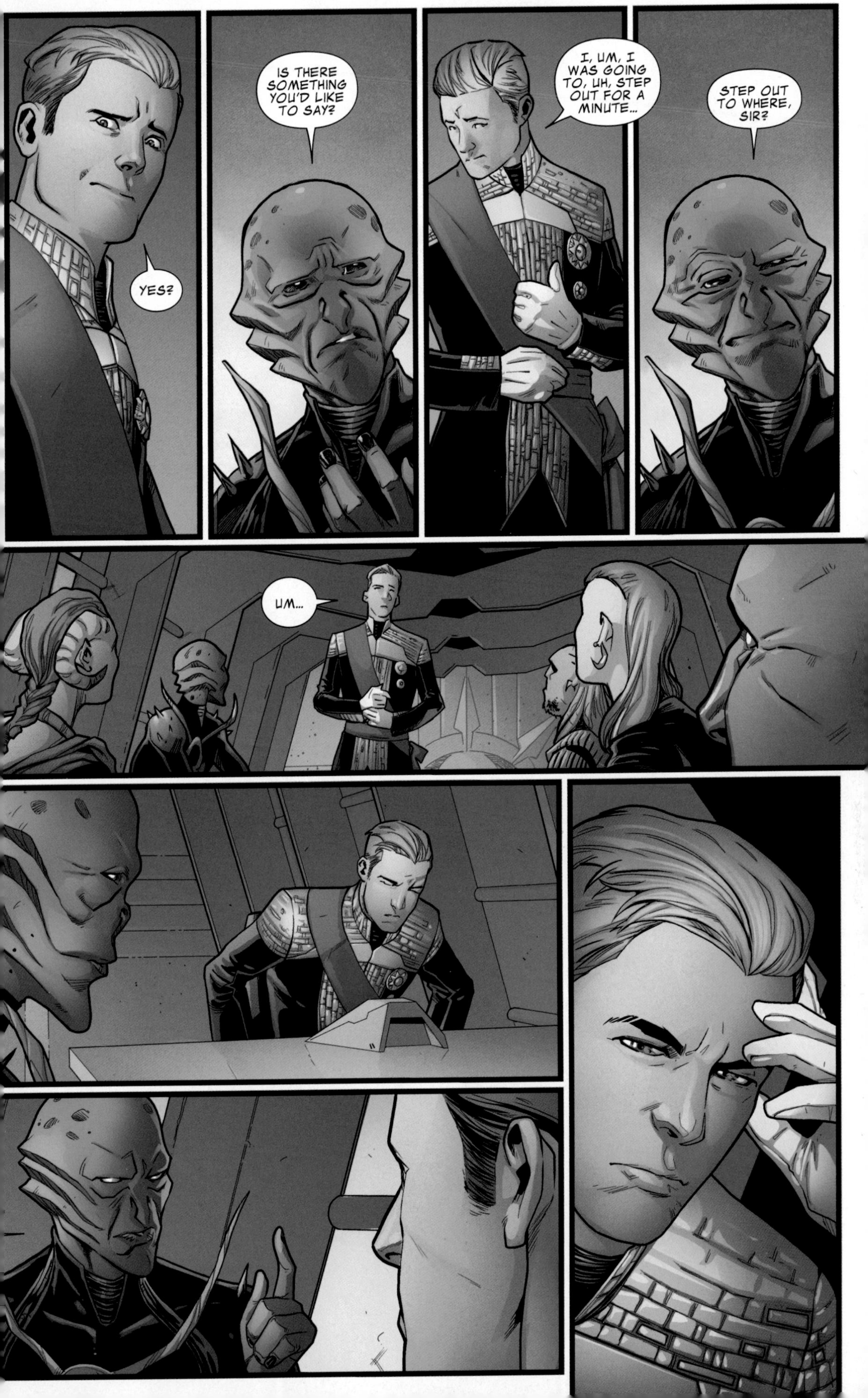
YES?
IS THERE SOMETHING YOU'D LIKE TO SAY?
I, UM, I WAS GOING TO, UH, STEP OUT FOR A MINUTE...
STEP OUT TO WHERE, SIR?
UM...

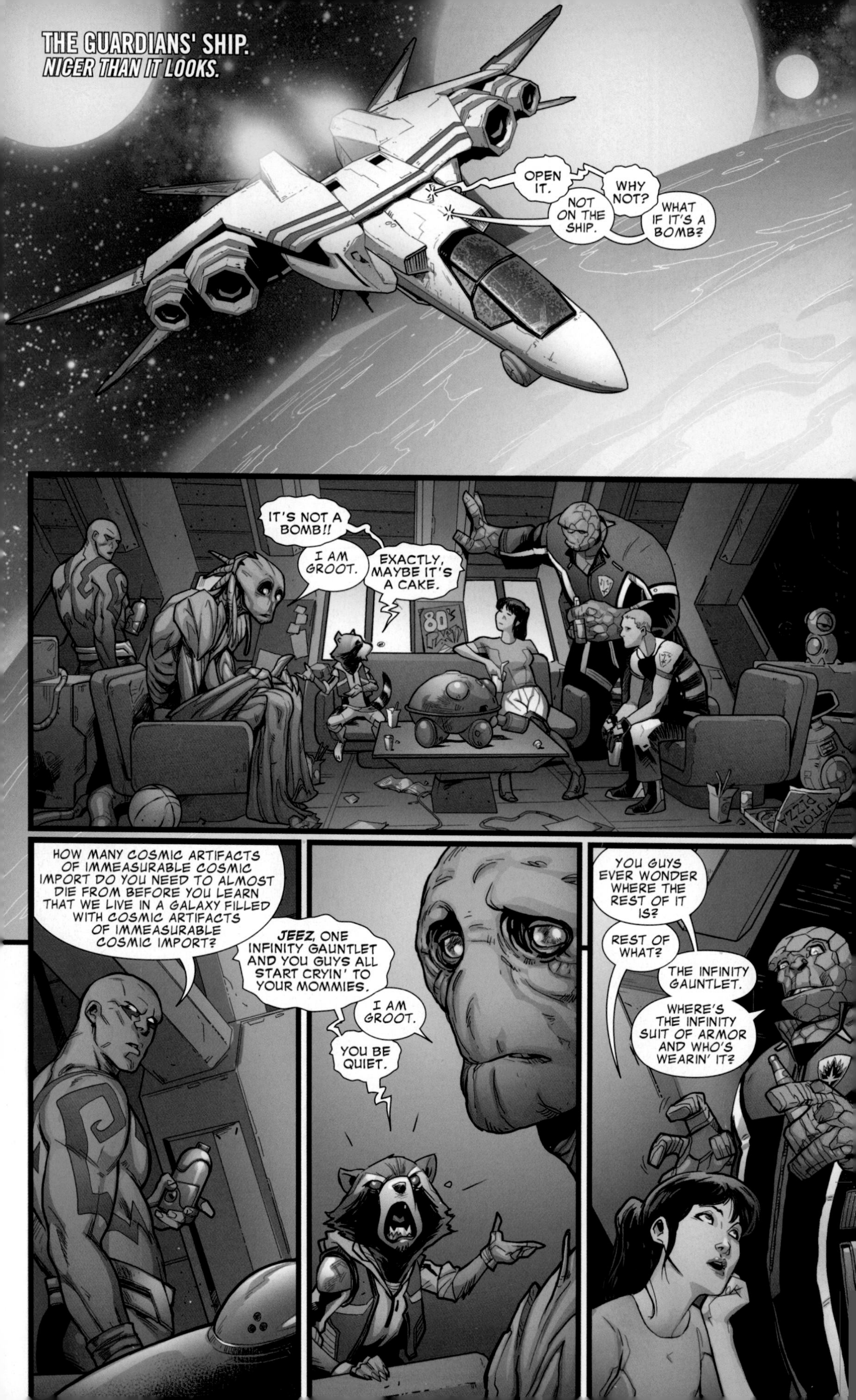
THE GUARDIANS' SHIP.
NICER THAN IT LOOKS.
OPEN IT.
NOT ON THE SHIP.
WHY NOT?
WHAT IF IT'S A BOMB?
IT'S NOT A BOMB!!
I AM GROOT.
EXACTLY, MAYBE IT'S A CAKE.
80'S
HOW MANY COSMIC ARTIFACTS OF IMMEASURABLE COSMIC IMPORT DO YOU NEED TO ALMOST DIE FROM BEFORE YOU LEARN THAT WE LIVE IN A GALAXY FILLED WITH COSMIC ARTIFACTS OF IMMEASURABLE COSMIC IMPORT?
JEEZ, ONE INFINITY GAUNTLET AND YOU GUYS ALL START CRYIN' TO YOUR MOMMIES.
I AM GROOT.
YOU BE QUIET.
YOU GUYS EVER WONDER WHERE THE REST OF IT IS?
REST OF WHAT?
THE INFINITY GAUNTLET.
WHERE'S THE INFINITY SUIT OF ARMOR AND WHO'S WEARIN' IT?

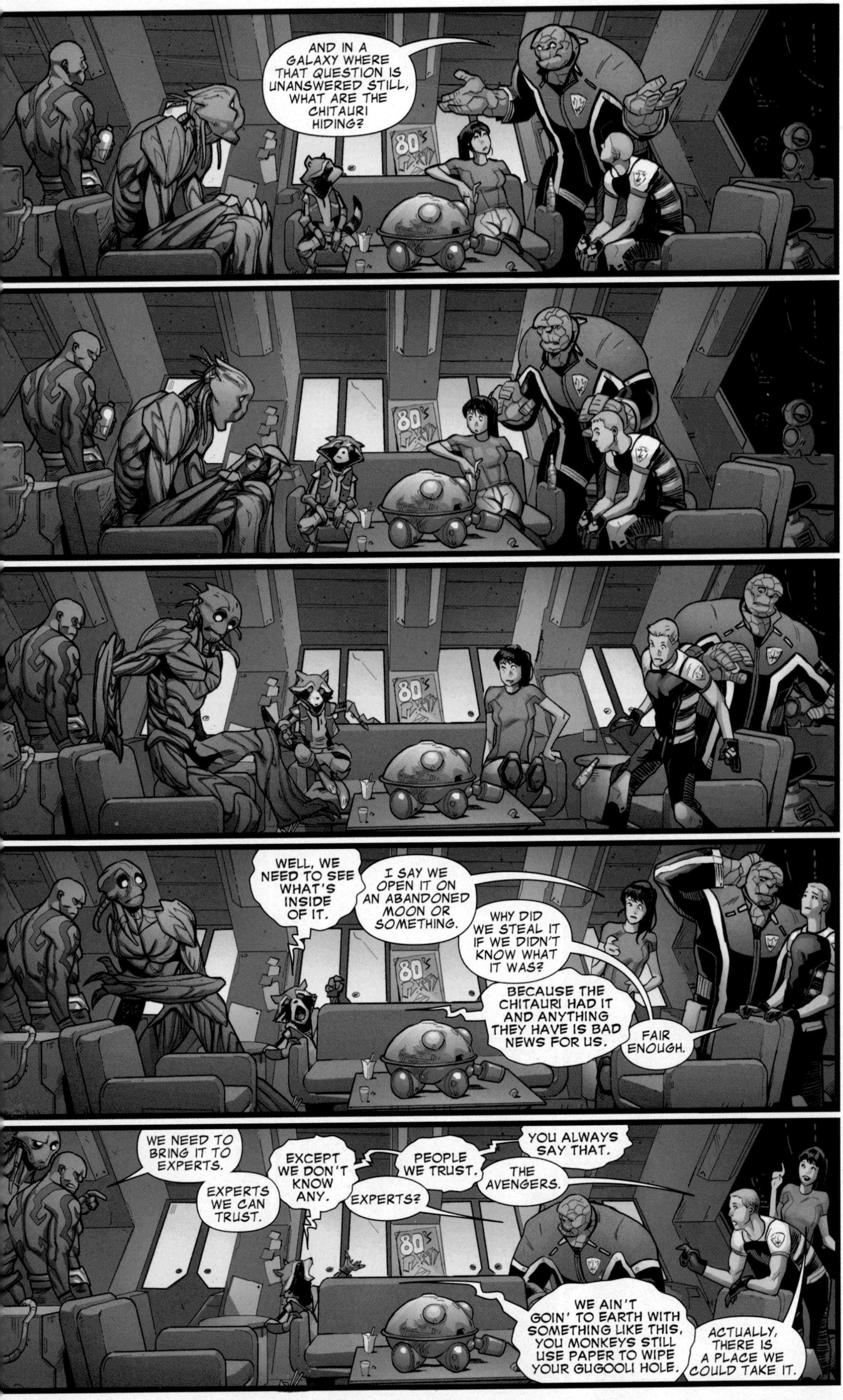
AND IN A GALAXY WHERE THAT QUESTION IS UNANSWERED STILL, WHAT ARE THE CHITAURI HIDING?
80's
80's
80's
WELL, WE NEED TO SEE WHAT'S INSIDE OF IT.
I SAY WE OPEN IT ON AN ABANDONED MOON OR SOMETHING.
WHY DID WE STEAL IT IF WE DIDN'T KNOW WHAT IT WAS?
BECAUSE THE CHITAURI HAD IT AND ANYTHING THEY HAVE IS BAD NEWS FOR US.
FAIR ENOUGH.
80's
WE NEED TO BRING IT TO EXPERTS.
EXPERTS WE CAN TRUST.
EXCEPT WE DON'T KNOW ANY.
PEOPLE WE TRUST.
YOU ALWAYS SAY THAT.
EXPERTS?
THE AVENGERS.
80's
WE AIN'T GOIN' TO EARTH WITH SOMETHING LIKE THIS, YOU MONKEYS STILL USE PAPER TO WIPE YOUR GUGOOLI HOLE.
ACTUALLY, THERE IS A PLACE WE COULD TAKE IT.

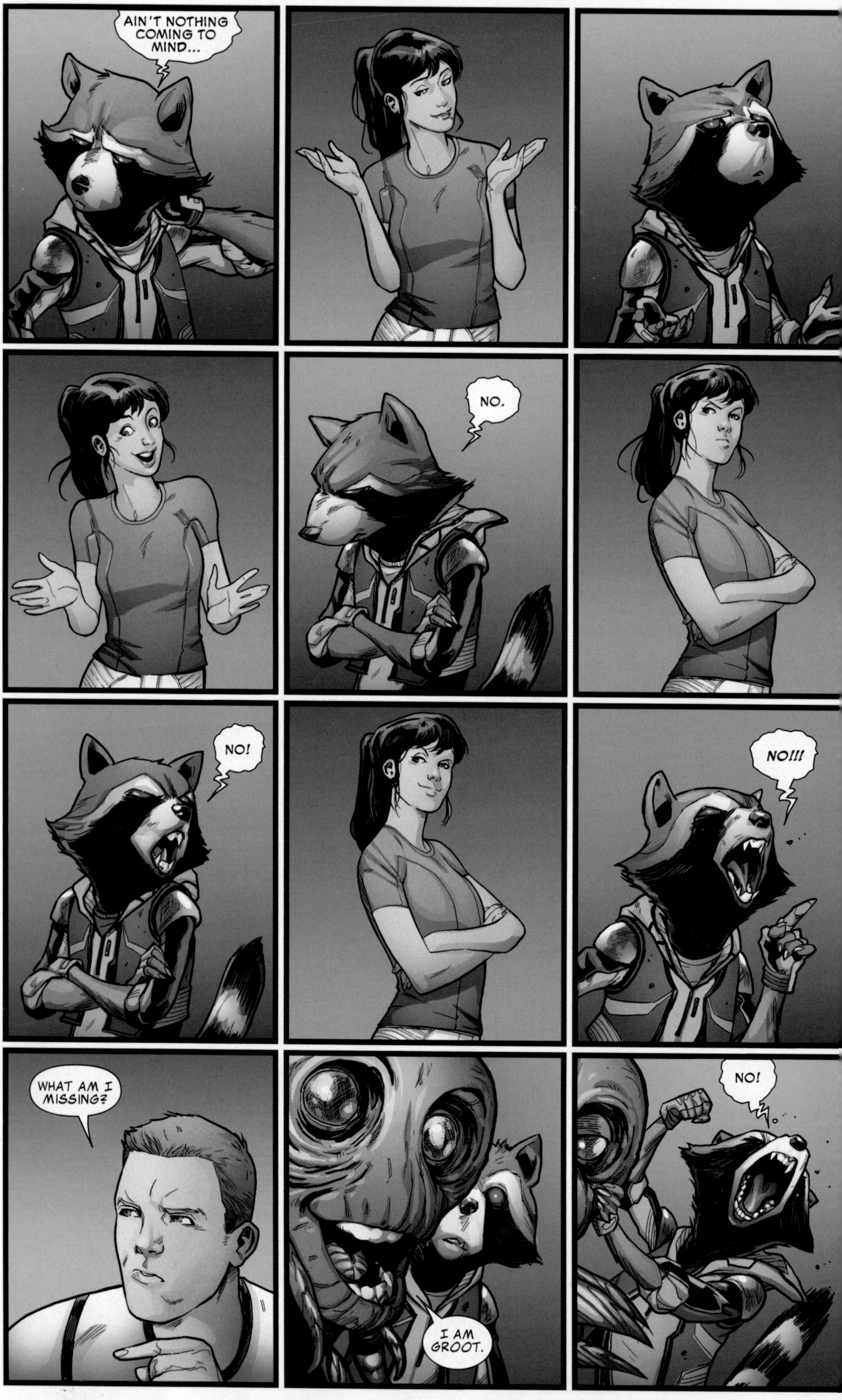
AIN'T NOTHING COMING TO MIND...
NO.
NO!
NO!!!
WHAT AM I MISSING?
I AM GROOT.
NO!

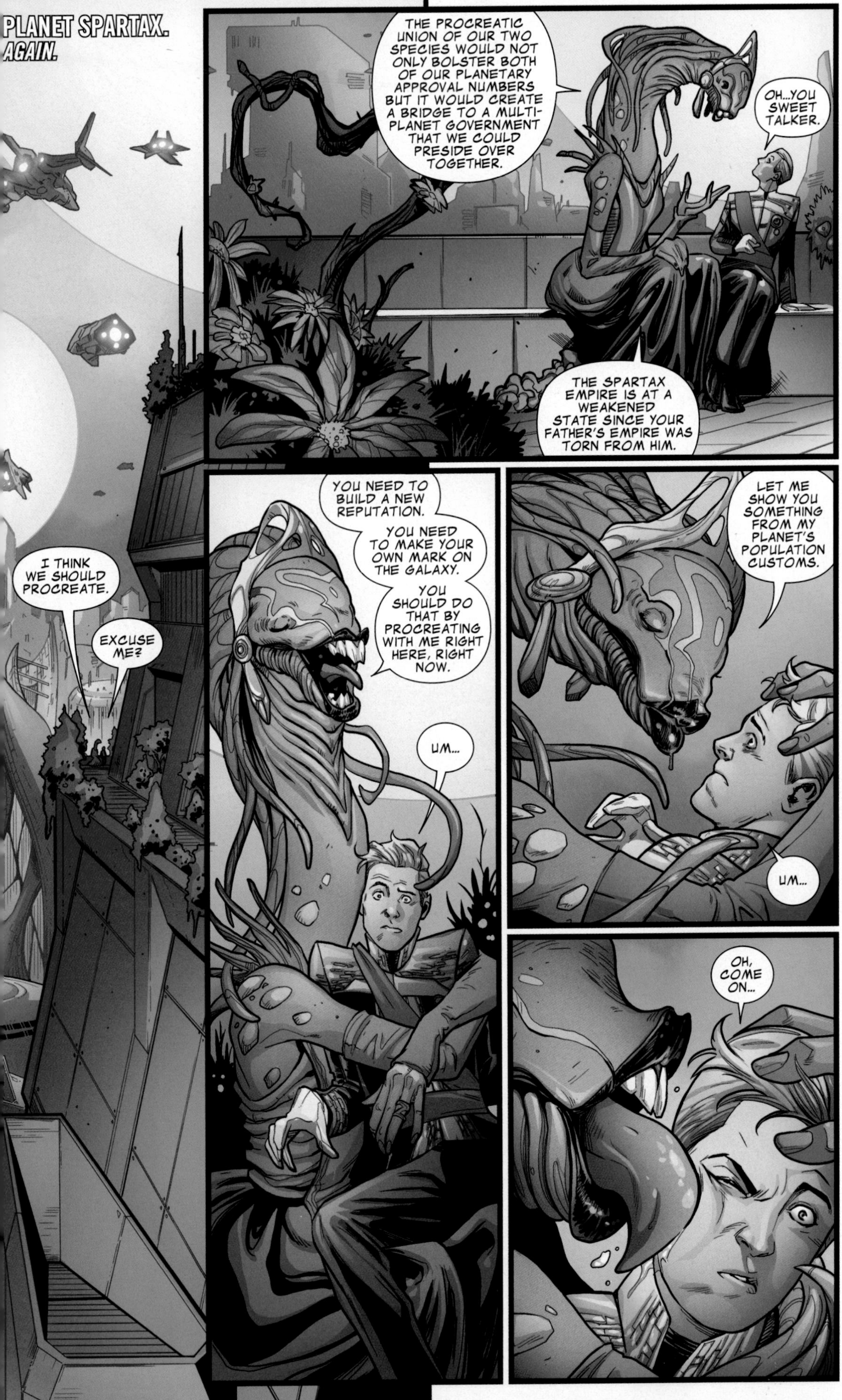
PLANET SPARTAX.
AGAIN.
THE PROCREATIC UNION OF OUR TWO SPECIES WOULD NOT ONLY BOLSTER BOTH OF OUR PLANETARY APPROVAL NUMBERS BUT IT WOULD CREATE A BRIDGE TO A MULTI-PLANET GOVERNMENT THAT WE COULD PRESIDE OVER TOGETHER.
OH...YOU SWEET TALKER.
THE SPARTAX EMPIRE IS AT A WEAKENED STATE SINCE YOUR FATHER'S EMPIRE WAS TORN FROM HIM.
I THINK WE SHOULD PROCREATE.
EXCUSE ME?
YOU NEED TO BUILD A NEW REPUTATION.
YOU NEED TO MAKE YOUR OWN MARK ON THE GALAXY.
YOU SHOULD DO THAT BY PROCREATING WITH ME RIGHT HERE, RIGHT NOW.
UM...
LET ME SHOW YOU SOMETHING FROM MY PLANET'S POPULATION CUSTOMS.
UM...
OH, COME ON...

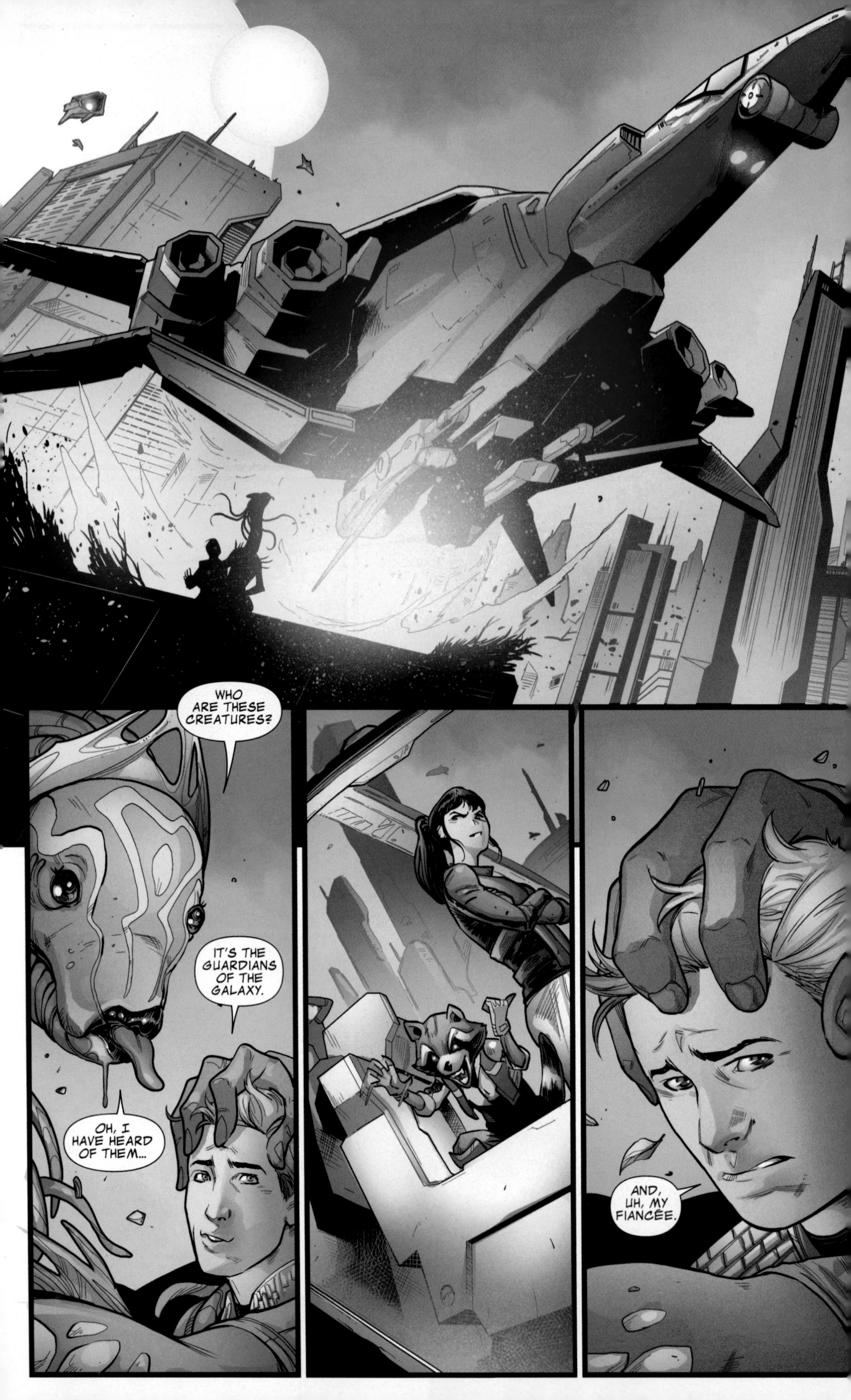
WHO ARE THESE CREATURES?
IT'S THE GUARDIANS OF THE GALAXY.
OH, I HAVE HEARD OF THEM...
AND, UH, MY FIANCÉE.

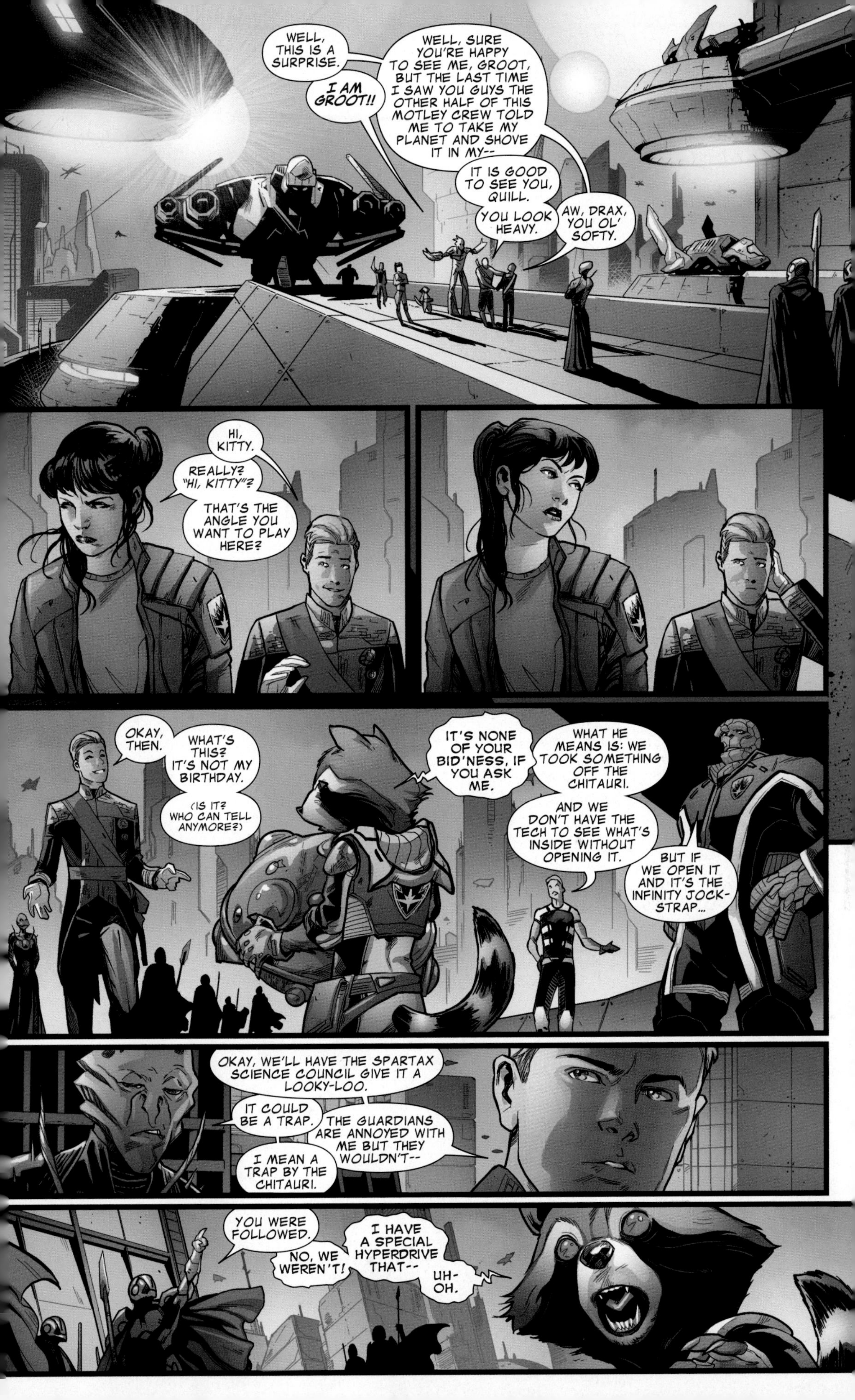
WELL, THIS IS A SURPRISE.
WELL, SURE YOU'RE HAPPY TO SEE ME, GROOT, BUT THE LAST TIME I SAW YOU GUYS THE OTHER HALF OF THIS MOTLEY CREW TOLD ME TO TAKE MY PLANET AND SHOVE IT IN MY--
I AM GROOT!!
IT IS GOOD TO SEE YOU, QUILL.
YOU LOOK HEAVY.
AW, DRAX, YOU OL' SOFTY.
HI, KITTY.
REALLY? "HI, KITTY"?
THAT'S THE ANGLE YOU WANT TO PLAY HERE?
OKAY, THEN.
WHAT'S THIS? IT'S NOT MY BIRTHDAY.
(IS IT? WHO CAN TELL ANYMORE?)
IT'S NONE OF YOUR BID'NESS, IF YOU ASK ME.
WHAT HE MEANS IS: WE TOOK SOMETHING OFF THE CHITAURI.
AND WE DON'T HAVE THE TECH TO SEE WHAT'S INSIDE WITHOUT OPENING IT.
BUT IF WE OPEN IT AND IT'S THE INFINITY JOCK-STRAP...
OKAY, WE'LL HAVE THE SPARTAX SCIENCE COUNCIL GIVE IT A LOOKY-LOO.
IT COULD BE A TRAP.
THE GUARDIANS ARE ANNOYED WITH ME BUT THEY WOULDN'T--
I MEAN A TRAP BY THE CHITAURI.
YOU WERE FOLLOWED.
NO, WE WEREN'T!
I HAVE A SPECIAL HYPERDRIVE THAT--
UH-OH.

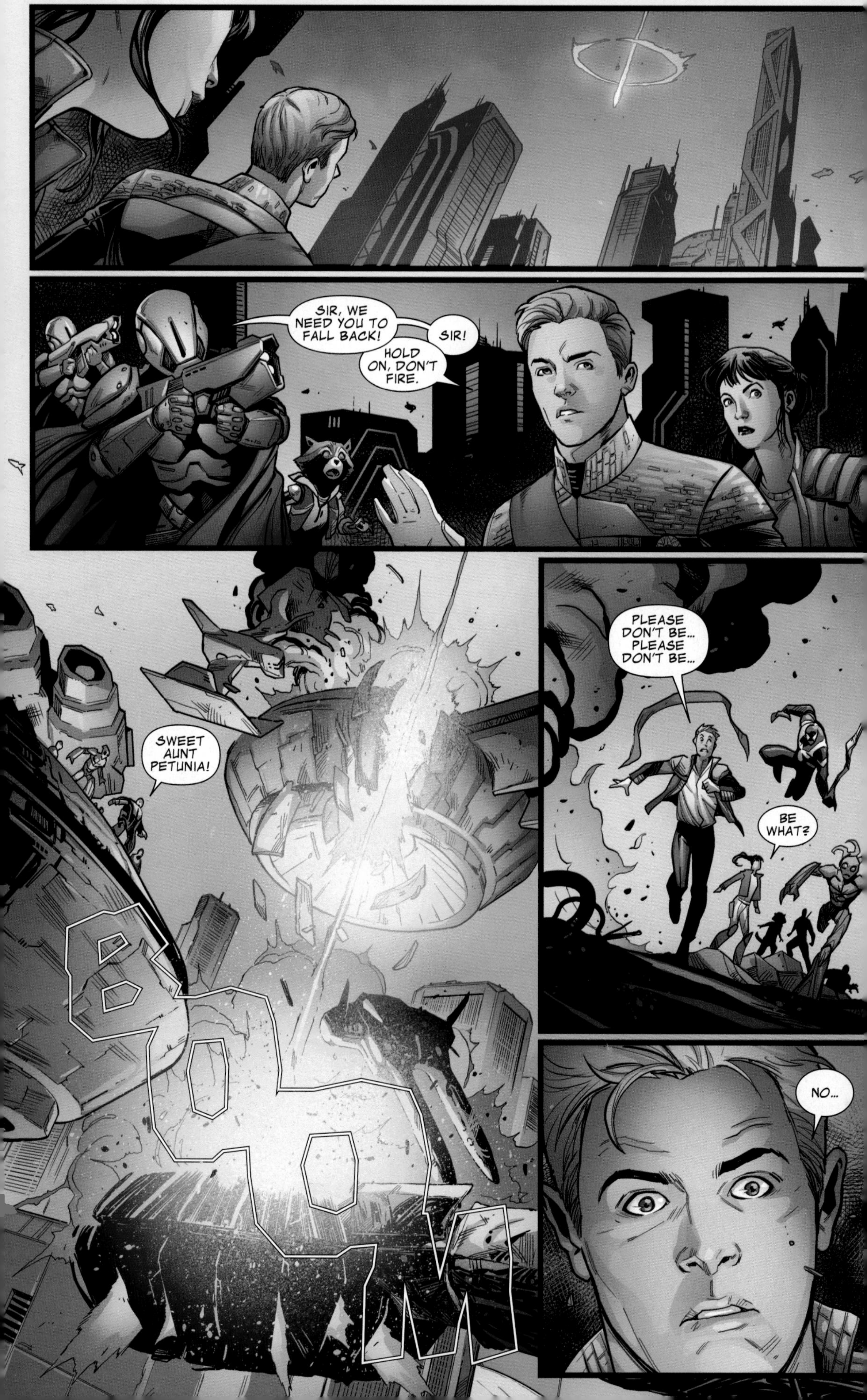
SIR, WE NEED YOU TO FALL BACK!
SIR!
HOLD ON, DON'T FIRE.
SWEET AUNT PETUNIA!
BOOM
PLEASE DON'T BE... PLEASE DON'T BE...
BE WHAT?
NO...

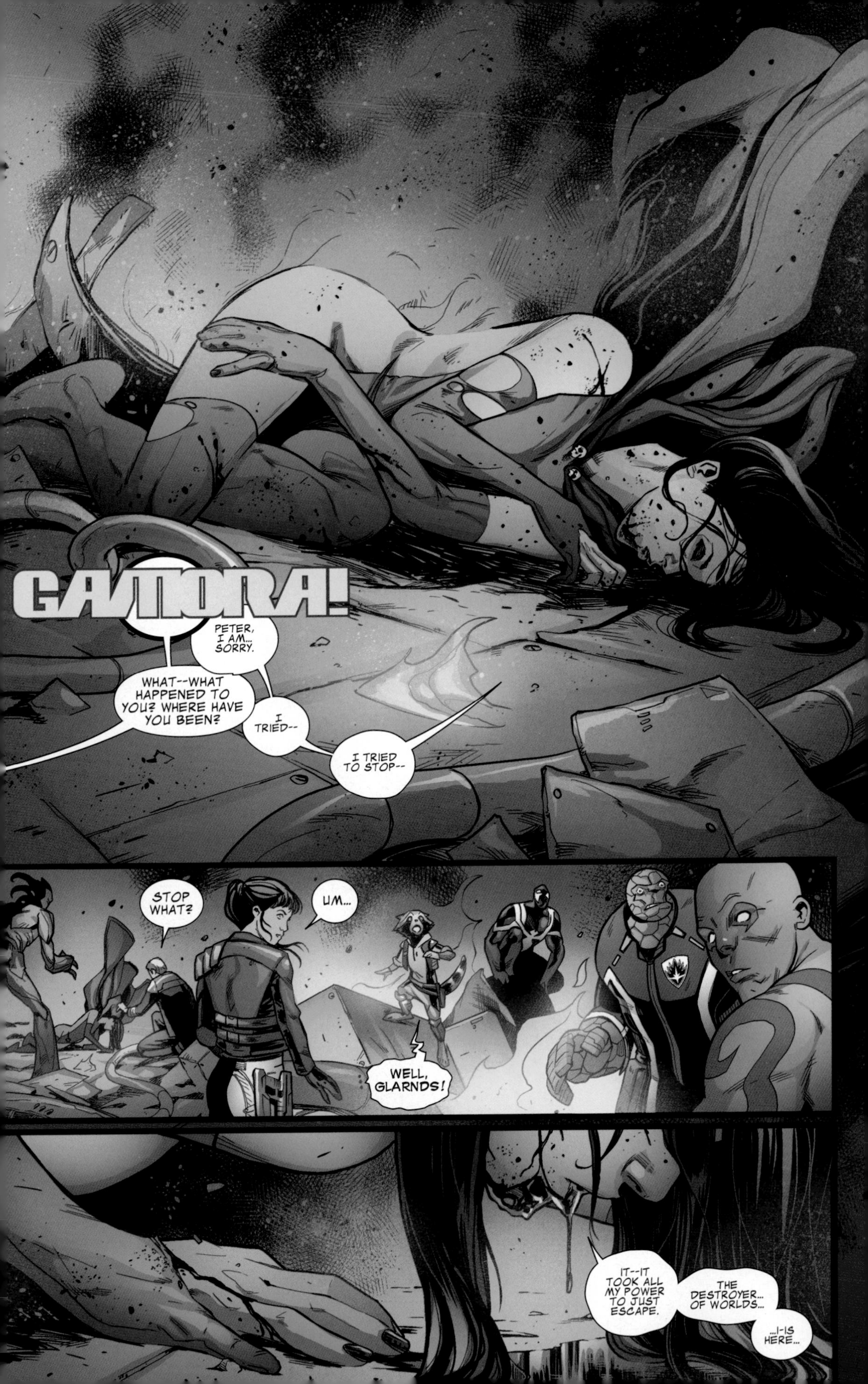
GAMORA!
PETER, I AM... SORRY.
WHAT--WHAT HAPPENED TO YOU? WHERE HAVE YOU BEEN?
I TRIED--
I TRIED TO STOP--
STOP WHAT?
UM...
WELL, GLARNDS!
IT--IT TOOK ALL MY POWER TO JUST ESCAPE.
THE DESTROYER... OF WORLDS...
...I-IS HERE...

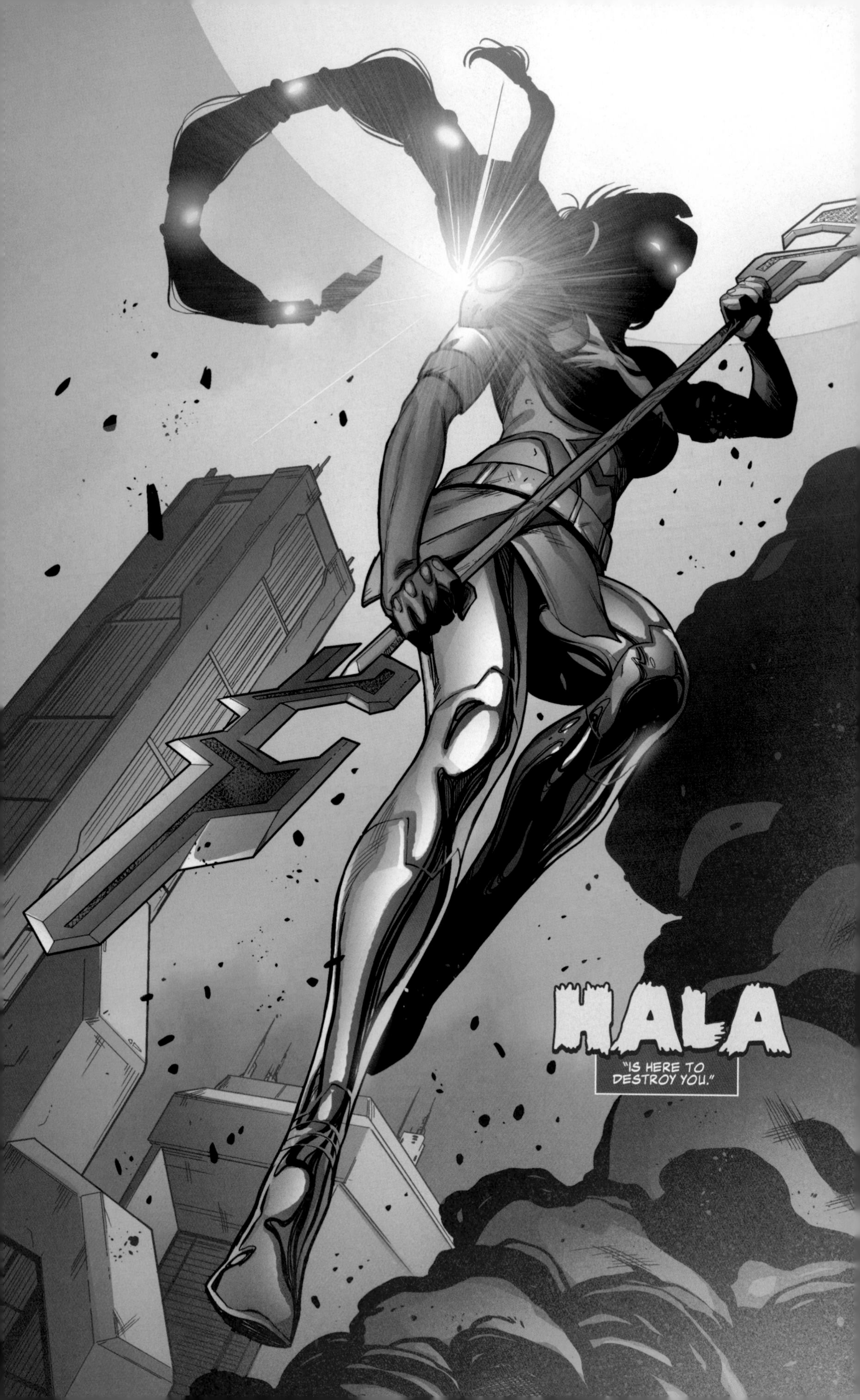
HALA
"IS HERE TO DESTROY YOU."

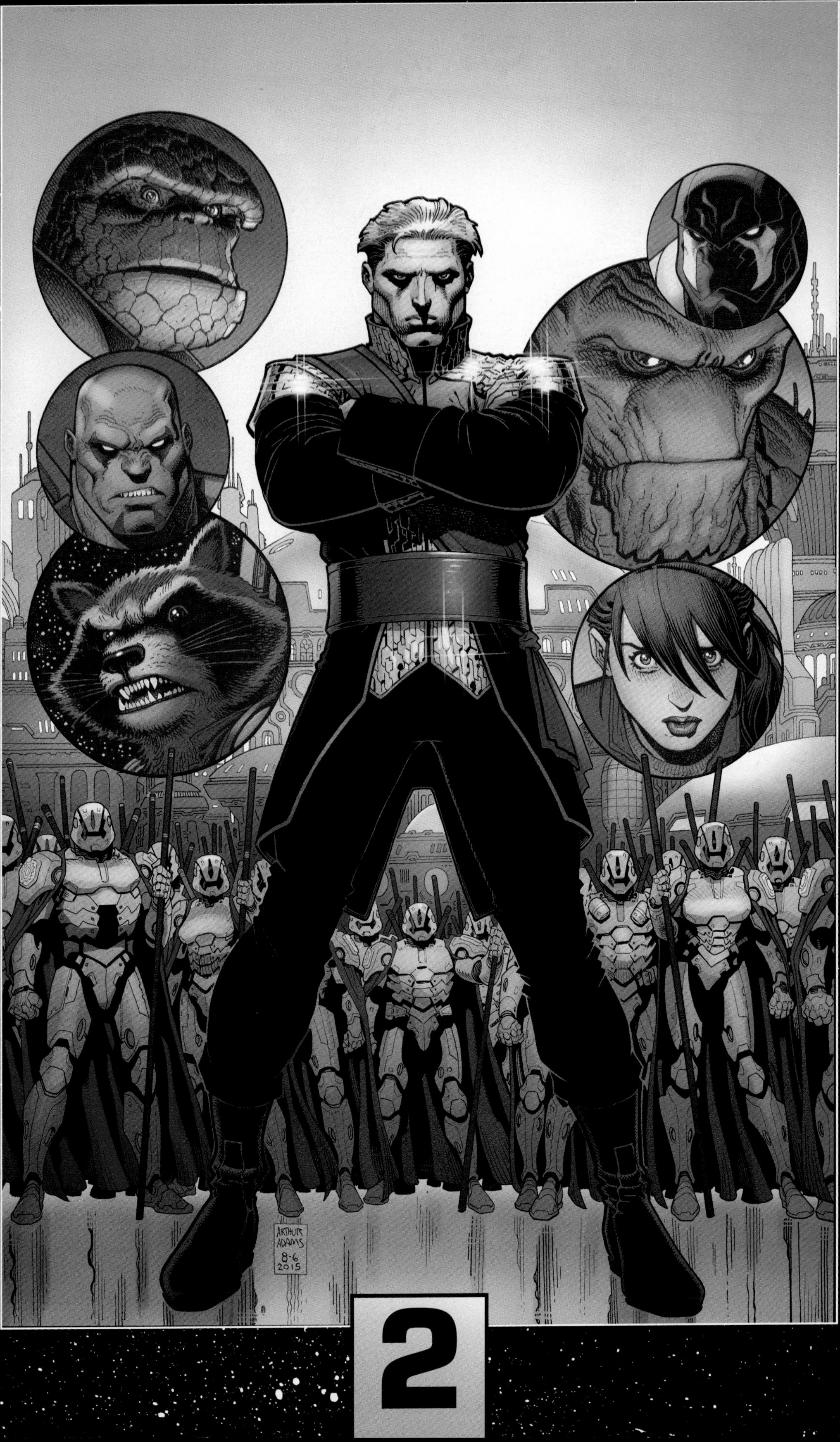
ARTHUR ADAMS 8-6 2015
2

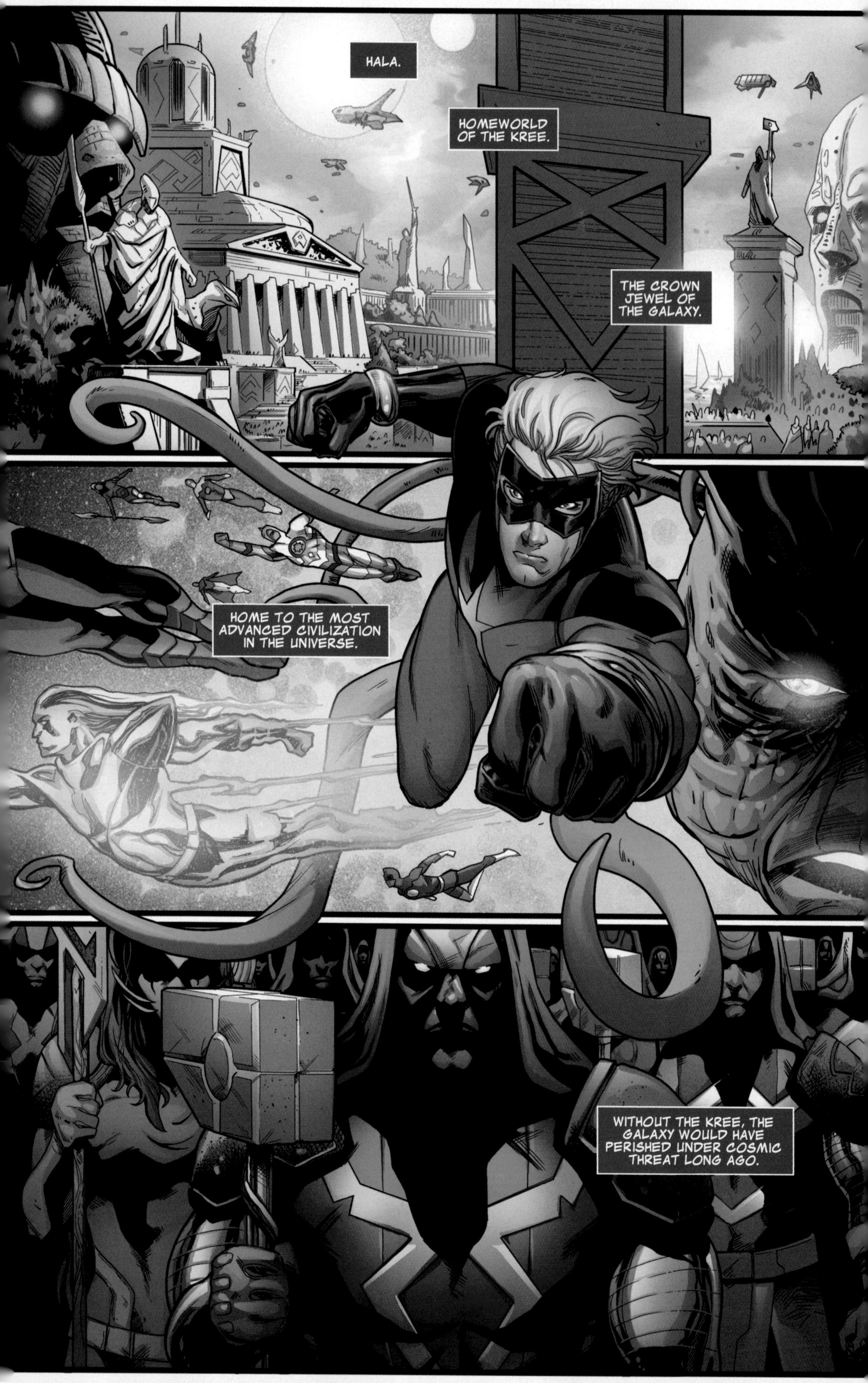
HALA.
HOMEWORLD OF THE KREE.
THE CROWN JEWEL OF THE GALAXY.
HOME TO THE MOST ADVANCED CIVILIZATION IN THE UNIVERSE.
WITHOUT THE KREE, THE GALAXY WOULD HAVE PERISHED UNDER COSMIC THREAT LONG AGO.

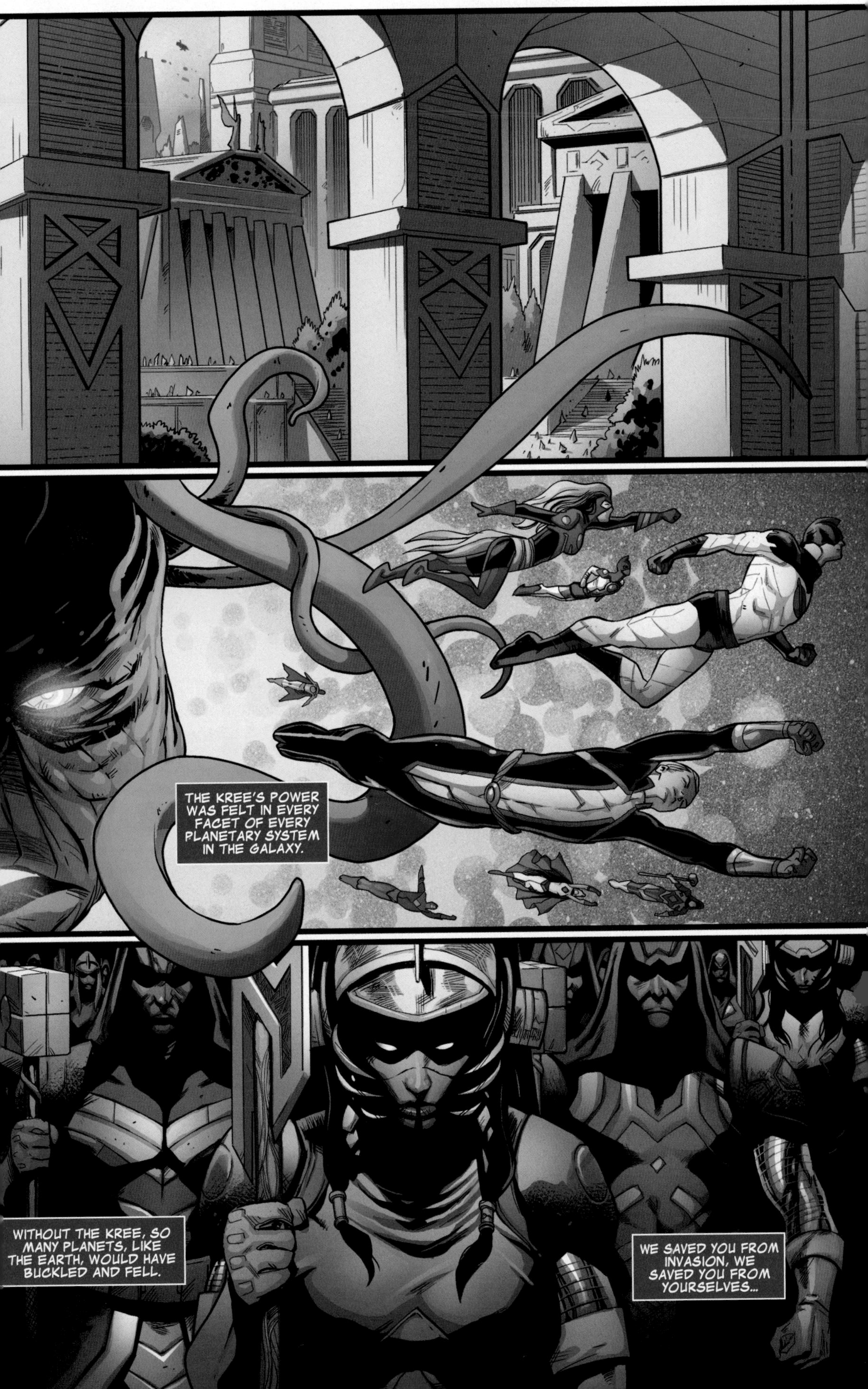
THE KREE'S POWER WAS FELT IN EVERY FACET OF EVERY PLANETARY SYSTEM IN THE GALAXY.
WITHOUT THE KREE, SO MANY PLANETS, LIKE THE EARTH, WOULD HAVE BUCKLED AND FELL.
WE SAVED YOU FROM INVASION, WE SAVED YOU FROM YOURSELVES...

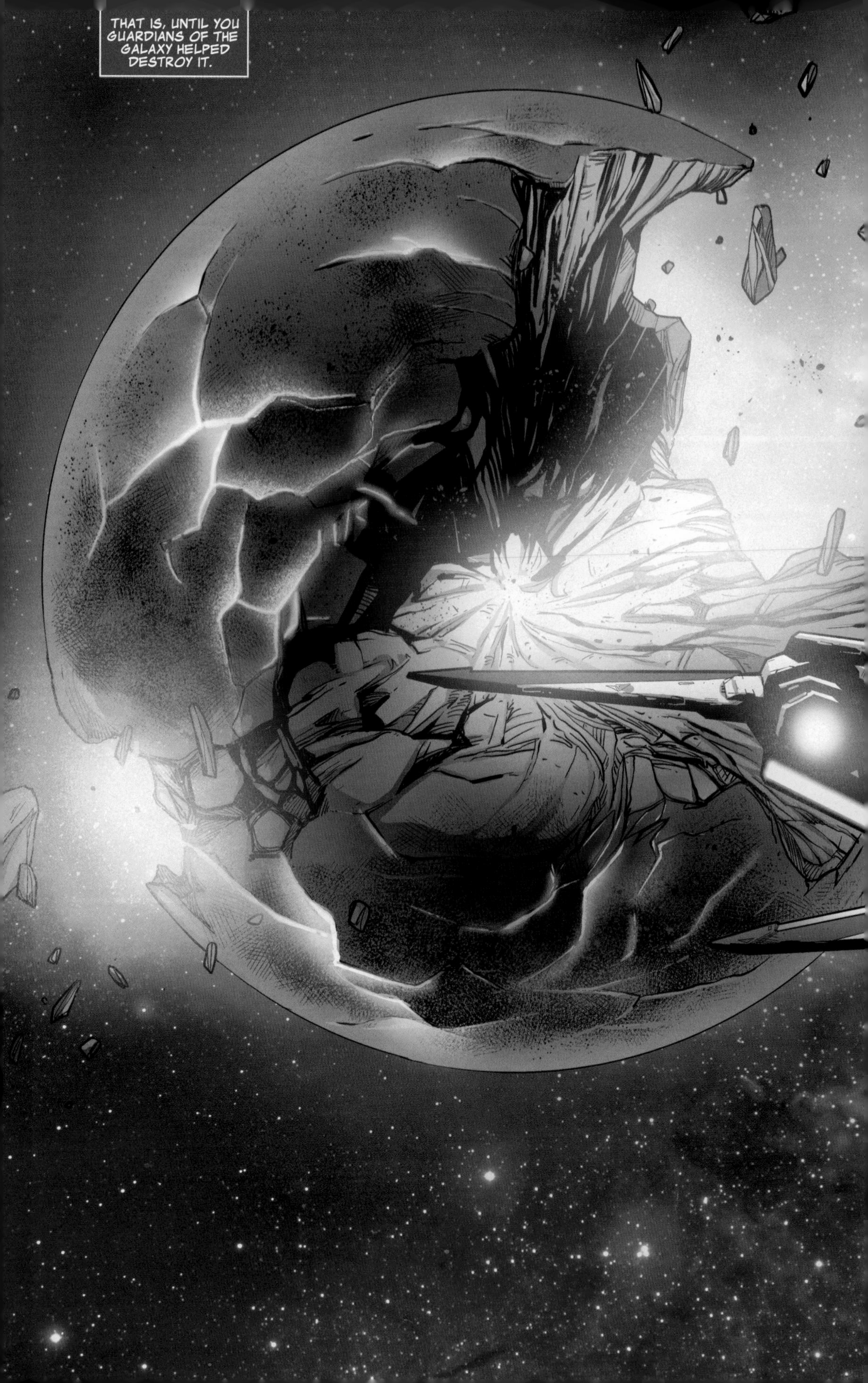
THAT IS, UNTIL YOU GUARDIANS OF THE GALAXY HELPED DESTROY IT.

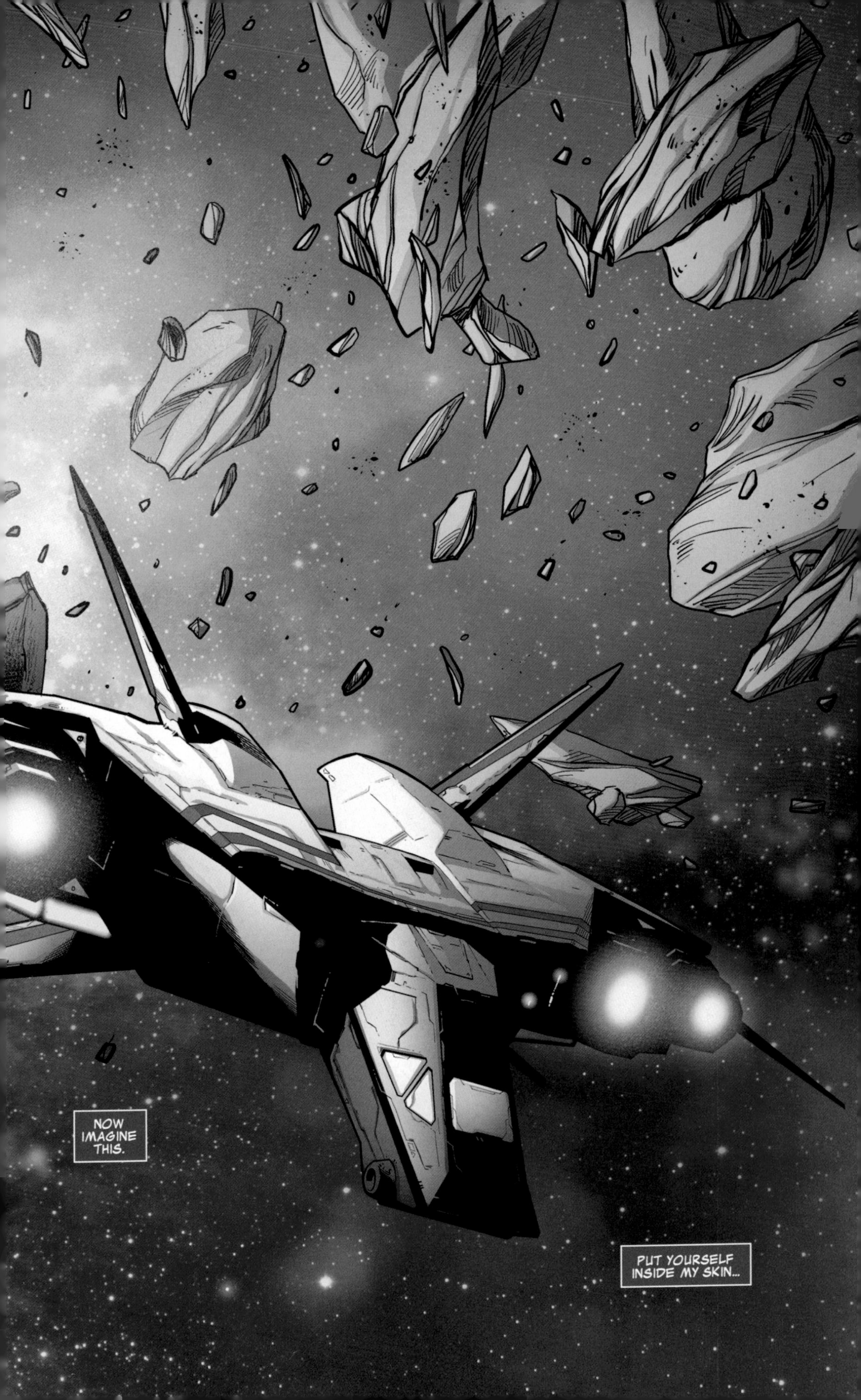
NOW IMAGINE THIS.
PUT YOURSELF INSIDE MY SKIN...

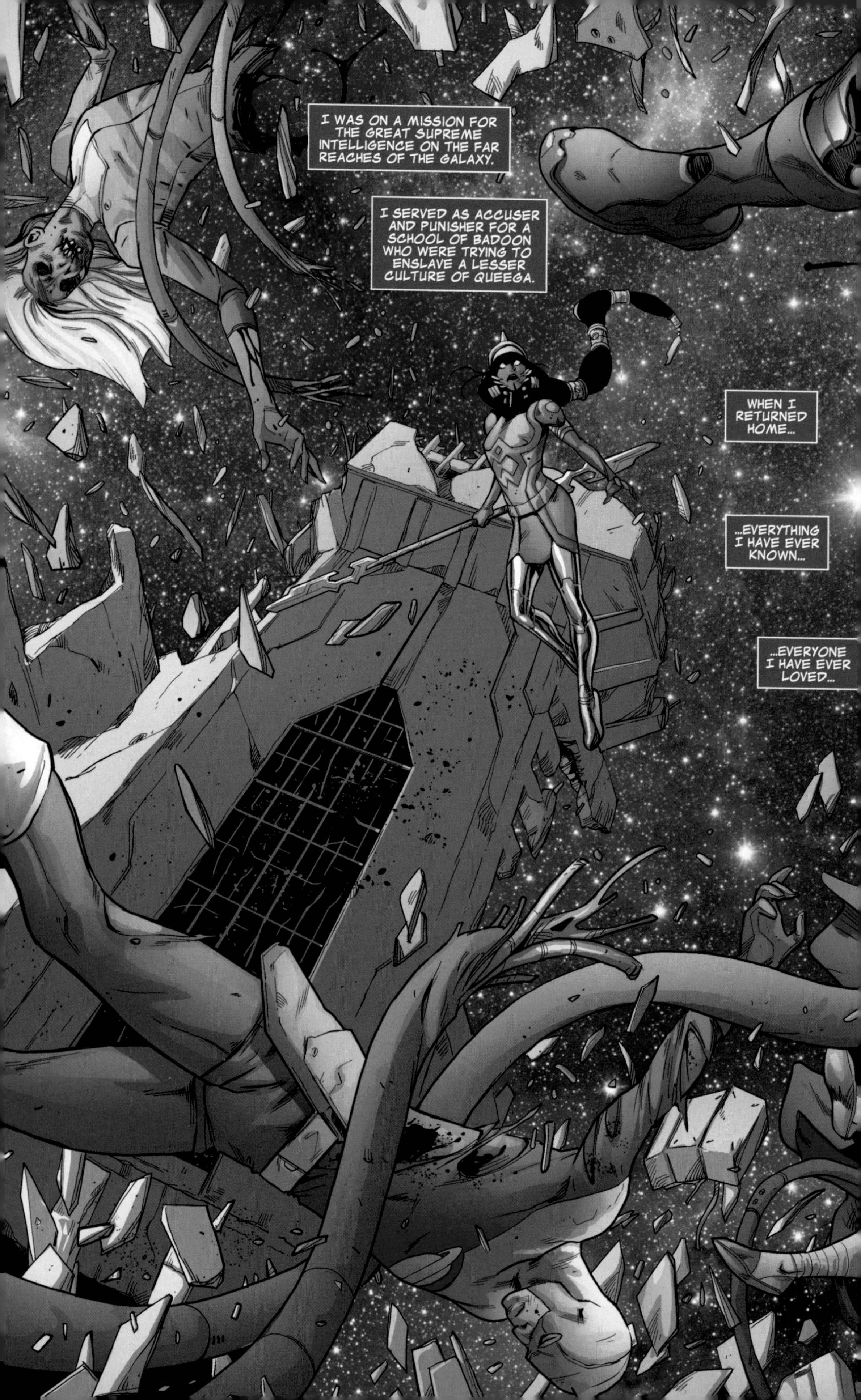
I WAS ON A MISSION FOR THE GREAT SUPREME INTELLIGENCE ON THE FAR REACHES OF THE GALAXY.
I SERVED AS ACCUSER AND PUNISHER FOR A SCHOOL OF BADOON WHO WERE TRYING TO ENSLAVE A LESSER CULTURE OF QUEEGA.
WHEN I RETURNED HOME...
...EVERYTHING I HAVE EVER KNOWN...
...EVERYONE I HAVE EVER LOVED...

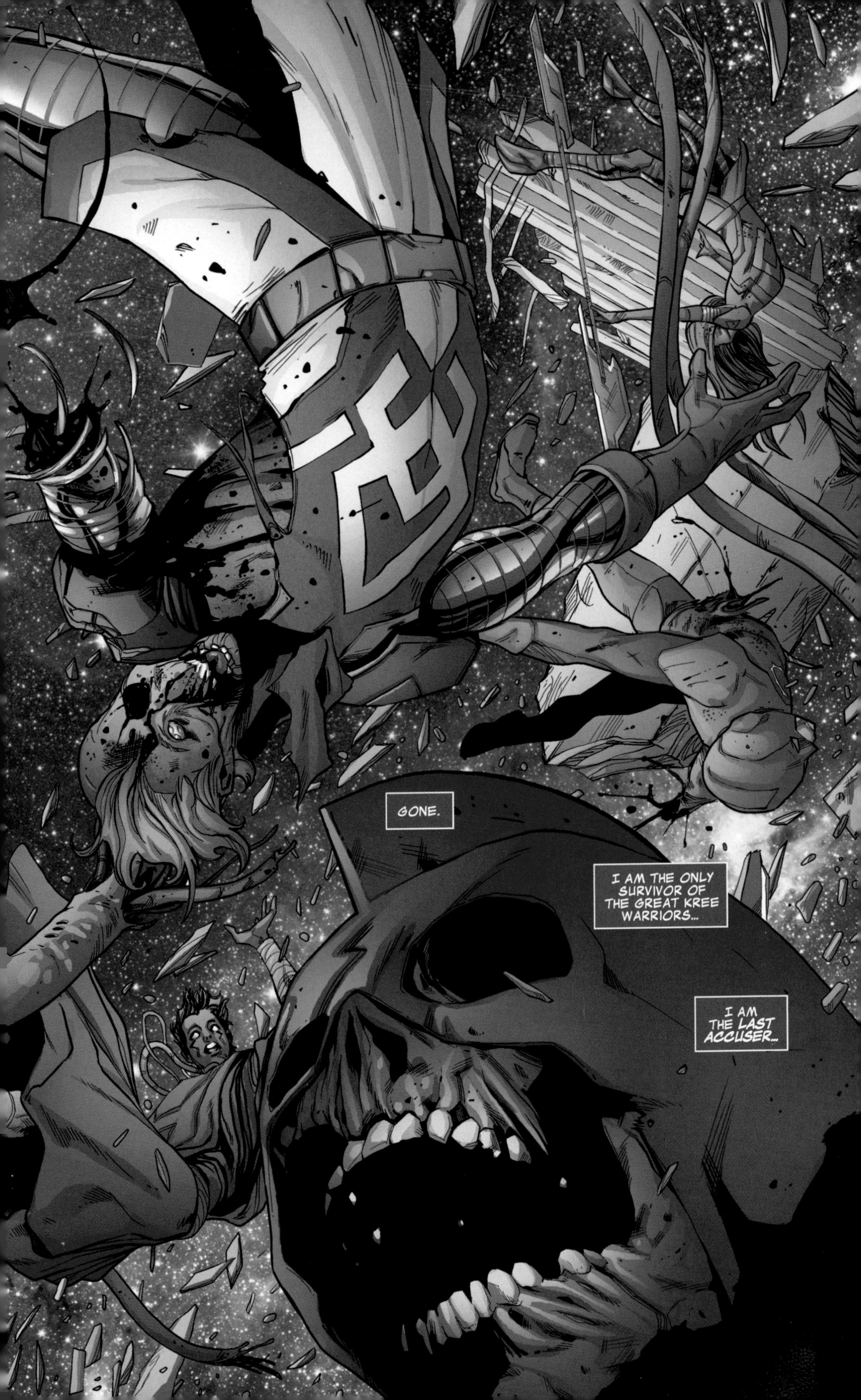
GONE.
I AM THE ONLY SURVIVOR OF THE GREAT KREE WARRIORS...
I AM THE LAST ACCUSER...

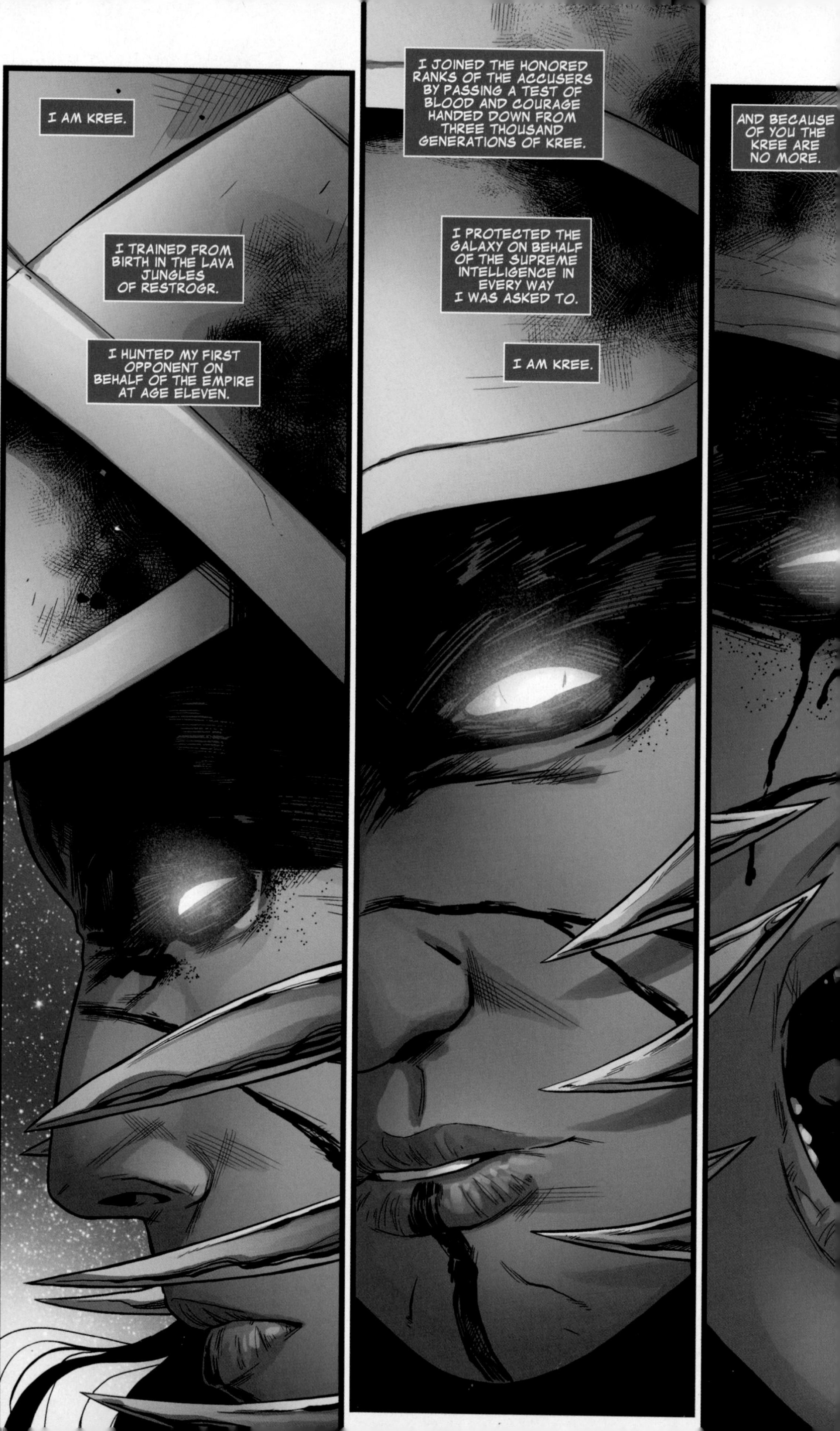
I AM KREE.
I TRAINED FROM BIRTH IN THE LAVA JUNGLES OF RESTROGR.
I HUNTED MY FIRST OPPONENT ON BEHALF OF THE EMPIRE AT AGE ELEVEN.
I JOINED THE HONORED RANKS OF THE ACCUSERS BY PASSING A TEST OF BLOOD AND COURAGE HANDED DOWN FROM THREE THOUSAND GENERATIONS OF KREE.
I PROTECTED THE GALAXY ON BEHALF OF THE SUPREME INTELLIGENCE IN EVERY WAY I WAS ASKED TO.
I AM KREE.
AND BECAUSE OF YOU THE KREE ARE NO MORE.

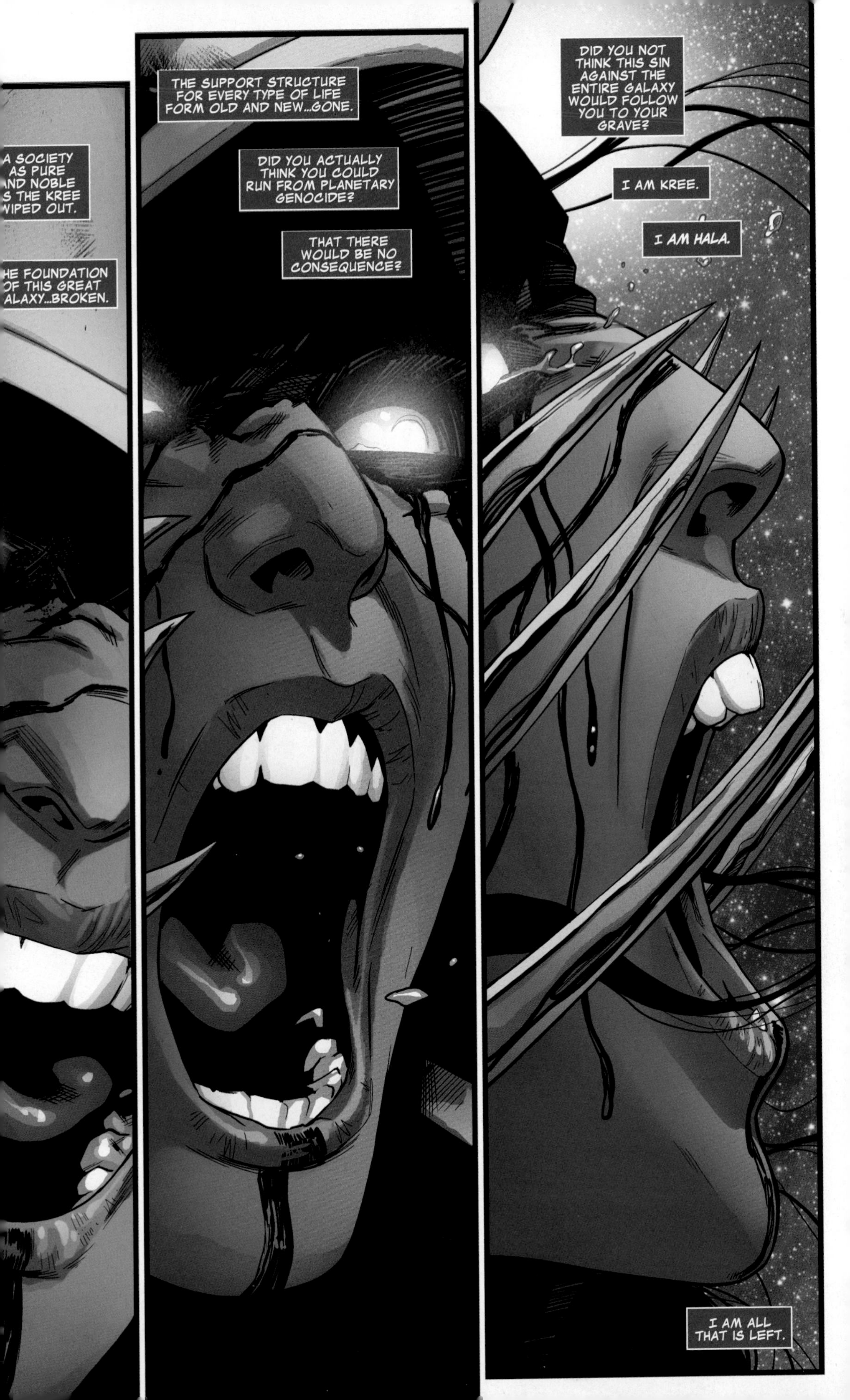
A SOCIETY AS PURE AND NOBLE S THE KREE WIPED OUT.
HE FOUNDATION OF THIS GREAT ALAXY...BROKEN.
THE SUPPORT STRUCTURE FOR EVERY TYPE OF LIFE FORM OLD AND NEW...GONE.
DID YOU ACTUALLY THINK YOU COULD RUN FROM PLANETARY GENOCIDE?
THAT THERE WOULD BE NO CONSEQUENCE?
DID YOU NOT THINK THIS SIN AGAINST THE ENTIRE GALAXY WOULD FOLLOW YOU TO YOUR GRAVE?
I AM KREE.
I AM HALA.
I AM ALL THAT IS LEFT.

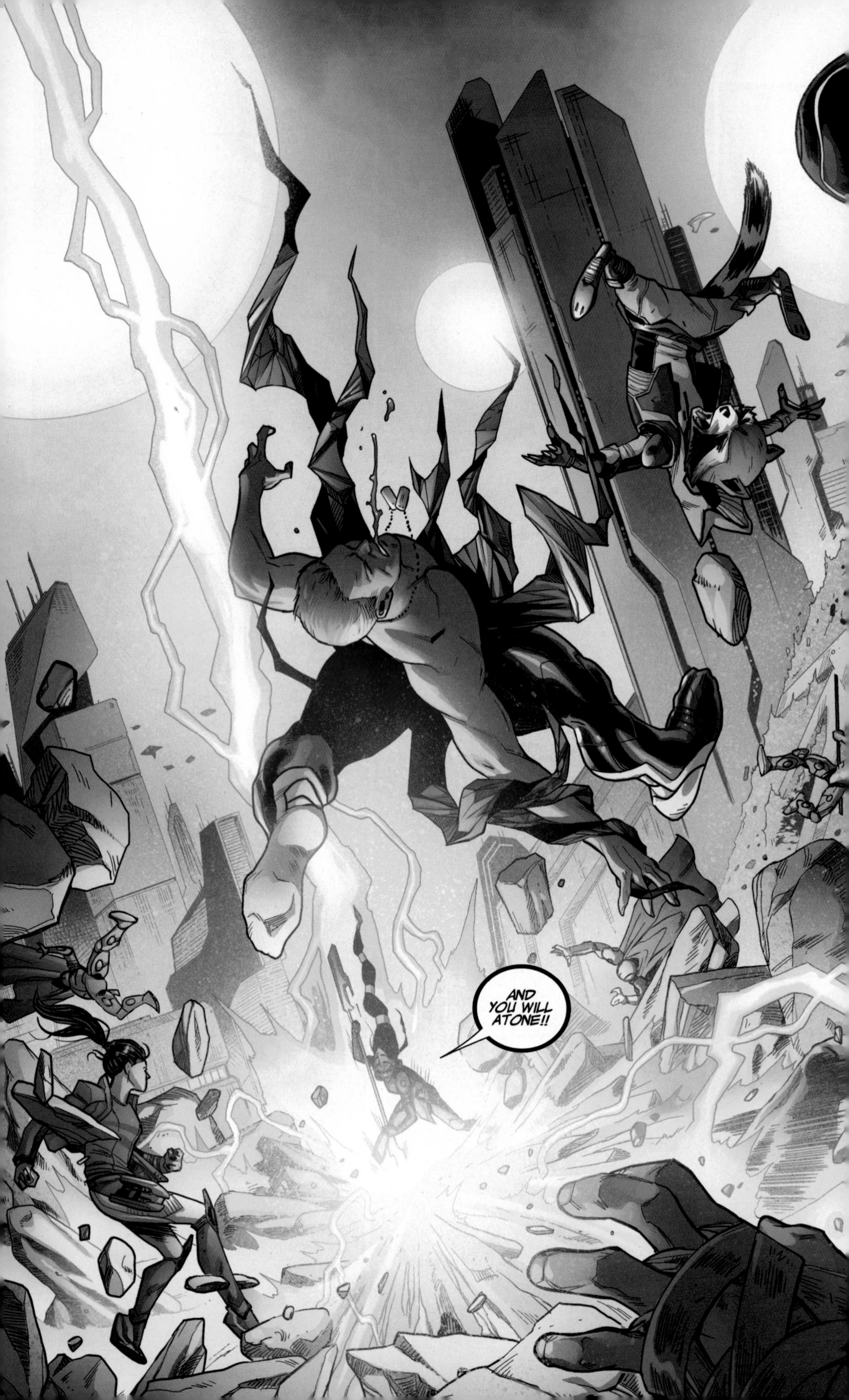
AND YOU WILL ATONE!!

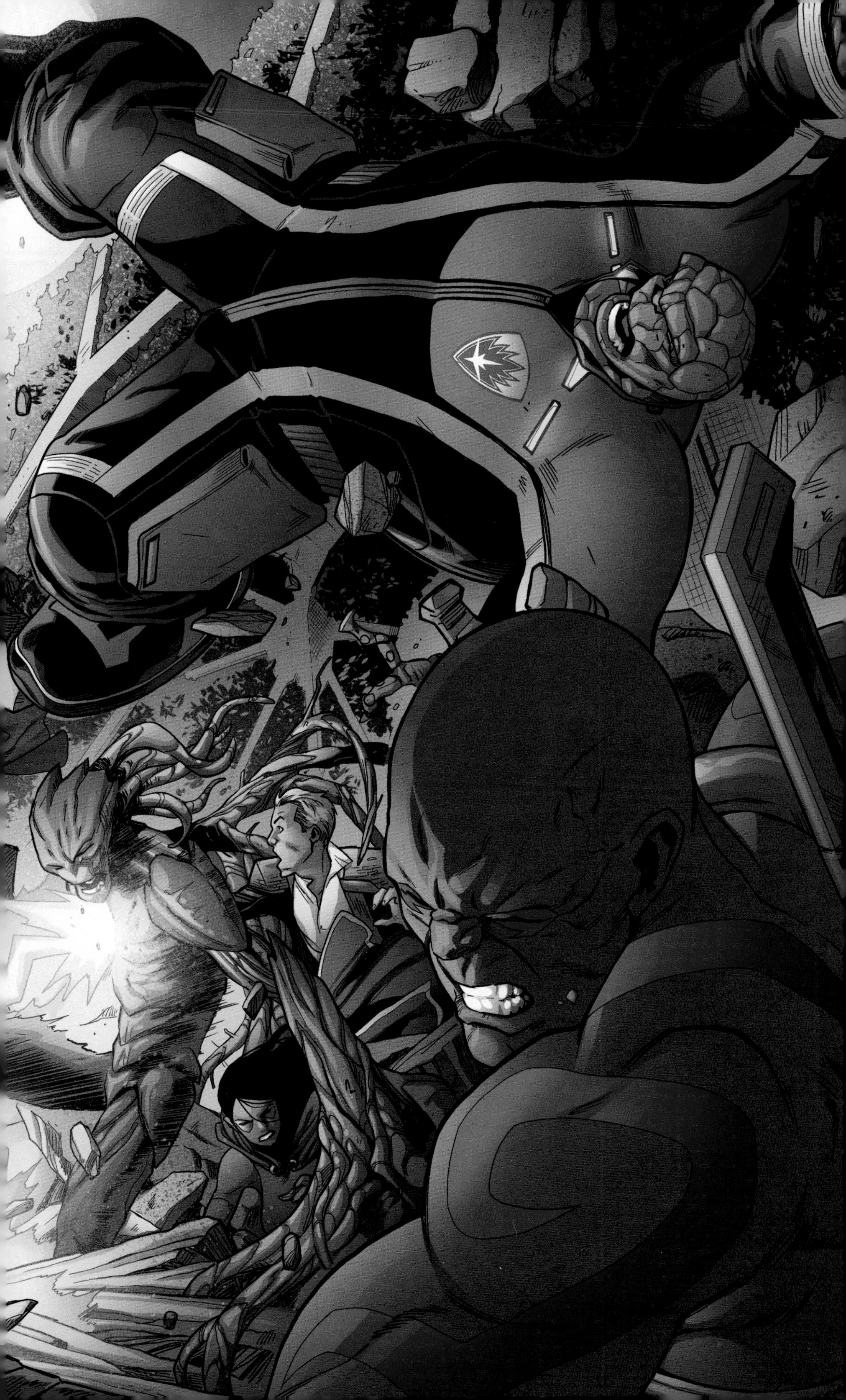

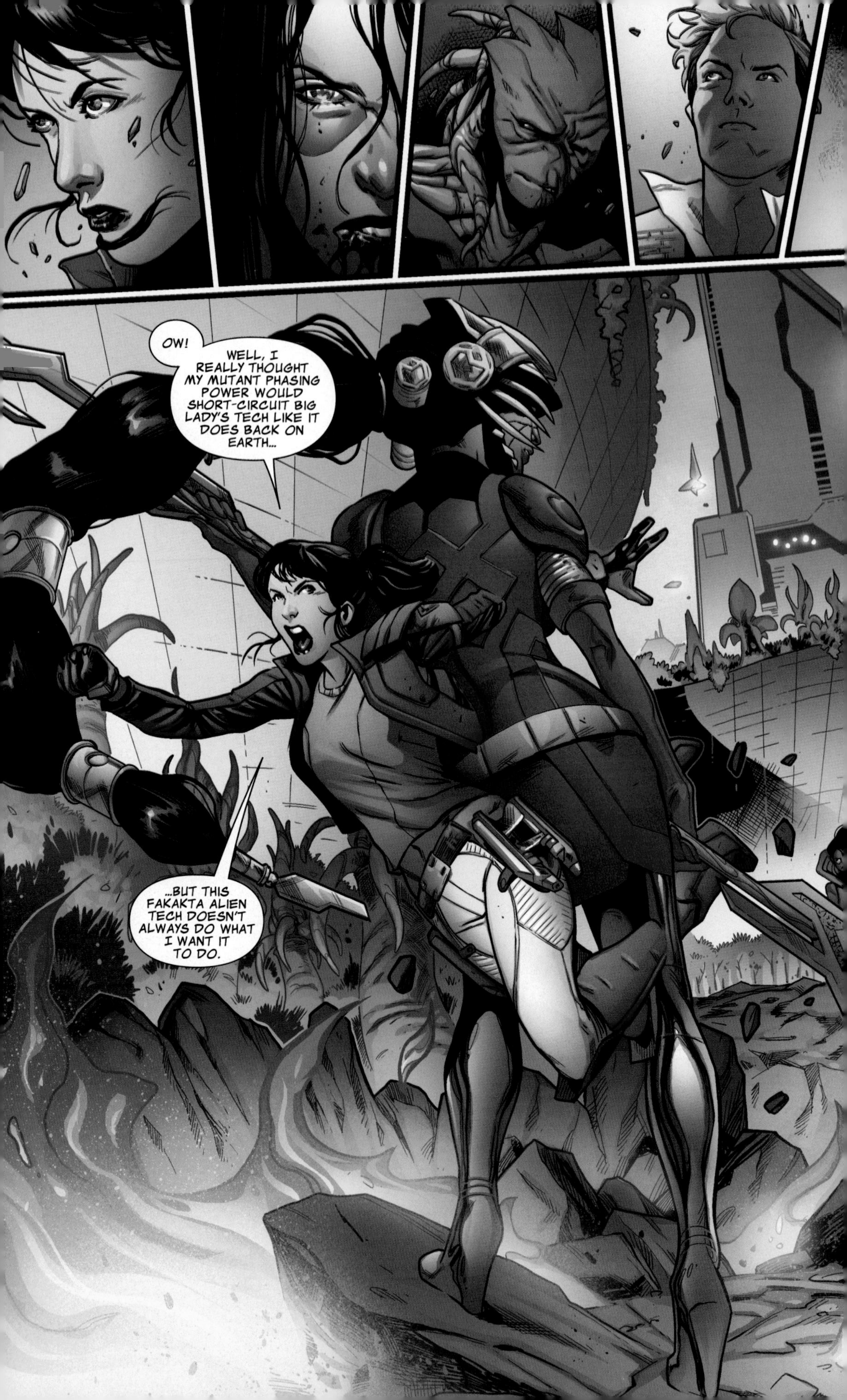
OW!
WELL, I REALLY THOUGHT MY MUTANT PHASING POWER WOULD SHORT-CIRCUIT BIG LADY'S TECH LIKE IT DOES BACK ON EARTH...
...BUT THIS FAKAKTA ALIEN TECH DOESN'T ALWAYS DO WHAT I WANT IT TO DO.

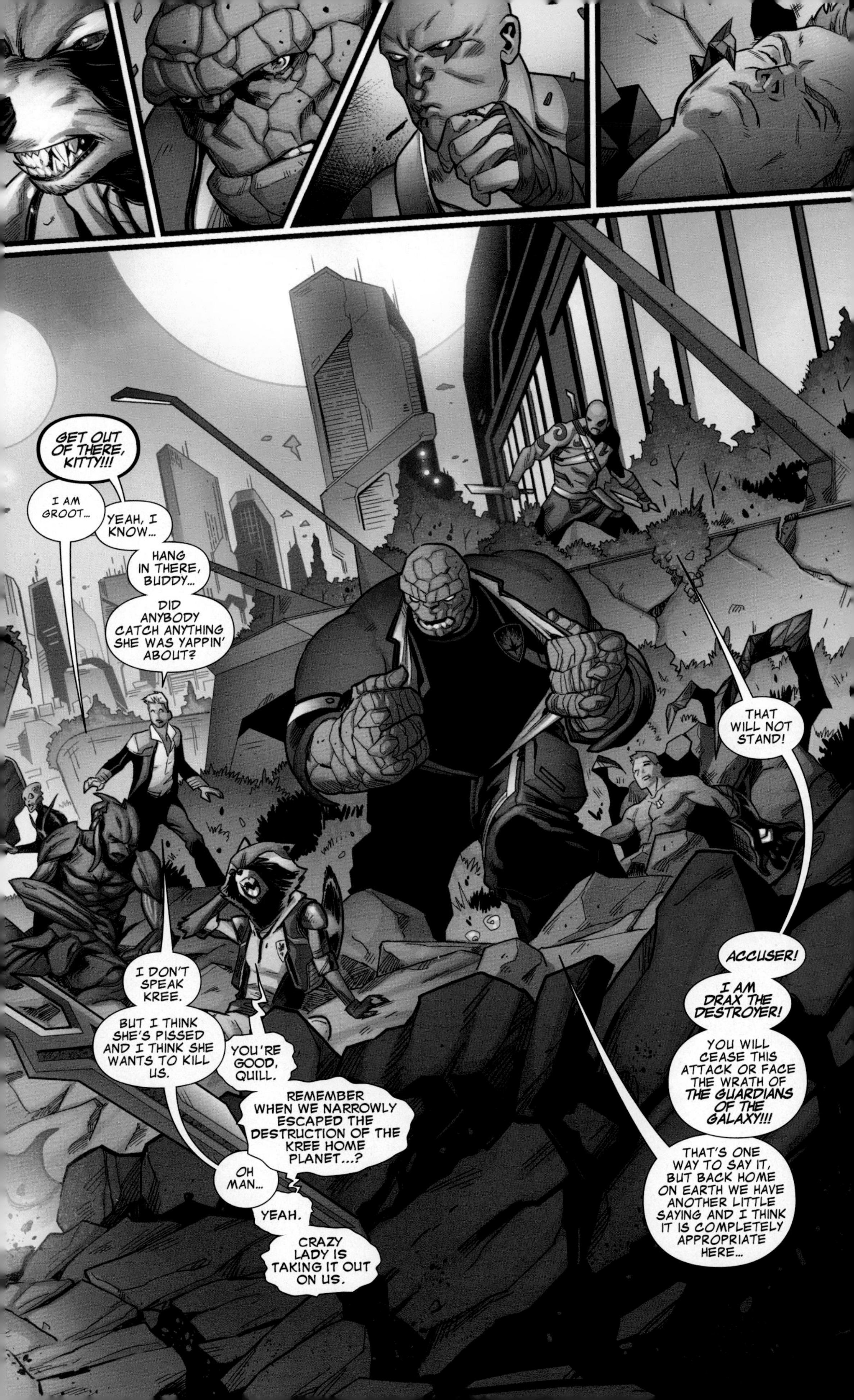
GET OUT OF THERE, KITTY!!!
I AM GROOT...
YEAH, I KNOW...
HANG IN THERE, BUDDY...
DID ANYBODY CATCH ANYTHING SHE WAS YAPPIN' ABOUT?
THAT WILL NOT STAND!
I DON'T SPEAK KREE.
BUT I THINK SHE'S PISSED AND I THINK SHE WANTS TO KILL US.
YOU'RE GOOD, QUILL.
REMEMBER WHEN WE NARROWLY ESCAPED THE DESTRUCTION OF THE KREE HOME PLANET...?
OH MAN...
YEAH.
CRAZY LADY IS TAKING IT OUT ON US.
ACCUSER!
I AM DRAX THE DESTROYER!
YOU WILL CEASE THIS ATTACK OR FACE THE WRATH OF THE GUARDIANS OF THE GALAXY!!!
THAT'S ONE WAY TO SAY IT, BUT BACK HOME ON EARTH WE HAVE ANOTHER LITTLE SAYING AND I THINK IT IS COMPLETELY APPROPRIATE HERE...

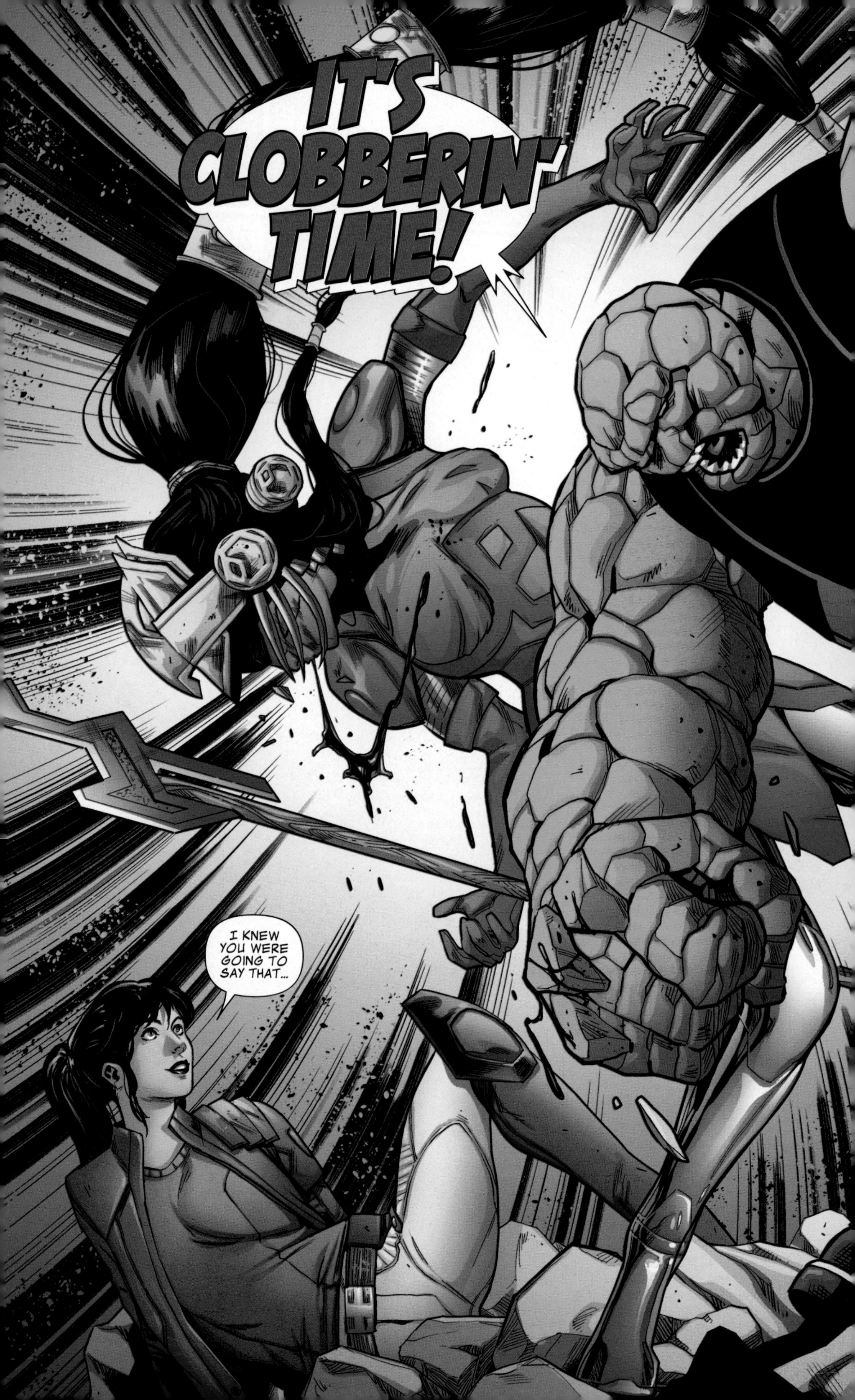
IT'S CLOBBERIN' TIME!
I KNEW YOU WERE GOING TO SAY THAT...

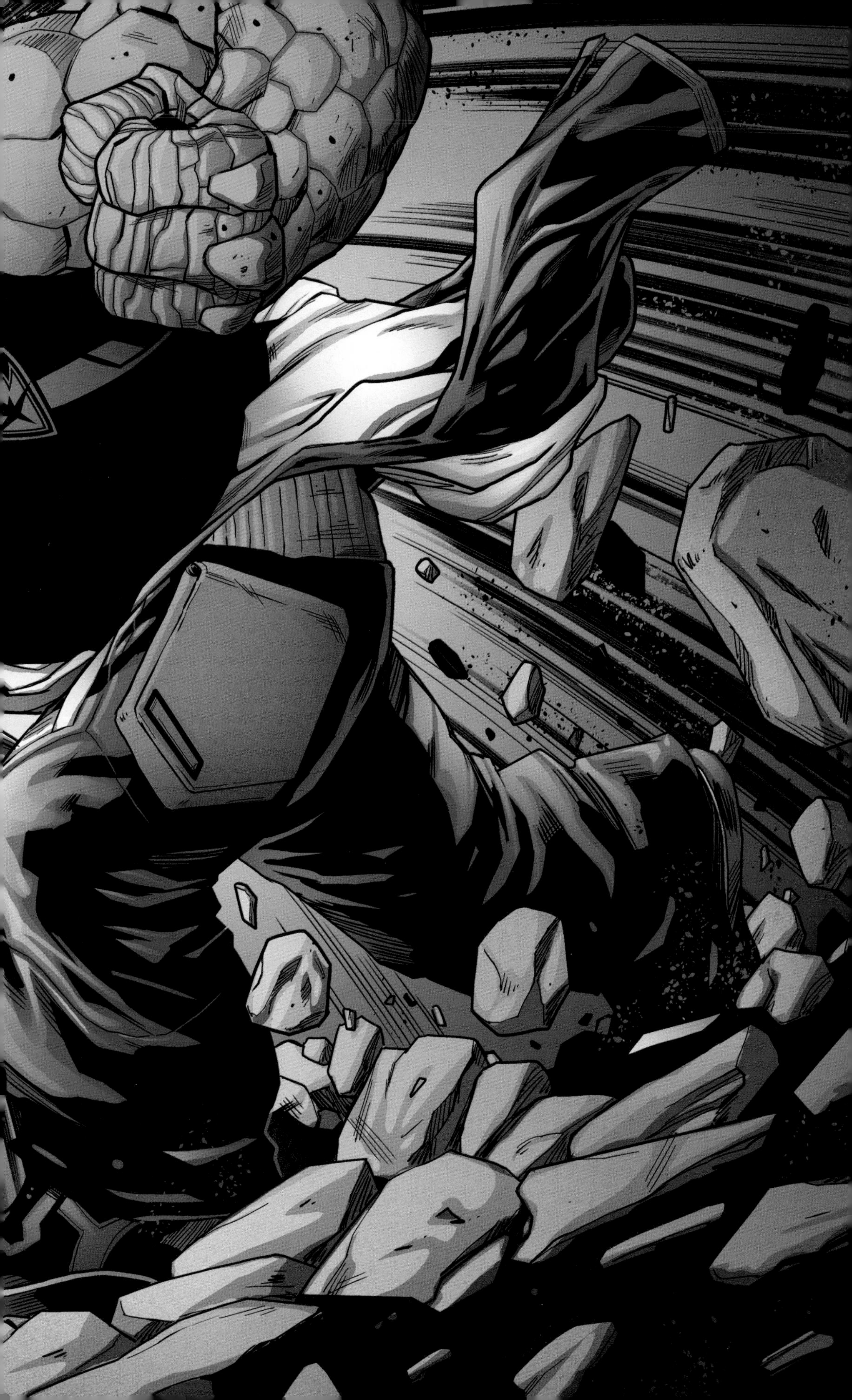

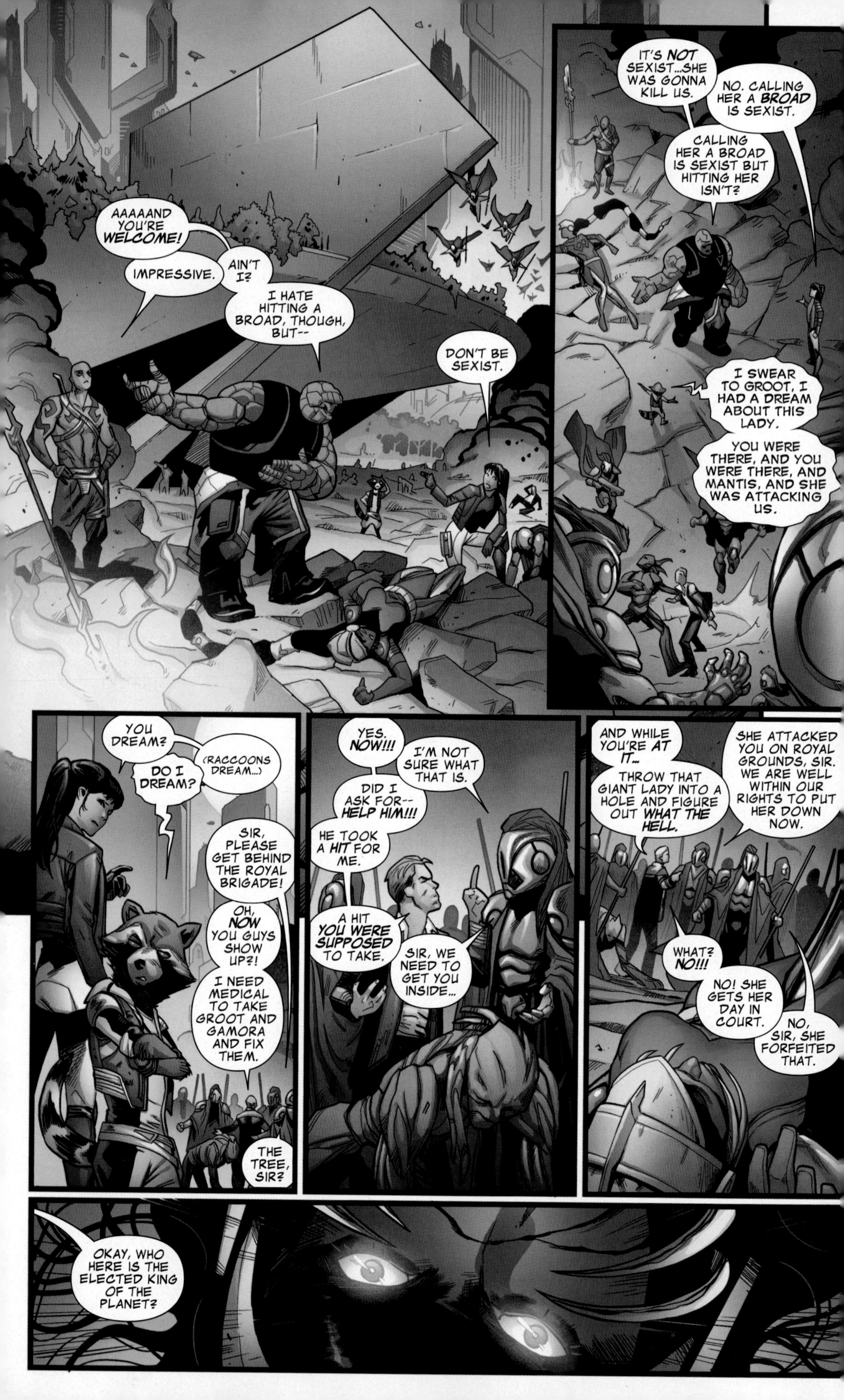
AAAAAND YOU'RE WELCOME!
IMPRESSIVE.
AIN'T I?
I HATE HITTING A BROAD, THOUGH, BUT--
DON'T BE SEXIST.
IT'S NOT SEXIST...SHE WAS GONNA KILL US.
NO. CALLING HER A BROAD IS SEXIST.
CALLING HER A BROAD IS SEXIST BUT HITTING HER ISN'T?
I SWEAR TO GROOT, I HAD A DREAM ABOUT THIS LADY.
YOU WERE THERE, AND YOU WERE THERE, AND MANTIS, AND SHE WAS ATTACKING US.
YOU DREAM?
(RACCOONS DREAM...)
DO I DREAM?
SIR, PLEASE GET BEHIND THE ROYAL BRIGADE!
OH, NOW YOU GUYS SHOW UP?!
I NEED MEDICAL TO TAKE GROOT AND GAMORA AND FIX THEM.
THE TREE, SIR?
YES. NOW!!!
I'M NOT SURE WHAT THAT IS.
DID I ASK FOR-- HELP HIM!!!
HE TOOK A HIT FOR ME.
A HIT YOU WERE SUPPOSED TO TAKE.
SIR, WE NEED TO GET YOU INSIDE...
AND WHILE YOU'RE AT IT...
THROW THAT GIANT LADY INTO A HOLE AND FIGURE OUT WHAT THE HELL.
SHE ATTACKED YOU ON ROYAL GROUNDS, SIR. WE ARE WELL WITHIN OUR RIGHTS TO PUT HER DOWN NOW.
WHAT? NO!!!
NO! SHE GETS HER DAY IN COURT.
NO, SIR, SHE FORFEITED THAT.
OKAY, WHO HERE IS THE ELECTED KING OF THE PLANET?

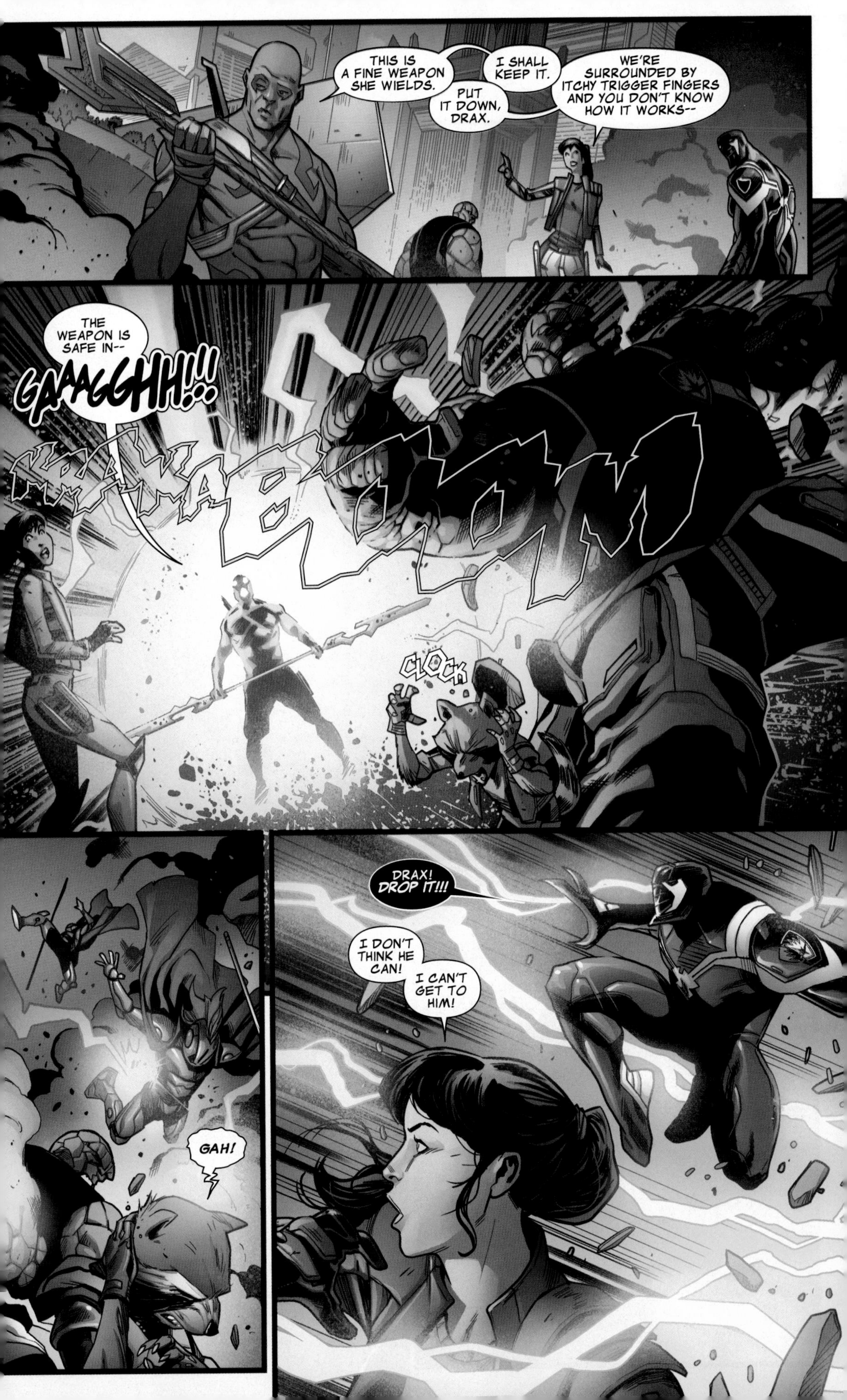
THIS IS A FINE WEAPON SHE WIELDS.
I SHALL KEEP IT.
PUT IT DOWN, DRAX.
WE'RE SURROUNDED BY ITCHY TRIGGER FINGERS AND YOU DON'T KNOW HOW IT WORKS--
THE WEAPON IS SAFE IN--
GAAAGGHH!!!
KRAKABOOM
CLOCK
GAH!
DRAX! DROP IT!!!
I DON'T THINK HE CAN!
I CAN'T GET TO HIM!

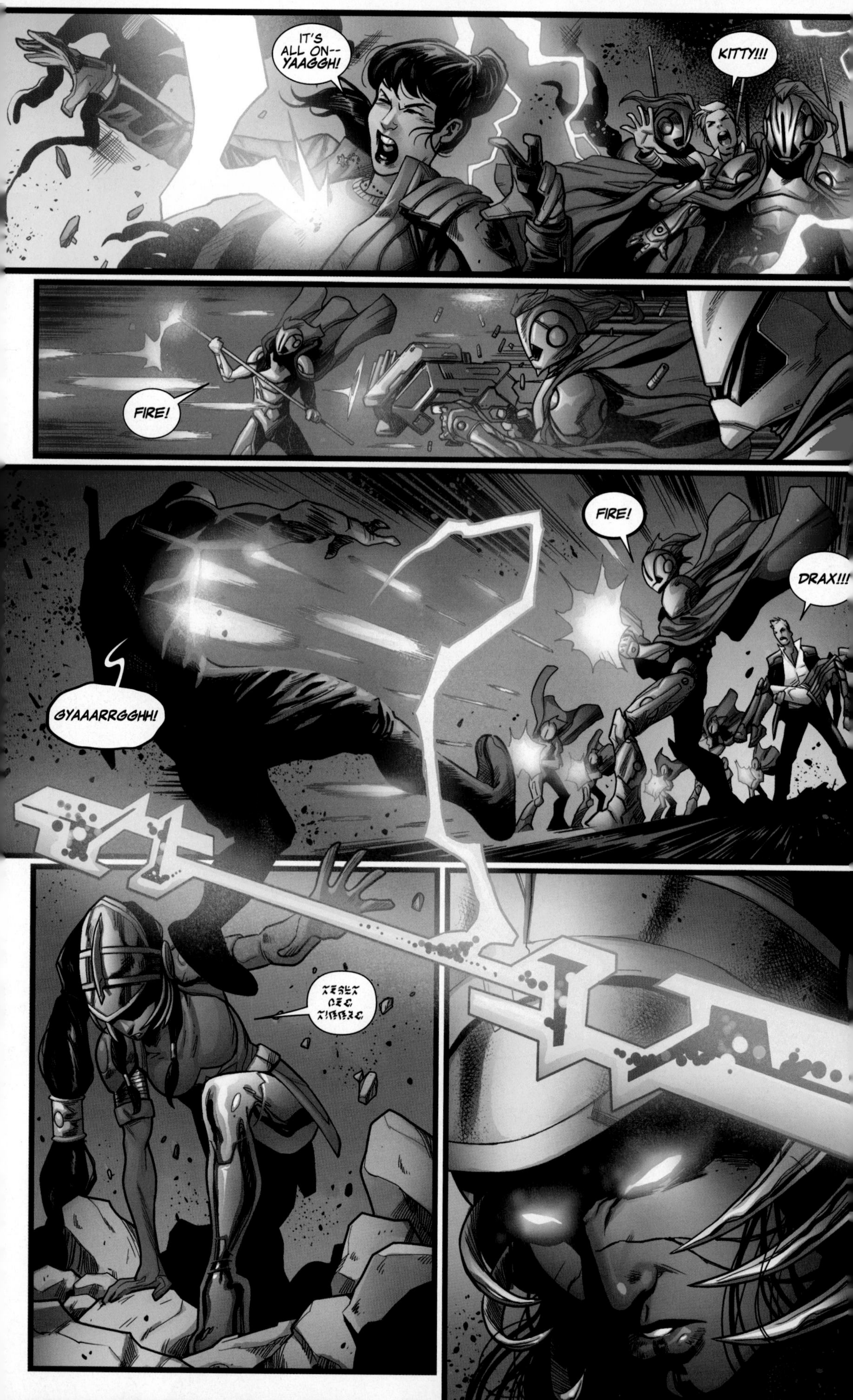
IT'S ALL ON-- YAAGGH!
KITTY!!!
FIRE!
FIRE!
DRAX!!!
GYAAARRGGHH!

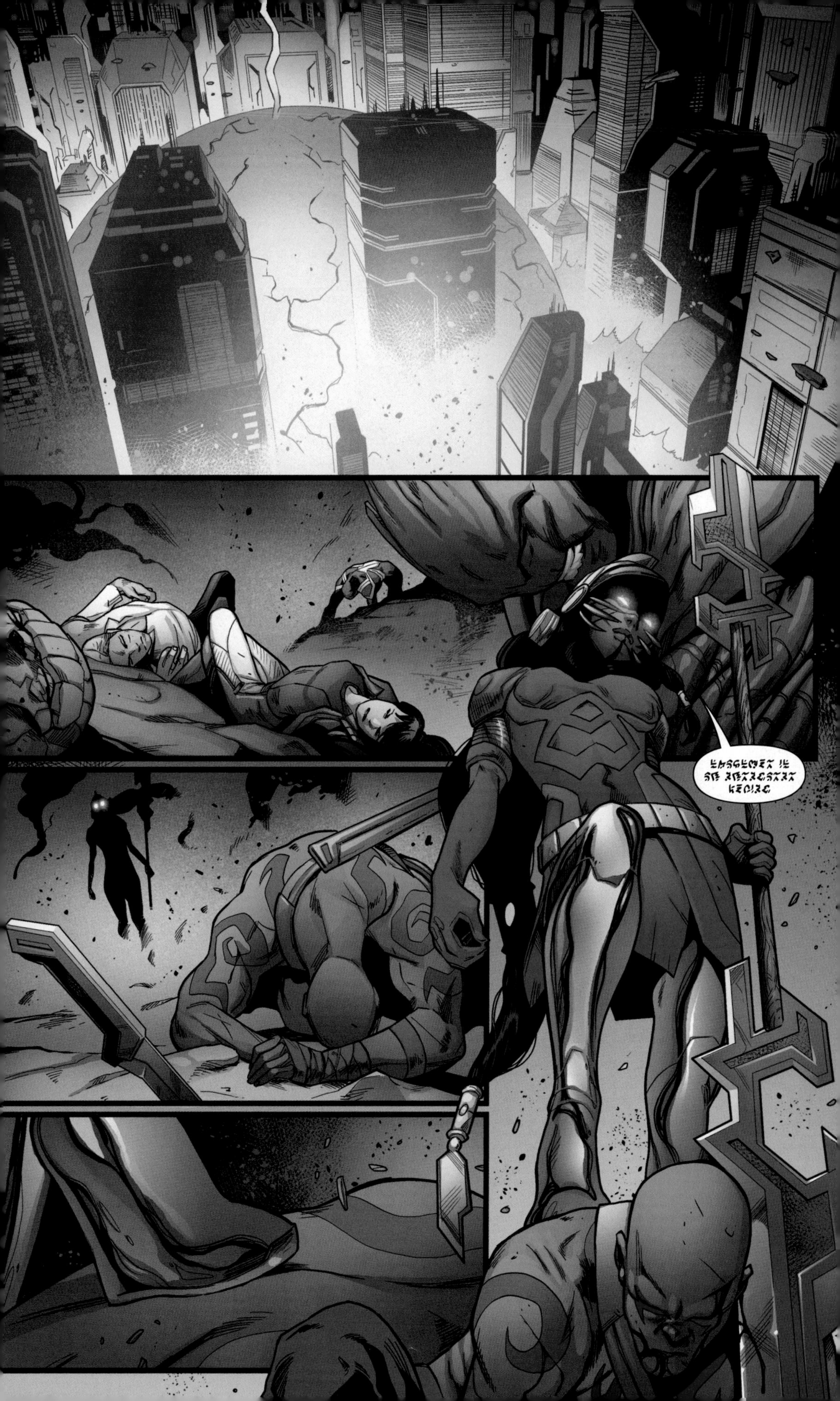

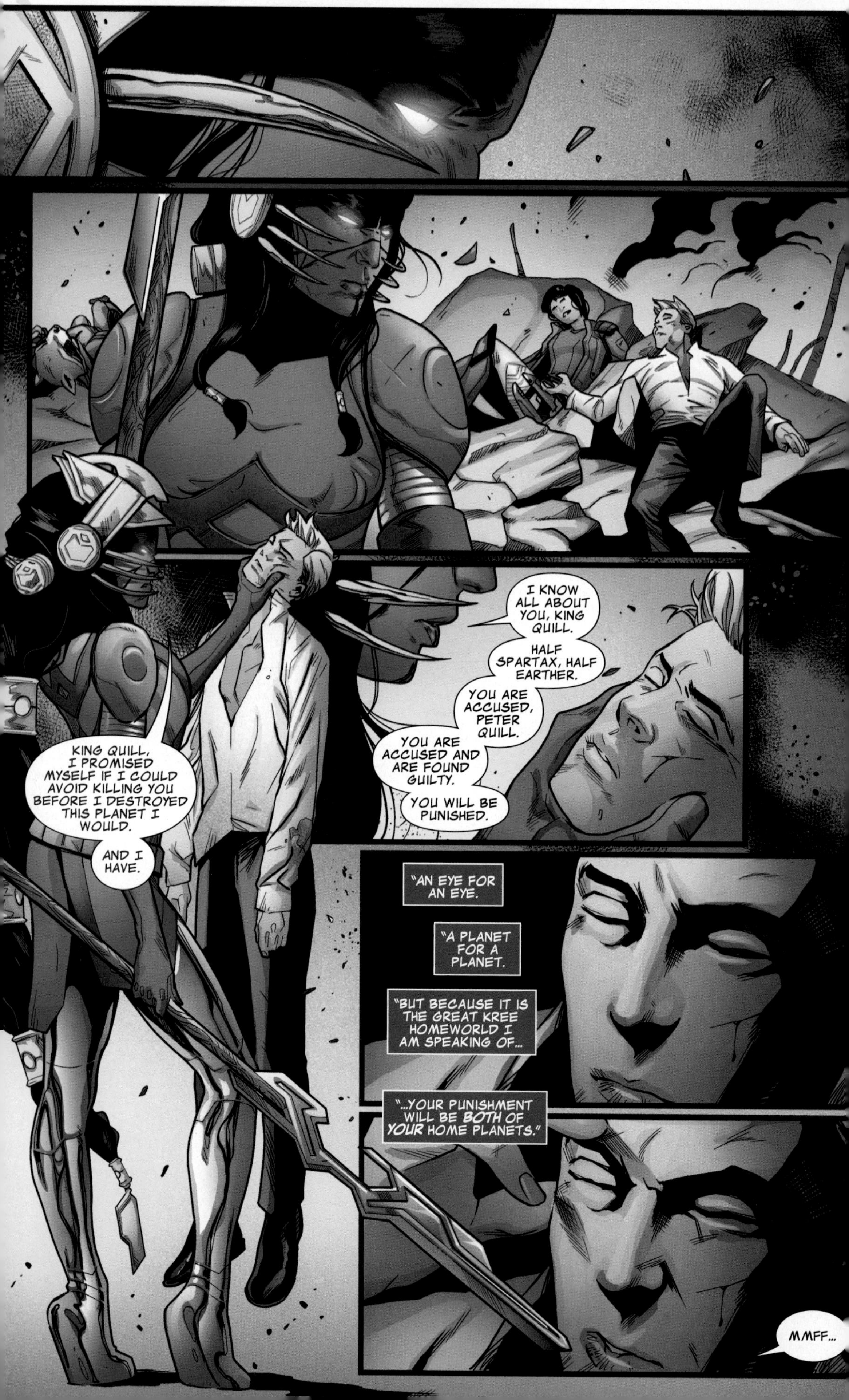
I KNOW ALL ABOUT YOU, KING QUILL.
HALF SPARTAX, HALF EARTHER.
YOU ARE ACCUSED, PETER QUILL.
YOU ARE ACCUSED AND ARE FOUND GUILTY.
YOU WILL BE PUNISHED.
KING QUILL, I PROMISED MYSELF IF I COULD AVOID KILLING YOU BEFORE I DESTROYED THIS PLANET I WOULD.
AND I HAVE.
"AN EYE FOR AN EYE.
"A PLANET FOR A PLANET.
"BUT BECAUSE IT IS THE GREAT KREE HOMEWORLD I AM SPEAKING OF...
"...YOUR PUNISHMENT WILL BE BOTH OF YOUR HOME PLANETS."
MMFF...

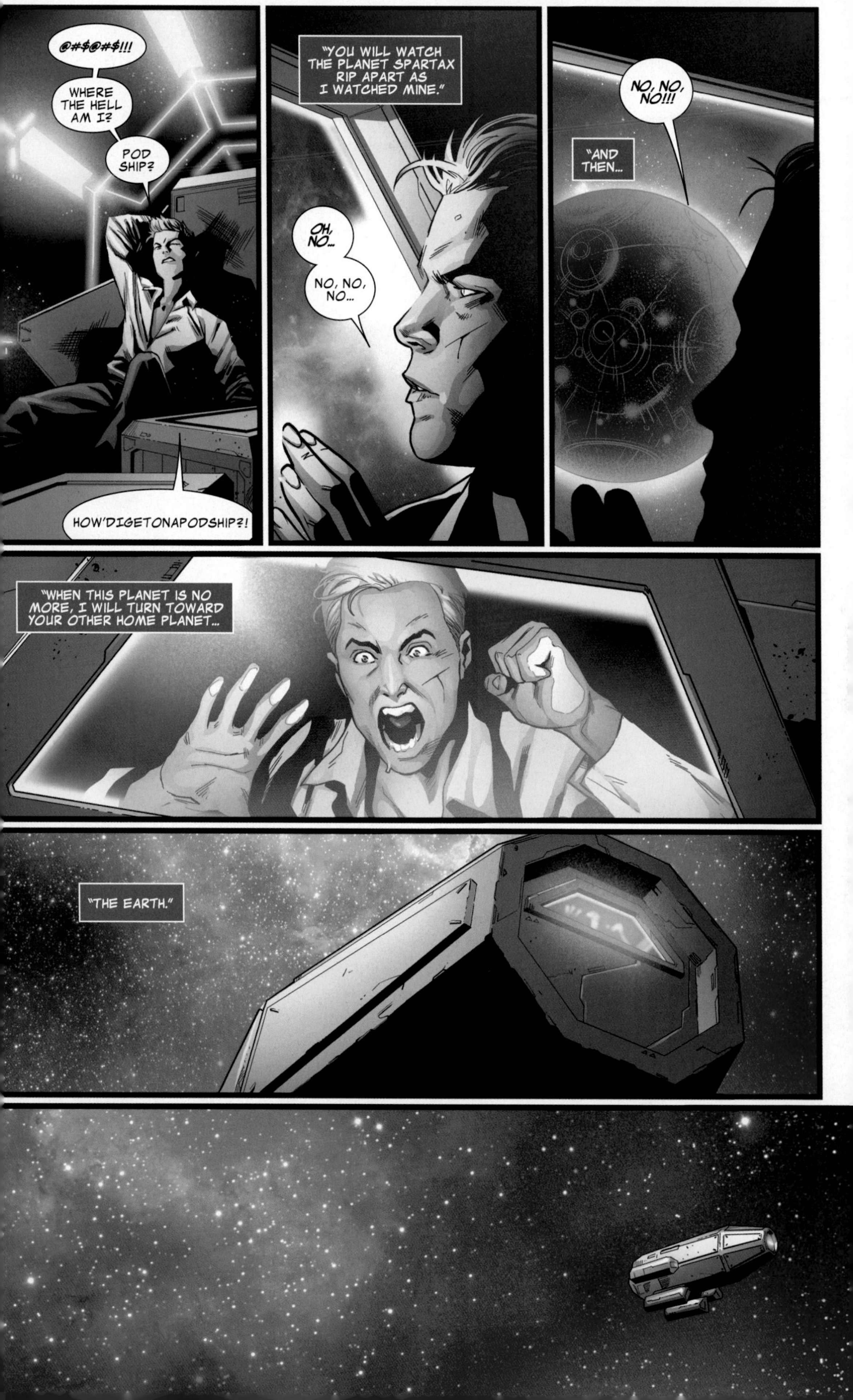
@#$@#$!!!
WHERE THE HELL AM I?
POD SHIP?
HOW'DIGETONAPODSHIP?!
"YOU WILL WATCH THE PLANET SPARTAX RIP APART AS I WATCHED MINE."
OH, NO...
NO, NO, NO...
"AND THEN...
NO, NO, NO!!!
"WHEN THIS PLANET IS NO MORE, I WILL TURN TOWARD YOUR OTHER HOME PLANET...
"THE EARTH."

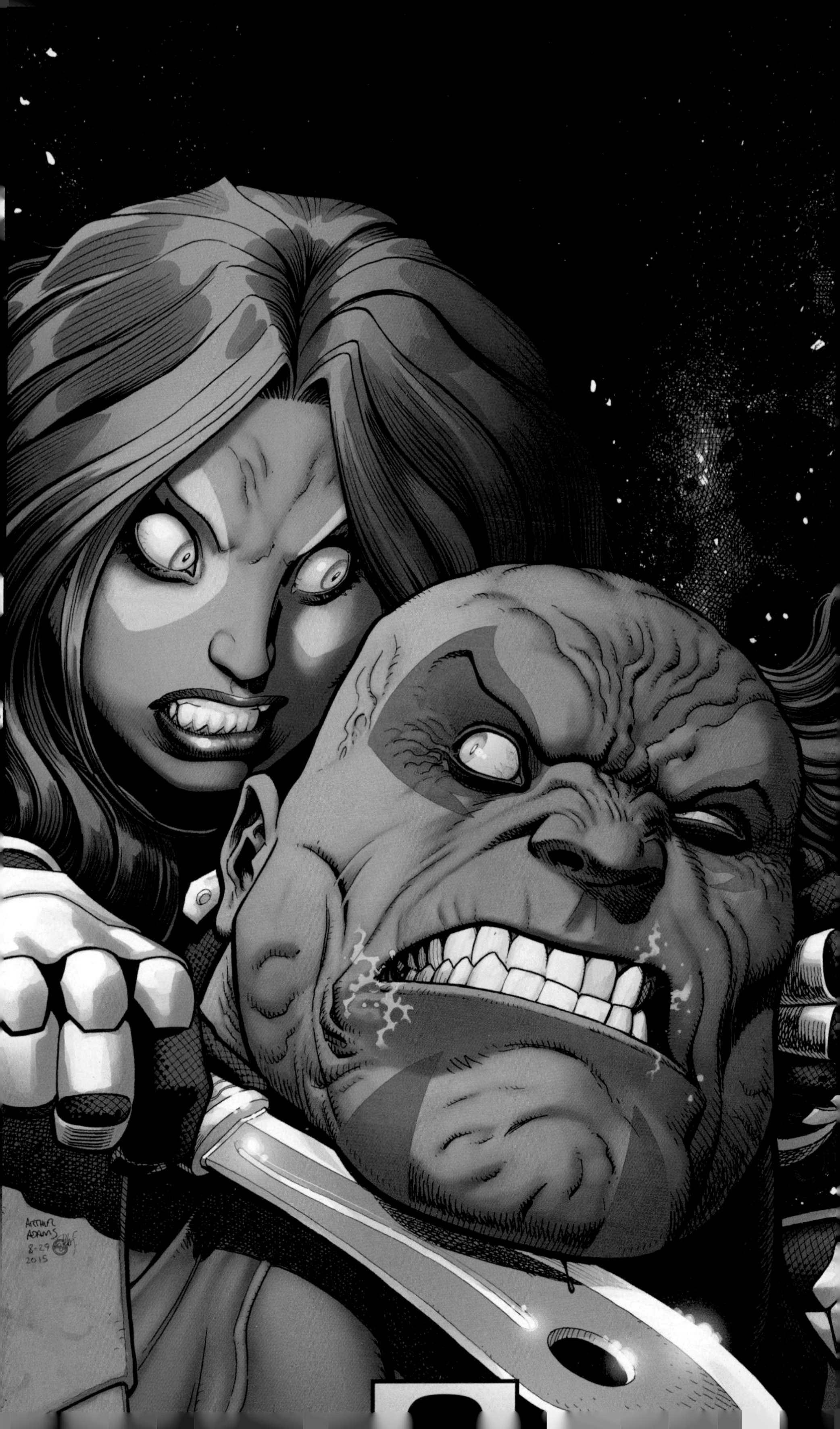
ARTHUR ADAMS
8-29
2015

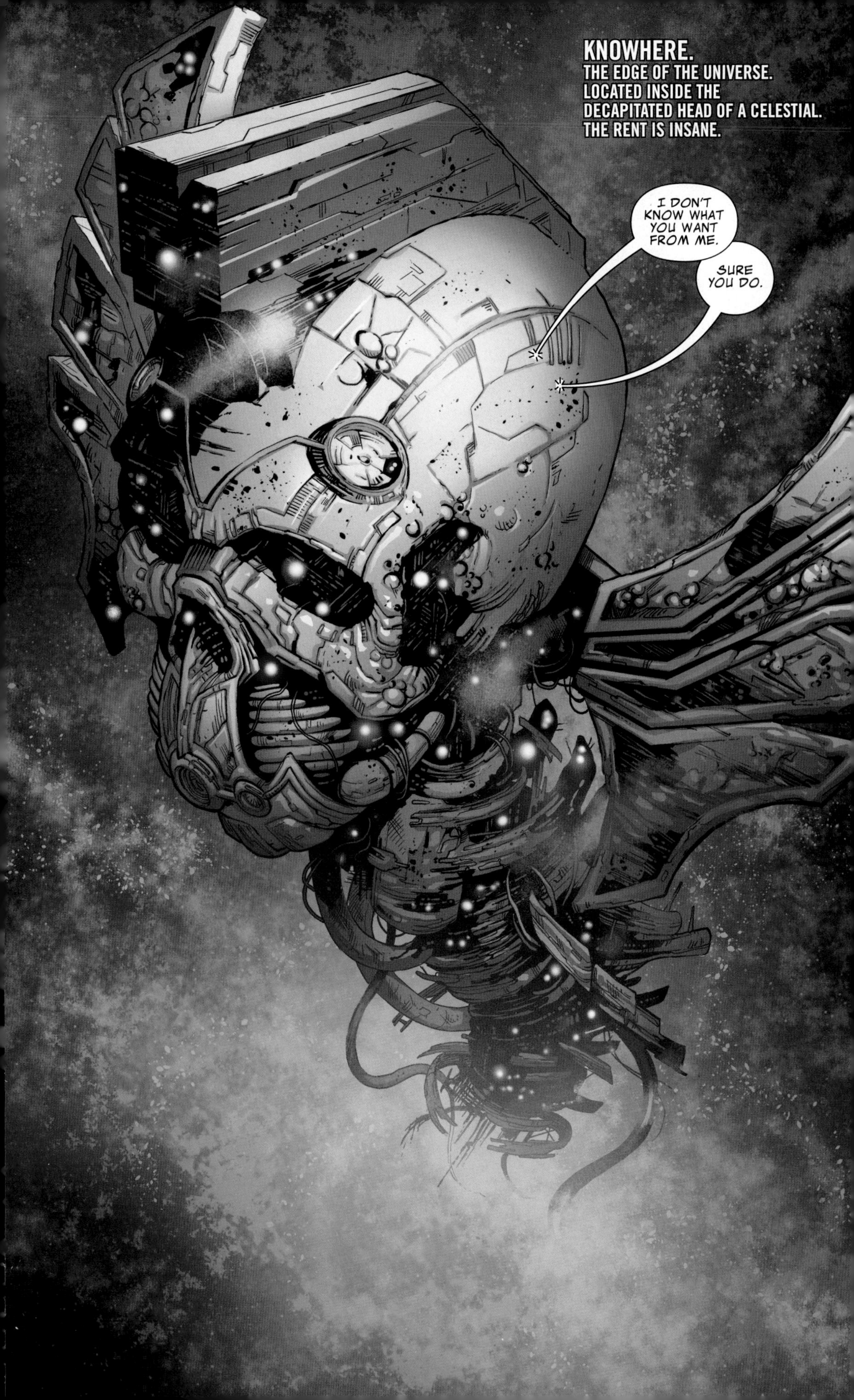
KNOWHERE.
THE EDGE OF THE UNIVERSE.
LOCATED INSIDE THE
DECAPITATED HEAD OF A CELESTIAL.
THE RENT IS INSANE.
I DON'T KNOW WHAT YOU WANT FROM ME.
SURE YOU DO.

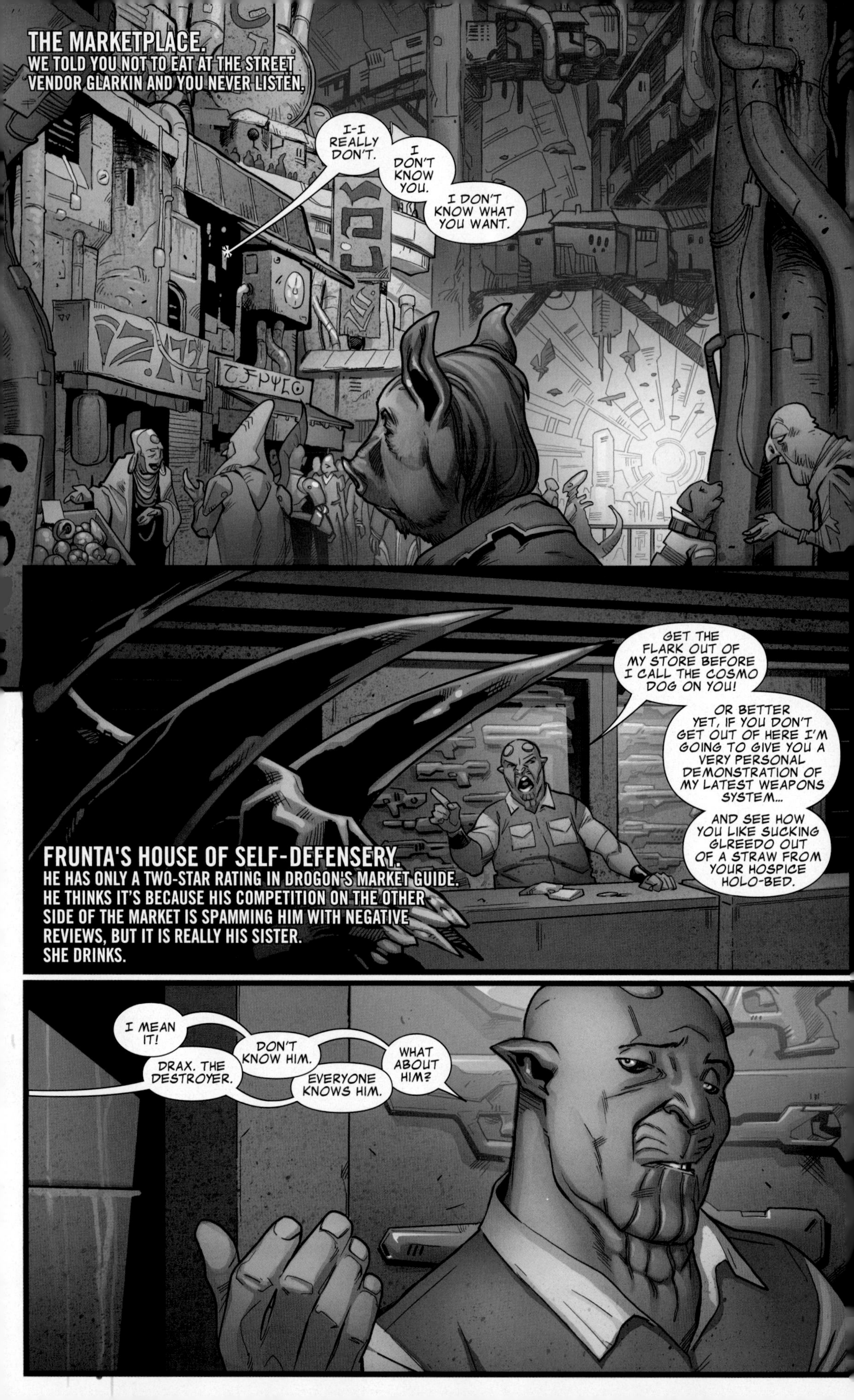
THE MARKETPLACE.
WE TOLD YOU NOT TO EAT AT THE STREET VENDOR GLARKIN AND YOU NEVER LISTEN.
I-I REALLY DON'T.
I DON'T KNOW YOU.
I DON'T KNOW WHAT YOU WANT.
FRUNTA'S HOUSE OF SELF-DEFENSERY.
HE HAS ONLY A TWO-STAR RATING IN DROGON'S MARKET GUIDE. HE THINKS IT'S BECAUSE HIS COMPETITION ON THE OTHER SIDE OF THE MARKET IS SPAMMING HIM WITH NEGATIVE REVIEWS, BUT IT IS REALLY HIS SISTER. SHE DRINKS.
GET THE FLARK OUT OF MY STORE BEFORE I CALL THE COSMO DOG ON YOU!
OR BETTER YET, IF YOU DON'T GET OUT OF HERE I'M GOING TO GIVE YOU A VERY PERSONAL DEMONSTRATION OF MY LATEST WEAPONS SYSTEM...
AND SEE HOW YOU LIKE SUCKING GLREEDO OUT OF A STRAW FROM YOUR HOSPICE HOLO-BED.
I MEAN IT!
DRAX. THE DESTROYER.
DON'T KNOW HIM.
EVERYONE KNOWS HIM.
WHAT ABOUT HIM?

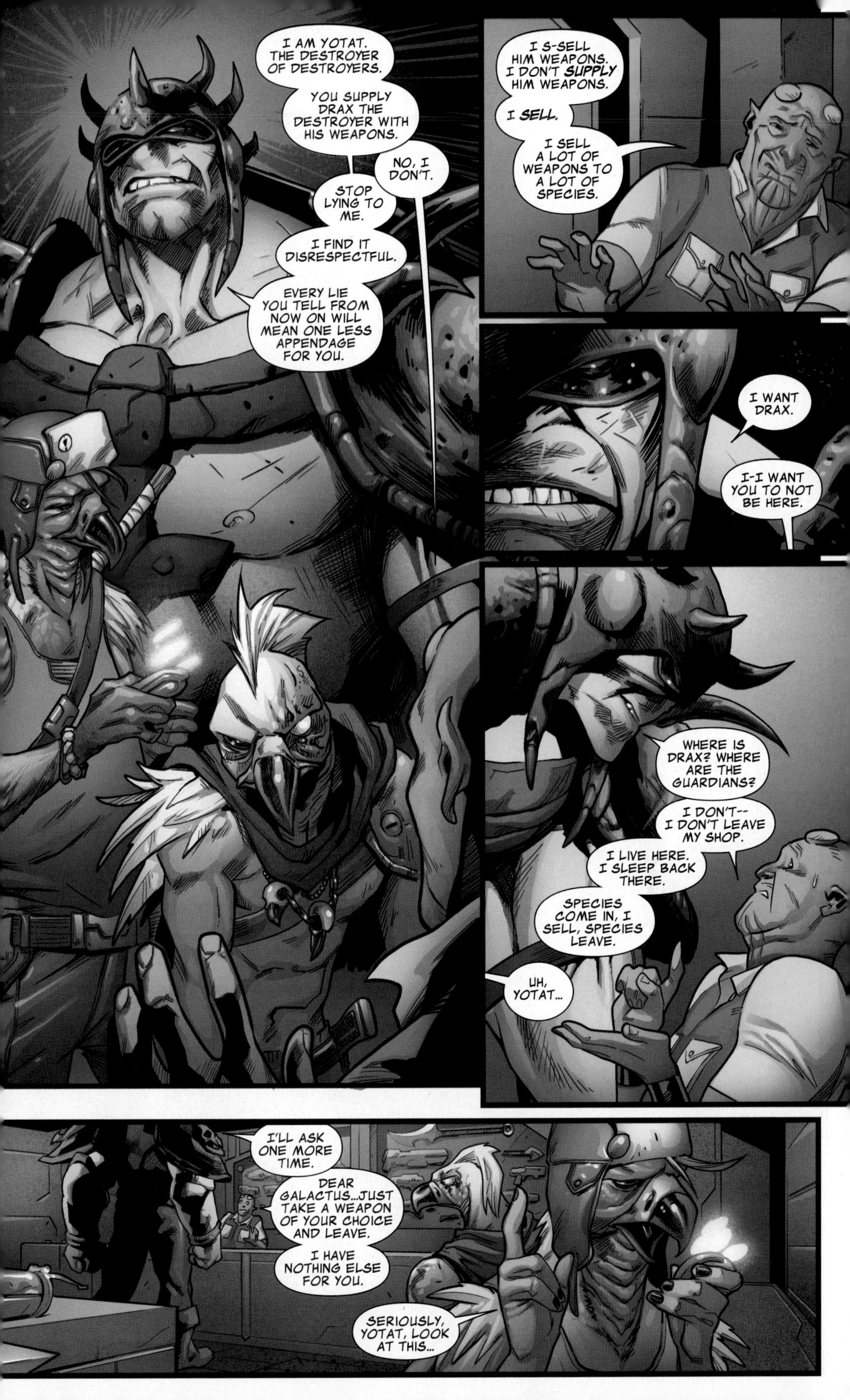
I AM YOTAT. THE DESTROYER OF DESTROYERS.
YOU SUPPLY DRAX THE DESTROYER WITH HIS WEAPONS.
NO, I DON'T.
STOP LYING TO ME.
I FIND IT DISRESPECTFUL.
EVERY LIE YOU TELL FROM NOW ON WILL MEAN ONE LESS APPENDAGE FOR YOU.
I S-SELL HIM WEAPONS. I DON'T SUPPLY HIM WEAPONS.
I SELL.
I SELL A LOT OF WEAPONS TO A LOT OF SPECIES.
I WANT DRAX.
I-I WANT YOU TO NOT BE HERE.
WHERE IS DRAX? WHERE ARE THE GUARDIANS?
I DON'T-- I DON'T LEAVE MY SHOP.
I LIVE HERE. I SLEEP BACK THERE.
SPECIES COME IN, I SELL, SPECIES LEAVE.
UH, YOTAT...
I'LL ASK ONE MORE TIME.
DEAR GALACTUS...JUST TAKE A WEAPON OF YOUR CHOICE AND LEAVE.
I HAVE NOTHING ELSE FOR YOU.
SERIOUSLY, YOTAT, LOOK AT THIS...

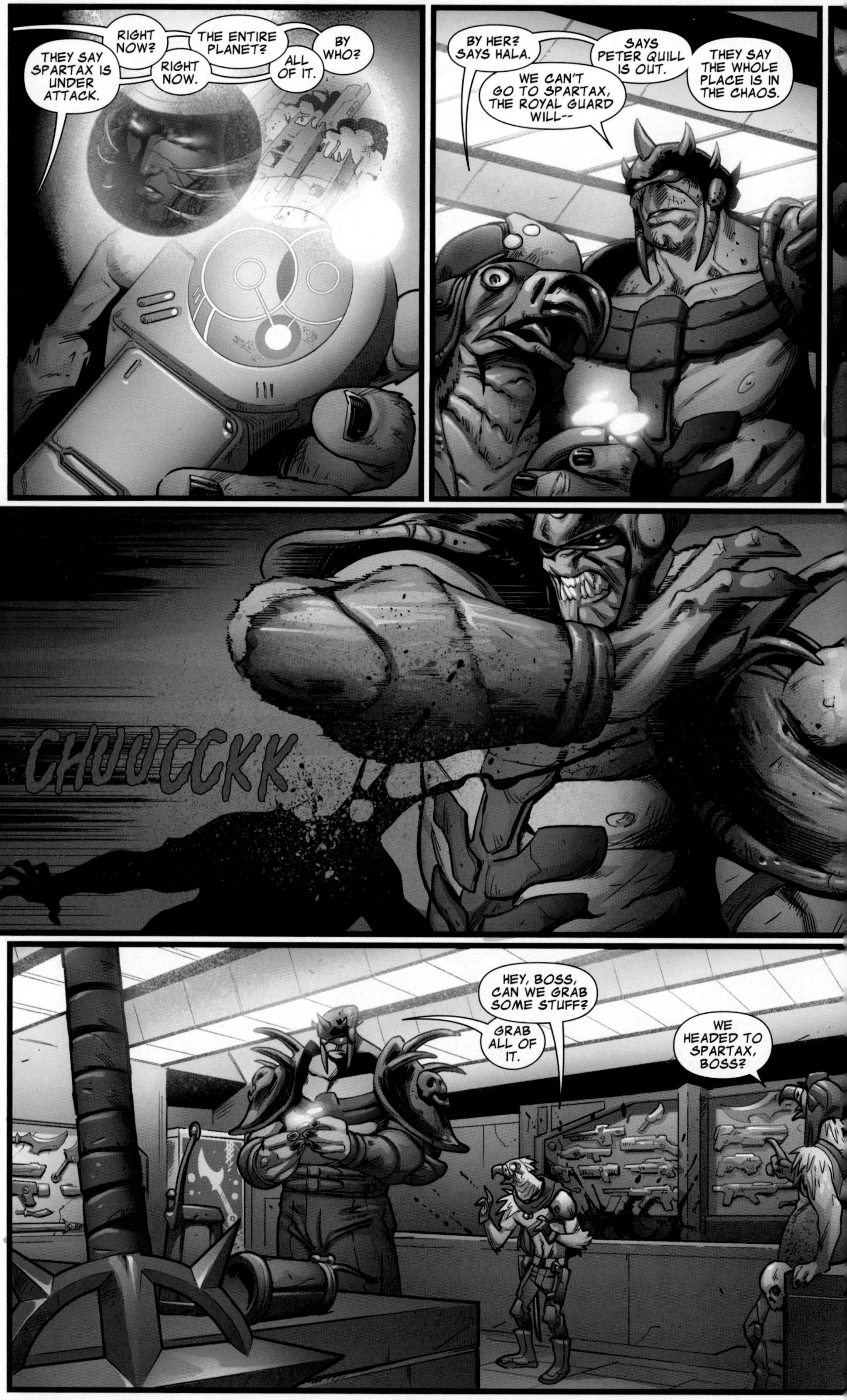
THEY SAY SPARTAX IS UNDER ATTACK.
RIGHT NOW?
RIGHT NOW.
THE ENTIRE PLANET?
ALL OF IT.
BY WHO?
BY HER? SAYS HALA.
WE CAN'T GO TO SPARTAX, THE ROYAL GUARD WILL--
SAYS PETER QUILL IS OUT.
THEY SAY THE WHOLE PLACE IS IN THE CHAOS.
CHUUCCKK
HEY, BOSS, CAN WE GRAB SOME STUFF?
GRAB ALL OF IT.
WE HEADED TO SPARTAX, BOSS?

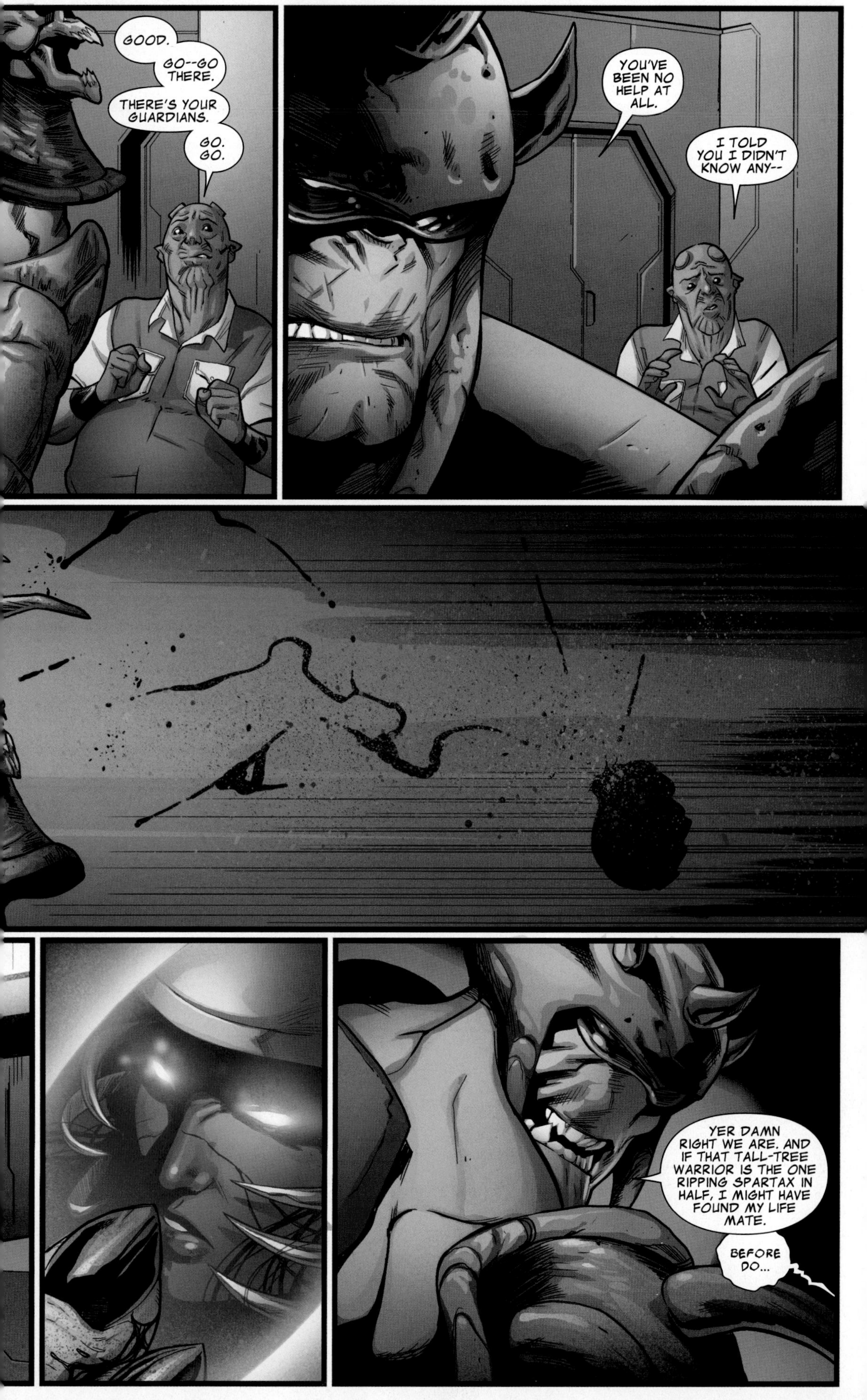
GOOD.
GO--GO THERE.
THERE'S YOUR GUARDIANS.
GO. GO.
YOU'VE BEEN NO HELP AT ALL.
I TOLD YOU I DIDN'T KNOW ANY--
YER DAMN RIGHT WE ARE. AND IF THAT TALL-TREE WARRIOR IS THE ONE RIPPING SPARTAX IN HALF, I MIGHT HAVE FOUND MY LIFE MATE.
BEFORE DO...

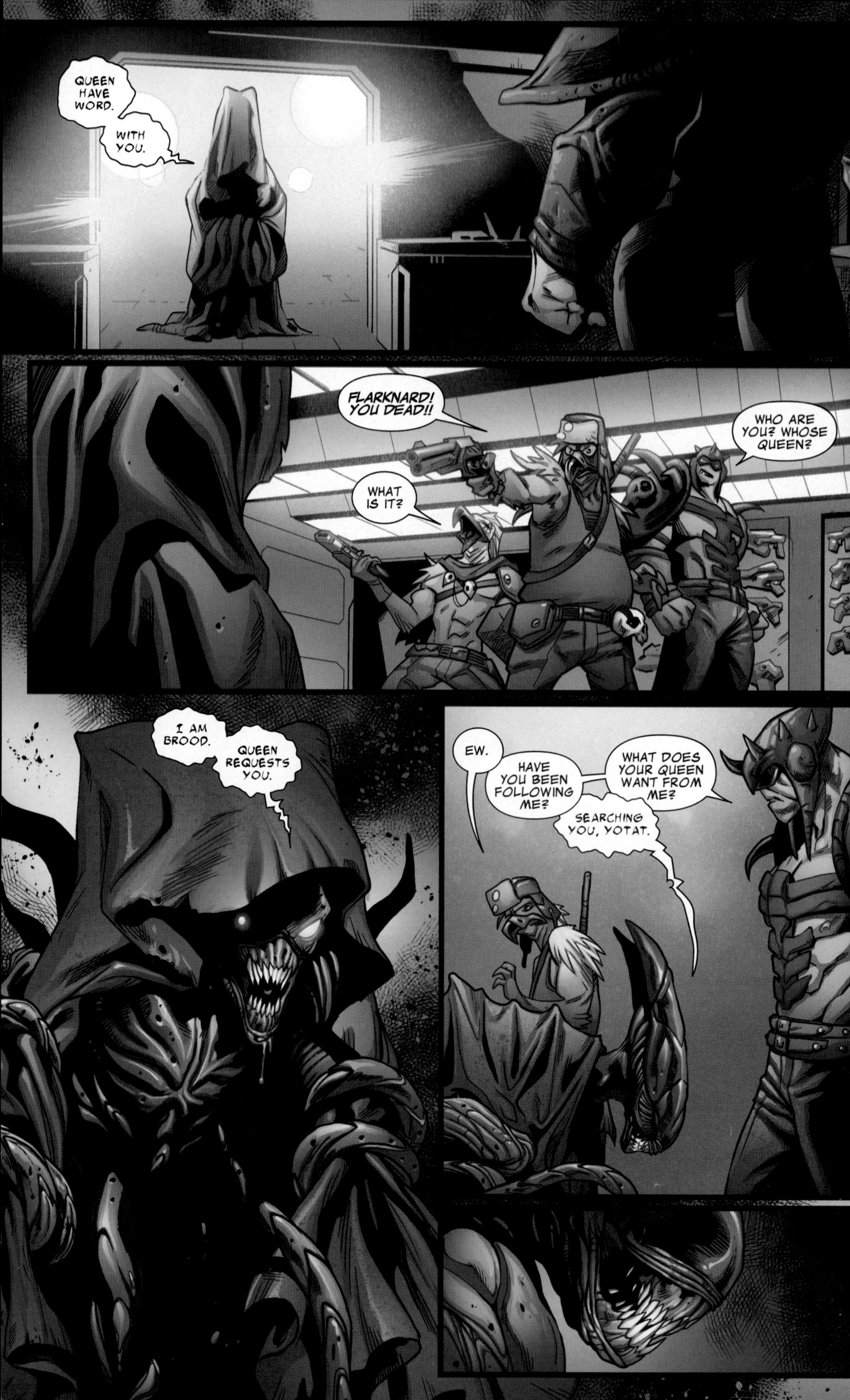
QUEEN HAVE WORD.
WITH YOU.
FLARKNARD! YOU DEAD!!
WHO ARE YOU? WHOSE QUEEN?
WHAT IS IT?
I AM BROOD.
QUEEN REQUESTS YOU.
EW.
HAVE YOU BEEN FOLLOWING ME?
WHAT DOES YOUR QUEEN WANT FROM ME?
SEARCHING YOU, YOTAT.

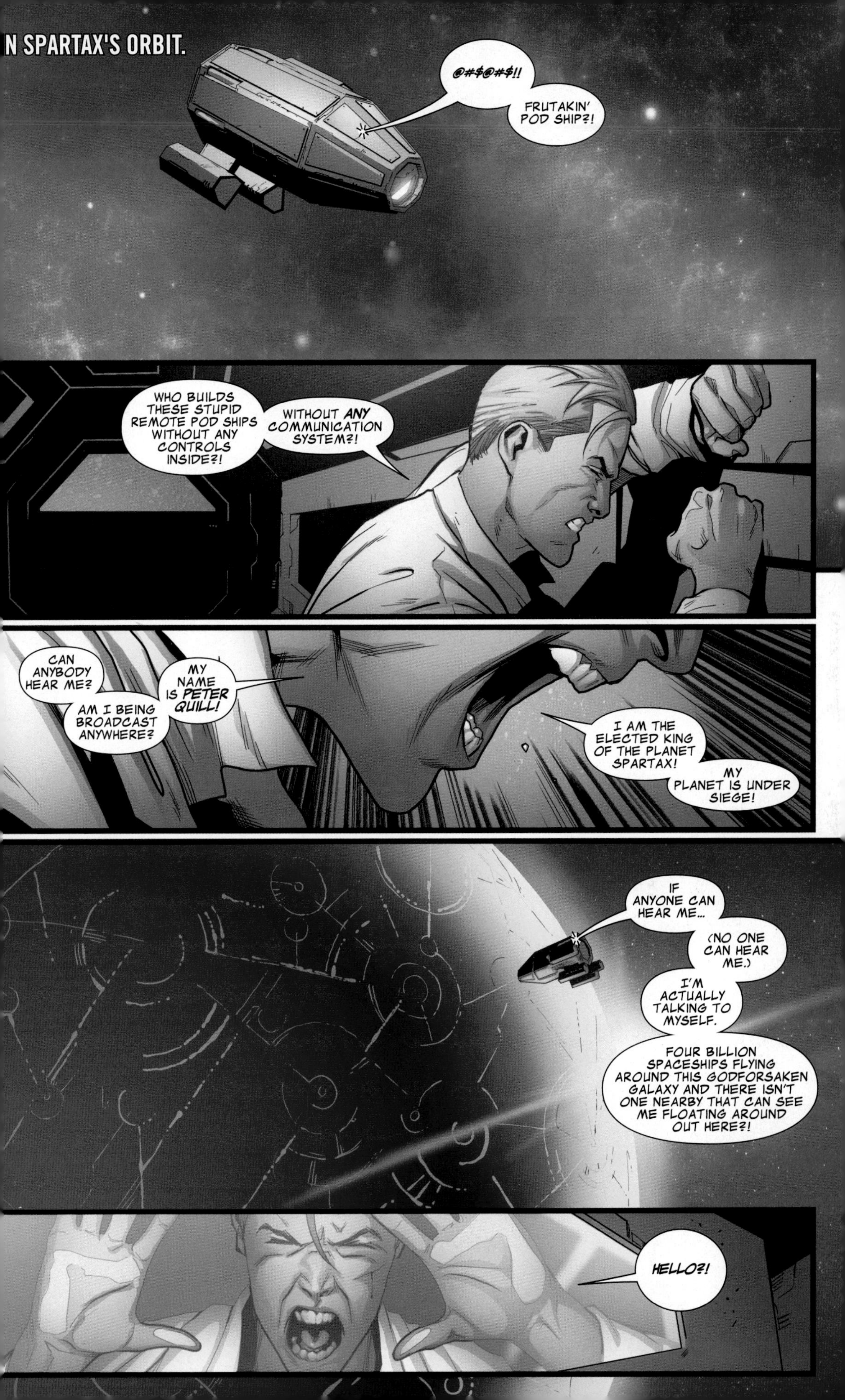
N SPARTAX'S ORBIT.
@#$@#$!!
FRUTAKIN' POD SHIP?!
WHO BUILDS THESE STUPID REMOTE POD SHIPS WITHOUT ANY CONTROLS INSIDE?!
WITHOUT ANY COMMUNICATION SYSTEM?!
CAN ANYBODY HEAR ME?
AM I BEING BROADCAST ANYWHERE?
MY NAME IS PETER QUILL!
I AM THE ELECTED KING OF THE PLANET SPARTAX!
MY PLANET IS UNDER SIEGE!
IF ANYONE CAN HEAR ME...
(NO ONE CAN HEAR ME.)
I'M ACTUALLY TALKING TO MYSELF.
FOUR BILLION SPACESHIPS FLYING AROUND THIS GODFORSAKEN GALAXY AND THERE ISN'T ONE NEARBY THAT CAN SEE ME FLOATING AROUND OUT HERE?!
HELLO?!

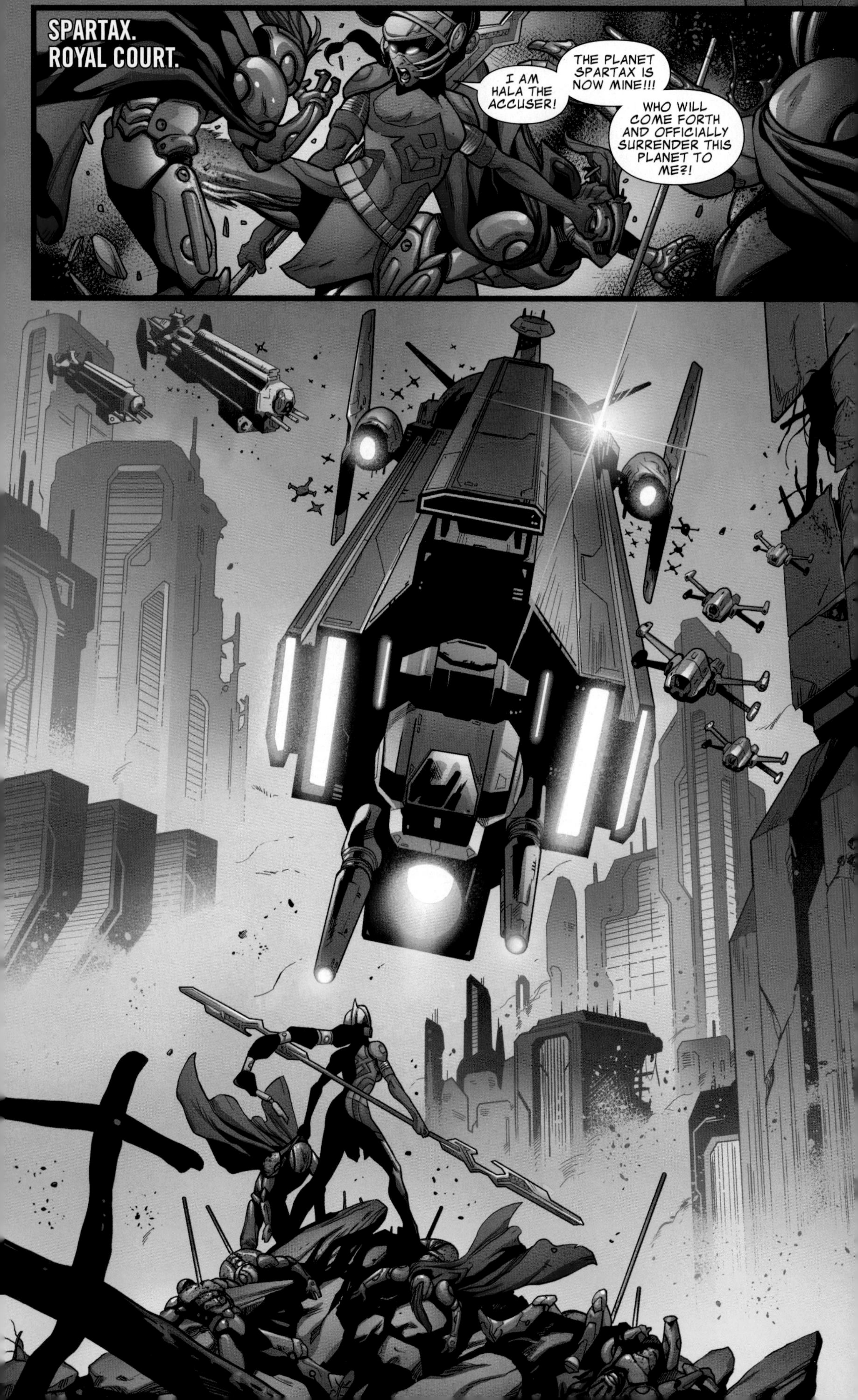
SPARTAX.
ROYAL COURT.
I AM HALA THE ACCUSER!
THE PLANET SPARTAX IS NOW MINE!!!
WHO WILL COME FORTH AND OFFICIALLY SURRENDER THIS PLANET TO ME?!

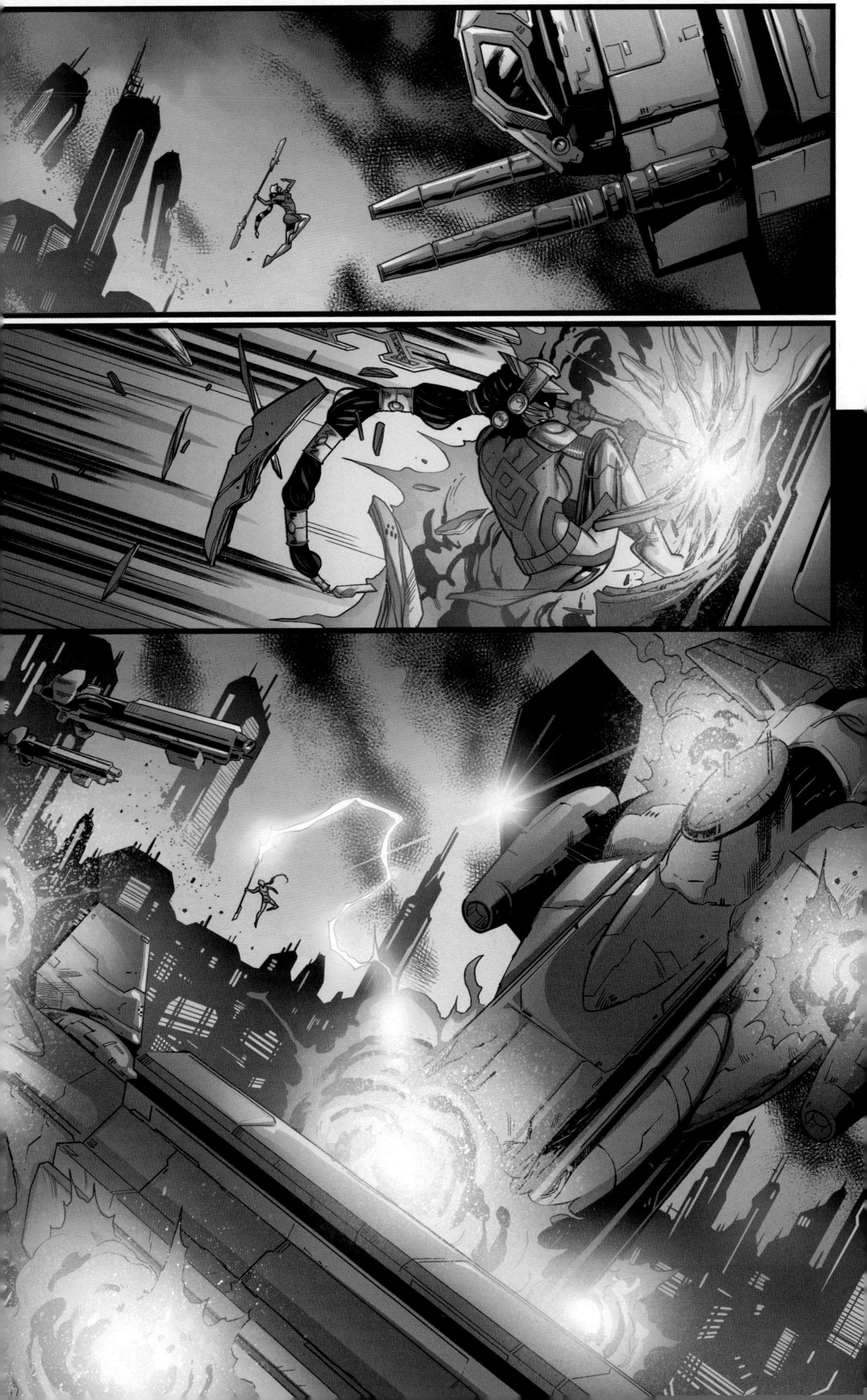

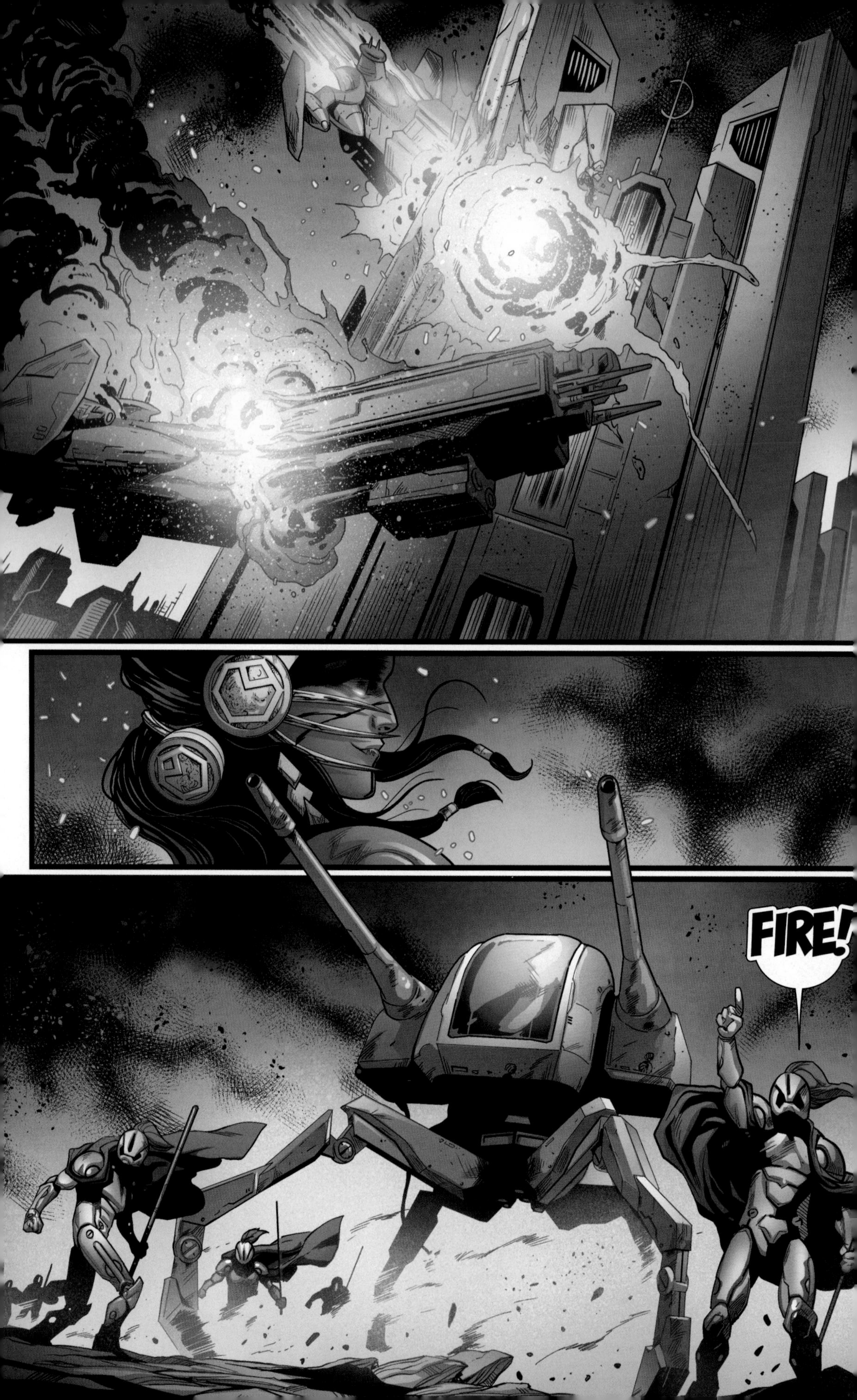
FIRE!

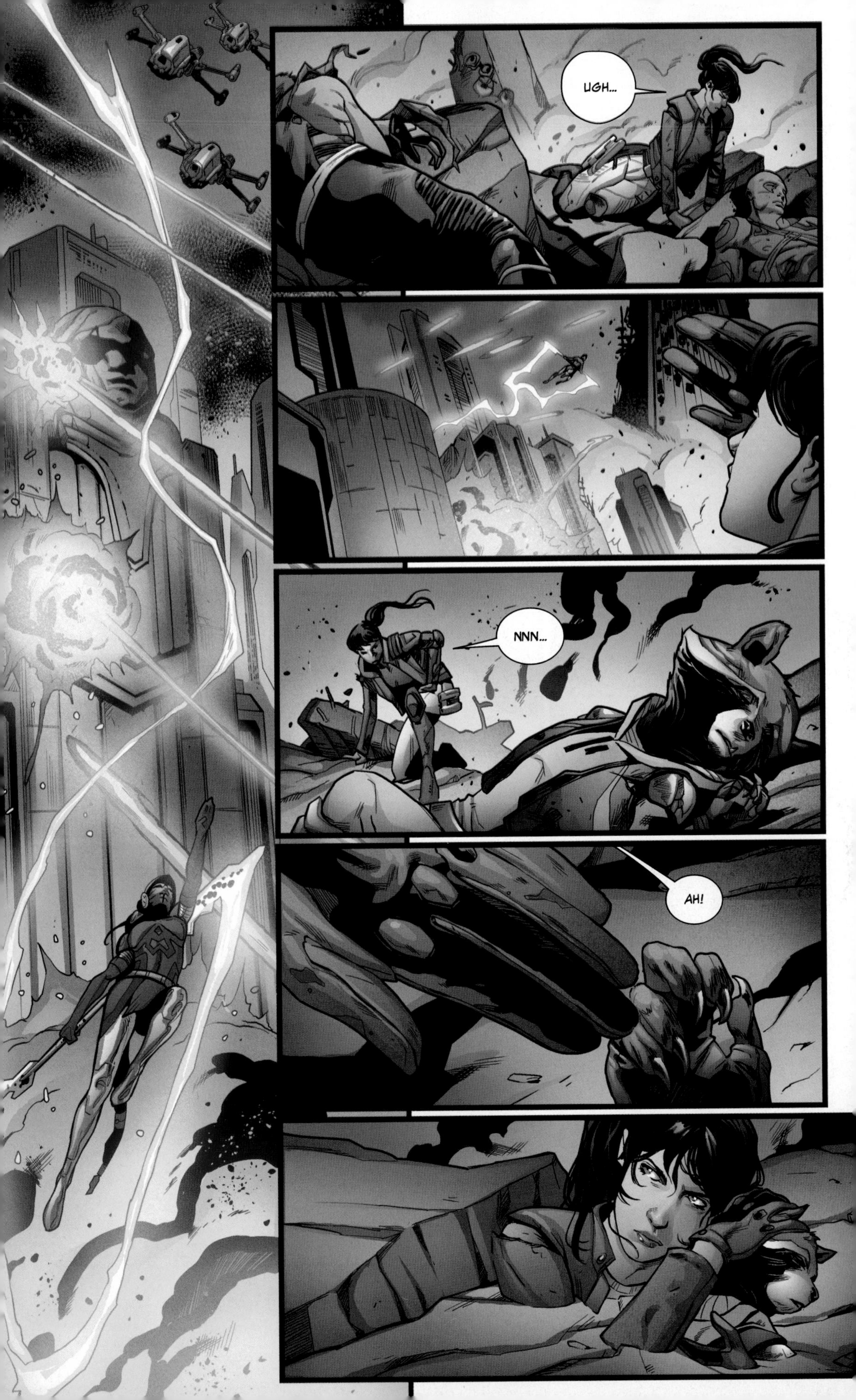
UGH...
NNN...
AH!

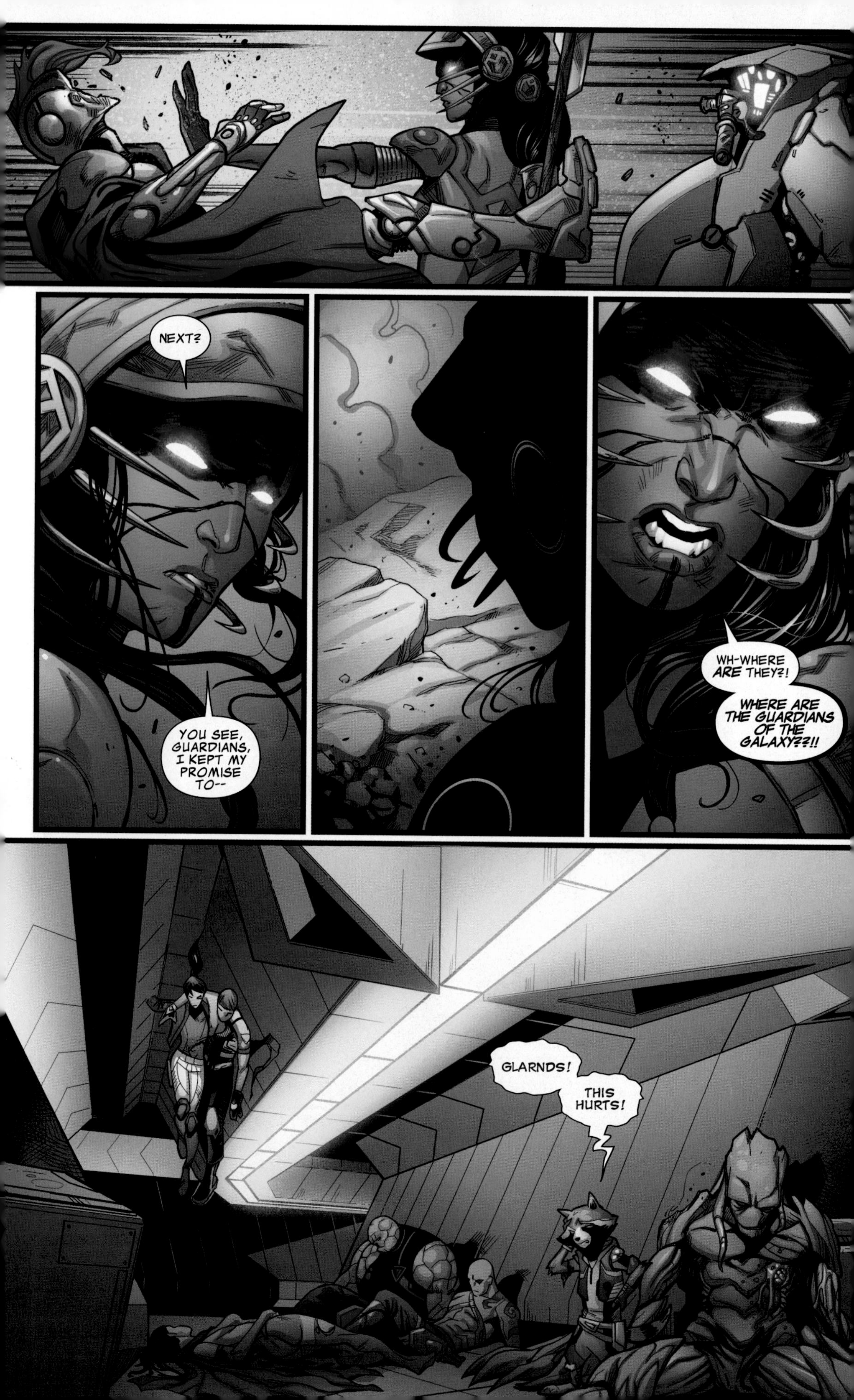
NEXT?
YOU SEE, GUARDIANS, I KEPT MY PROMISE TO--
WH-WHERE ARE THEY?!
WHERE ARE THE GUARDIANS OF THE GALAXY??!!
GLARNDS!
THIS HURTS!

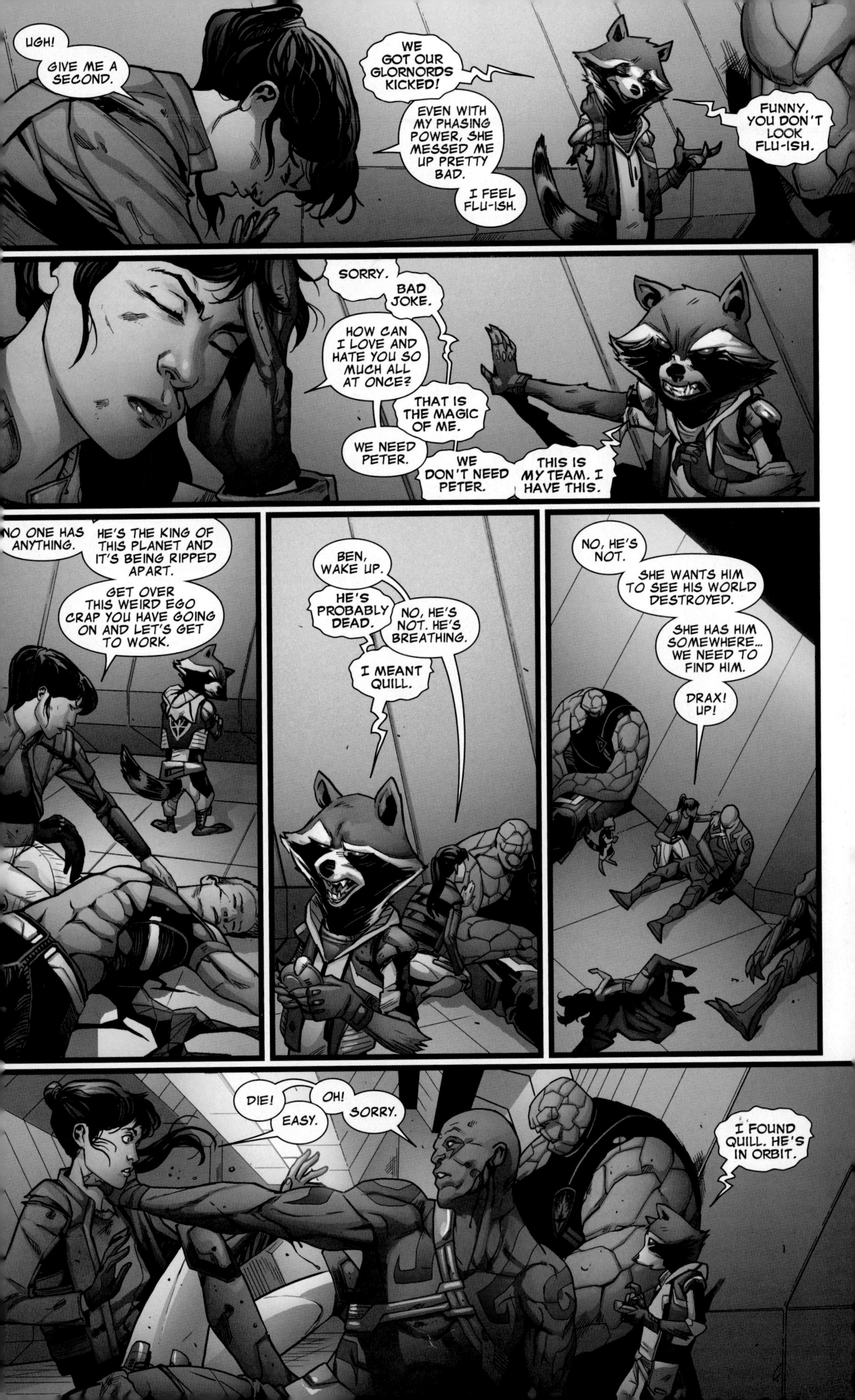
UGH!
GIVE ME A SECOND.
WE GOT OUR GLORNORDS KICKED!
EVEN WITH MY PHASING POWER, SHE MESSED ME UP PRETTY BAD.
I FEEL FLU-ISH.
FUNNY, YOU DON'T LOOK FLU-ISH.
SORRY.
BAD JOKE.
HOW CAN I LOVE AND HATE YOU SO MUCH ALL AT ONCE?
THAT IS THE MAGIC OF ME.
WE NEED PETER.
WE DON'T NEED PETER.
THIS IS MY TEAM. I HAVE THIS.
NO ONE HAS ANYTHING.
HE'S THE KING OF THIS PLANET AND IT'S BEING RIPPED APART.
GET OVER THIS WEIRD EGO CRAP YOU HAVE GOING ON AND LET'S GET TO WORK.
BEN, WAKE UP.
HE'S PROBABLY DEAD.
NO, HE'S NOT. HE'S BREATHING.
I MEANT QUILL.
NO, HE'S NOT.
SHE WANTS HIM TO SEE HIS WORLD DESTROYED.
SHE HAS HIM SOMEWHERE... WE NEED TO FIND HIM.
DRAX! UP!
DIE!
EASY.
OH!
SORRY.
I FOUND QUILL. HE'S IN ORBIT.

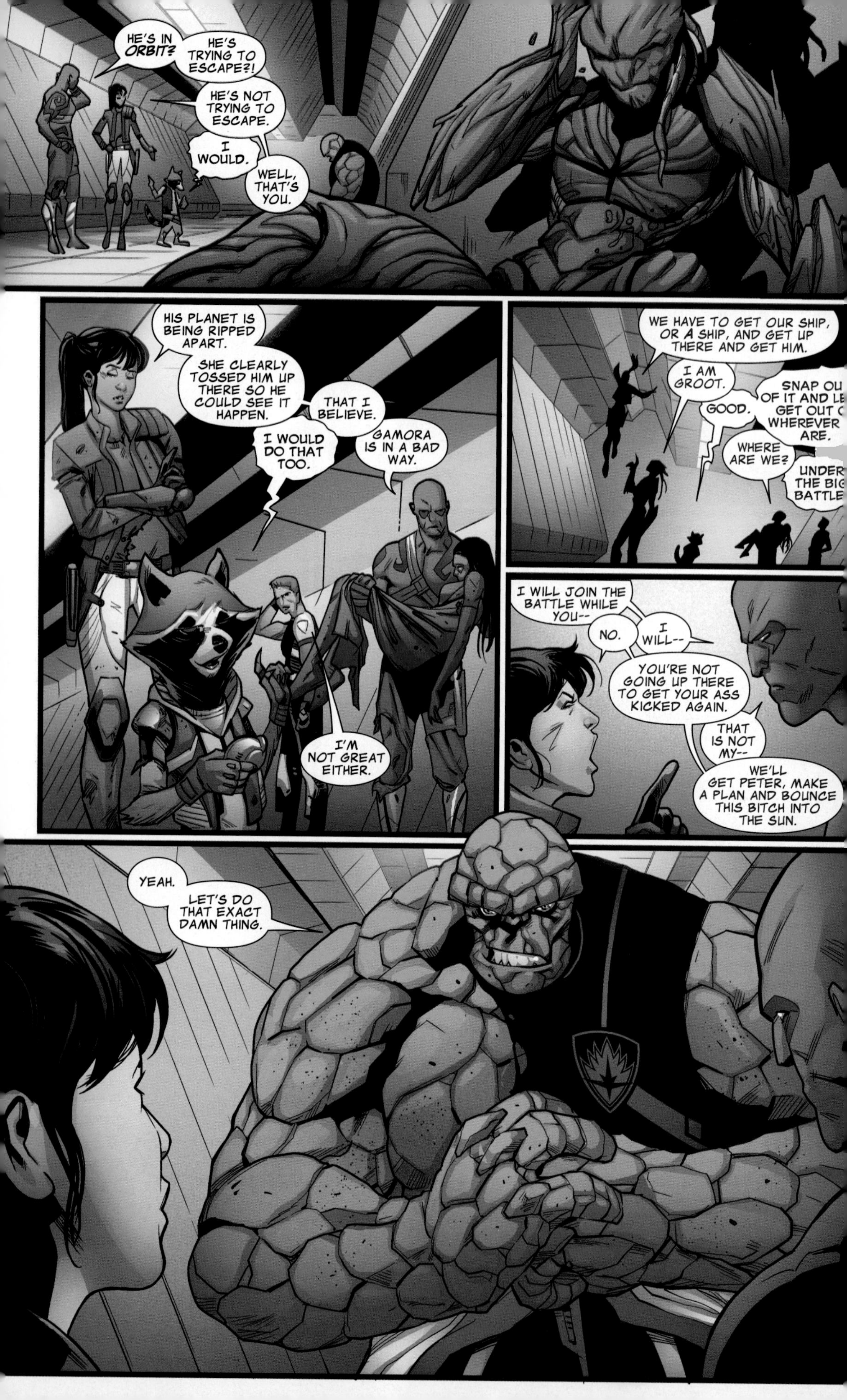

HE'S IN ORBIT?
HE'S TRYING TO ESCAPE?!
HE'S NOT TRYING TO ESCAPE.
I WOULD.
WELL, THAT'S YOU.
HIS PLANET IS BEING RIPPED APART.
SHE CLEARLY TOSSED HIM UP THERE SO HE COULD SEE IT HAPPEN.
THAT I BELIEVE.
I WOULD DO THAT TOO.
GAMORA IS IN A BAD WAY.
I'M NOT GREAT EITHER.
WE HAVE TO GET OUR SHIP, OR A SHIP, AND GET UP THERE AND GET HIM.
I AM GROOT.
GOOD.
SNAP OU OF IT AND LE GET OUT O WHEREVER ARE.
WHERE ARE WE?
UNDER THE BIG BATTLE
I WILL JOIN THE BATTLE WHILE YOU--
NO.
I WILL--
YOU'RE NOT GOING UP THERE TO GET YOUR ASS KICKED AGAIN.
THAT IS NOT MY--
WE'LL GET PETER, MAKE A PLAN AND BOUNCE THIS BITCH INTO THE SUN.
YEAH.
LET'S DO THAT EXACT DAMN THING.

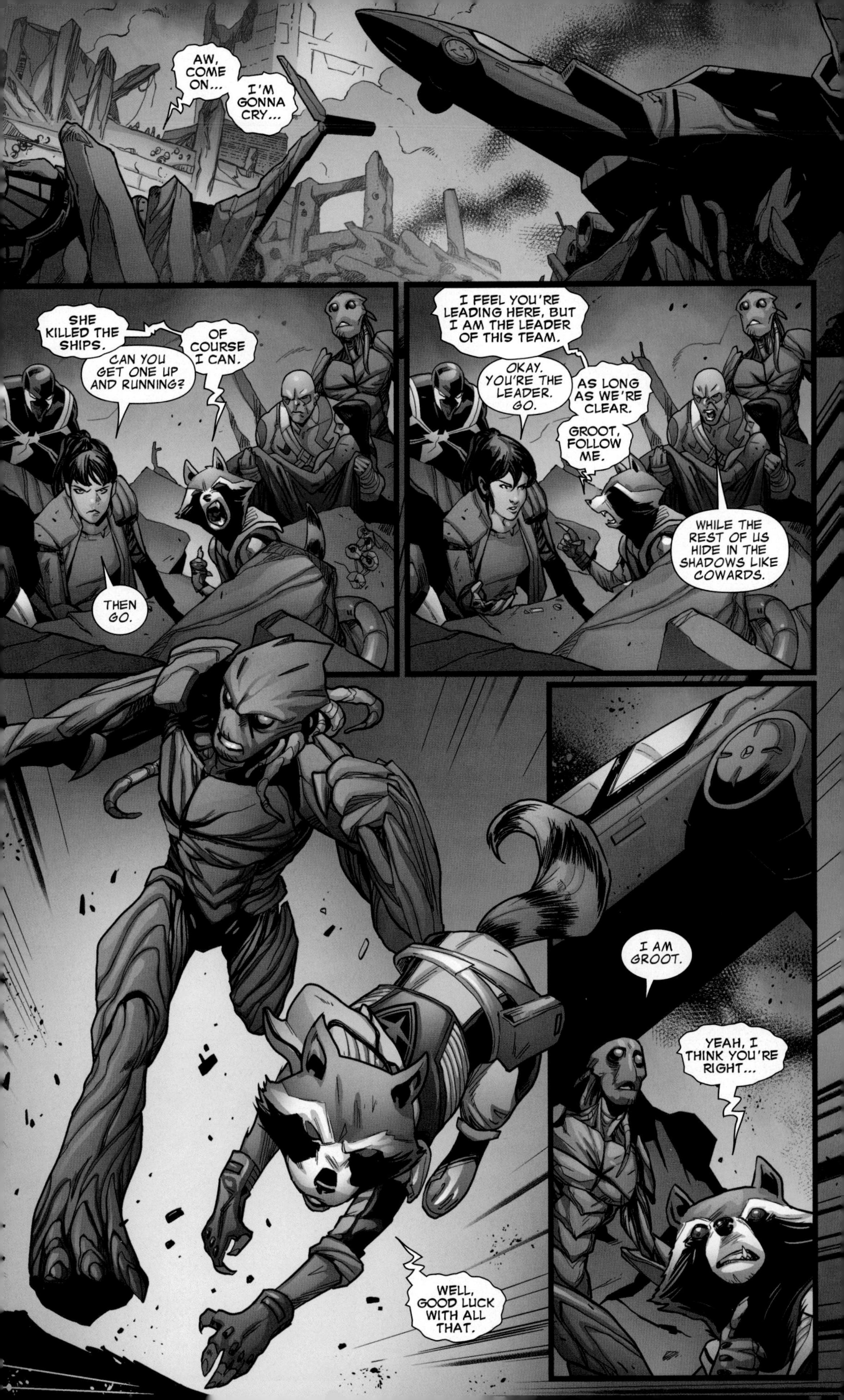
AW, COME ON...
I'M GONNA CRY...
SHE KILLED THE SHIPS.
CAN YOU GET ONE UP AND RUNNING?
OF COURSE I CAN.
THEN GO.
I FEEL YOU'RE LEADING HERE, BUT I AM THE LEADER OF THIS TEAM.
OKAY. YOU'RE THE LEADER. GO.
AS LONG AS WE'RE CLEAR.
GROOT, FOLLOW ME.
WHILE THE REST OF US HIDE IN THE SHADOWS LIKE COWARDS.
WELL, GOOD LUCK WITH ALL THAT.
I AM GROOT.
YEAH, I THINK YOU'RE RIGHT...

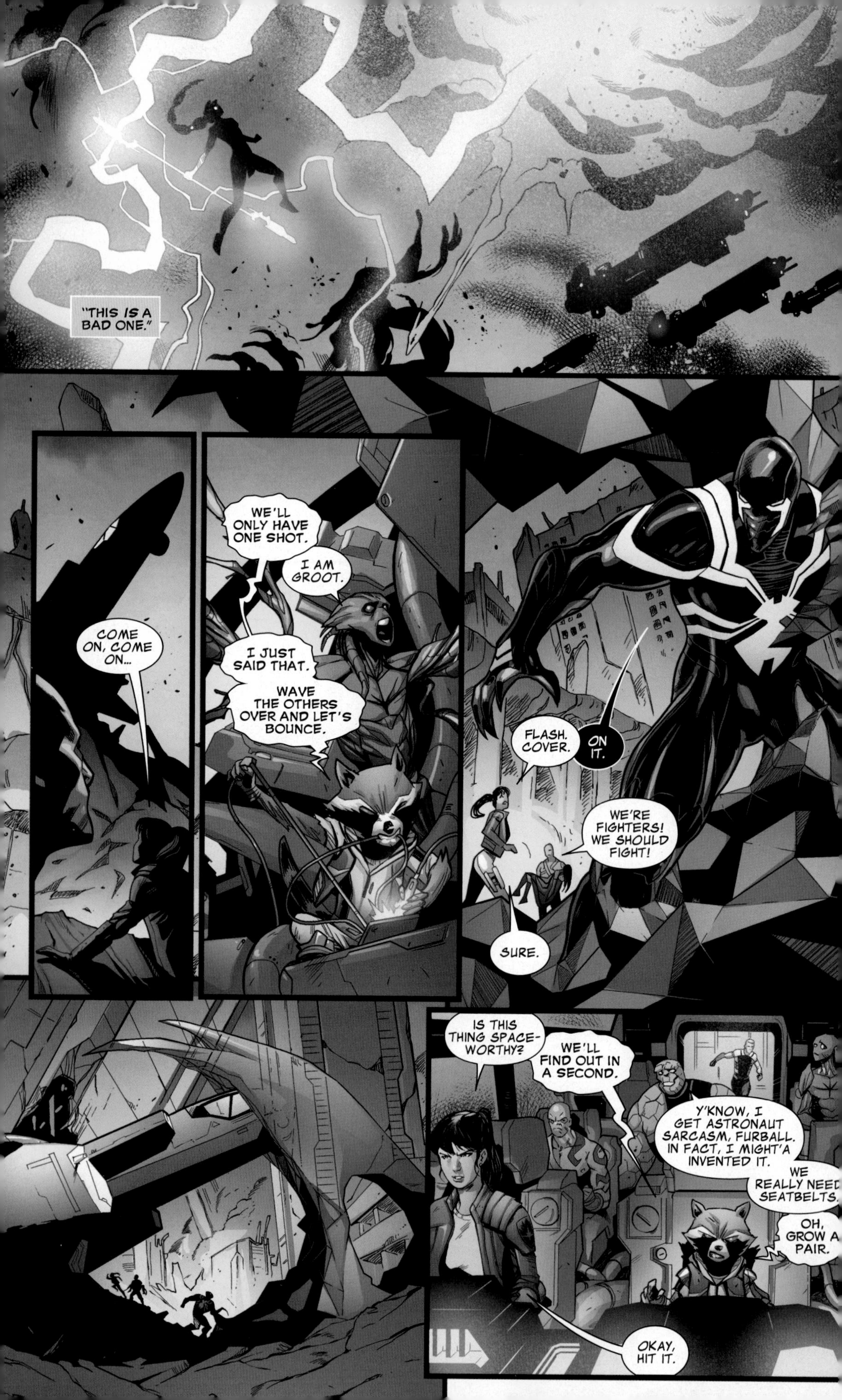

"THIS IS A BAD ONE."
COME ON, COME ON...
WE'LL ONLY HAVE ONE SHOT.
I AM GROOT.
I JUST SAID THAT.
WAVE THE OTHERS OVER AND LET'S BOUNCE.
FLASH. COVER.
ON IT.
WE'RE FIGHTERS! WE SHOULD FIGHT!
SURE.
IS THIS THING SPACE-WORTHY?
WE'LL FIND OUT IN A SECOND.
Y'KNOW, I GET ASTRONAUT SARCASM, FURBALL. IN FACT, I MIGHT'A INVENTED IT.
WE REALLY NEED SEATBELTS.
OH, GROW A PAIR.
OKAY, HIT IT.

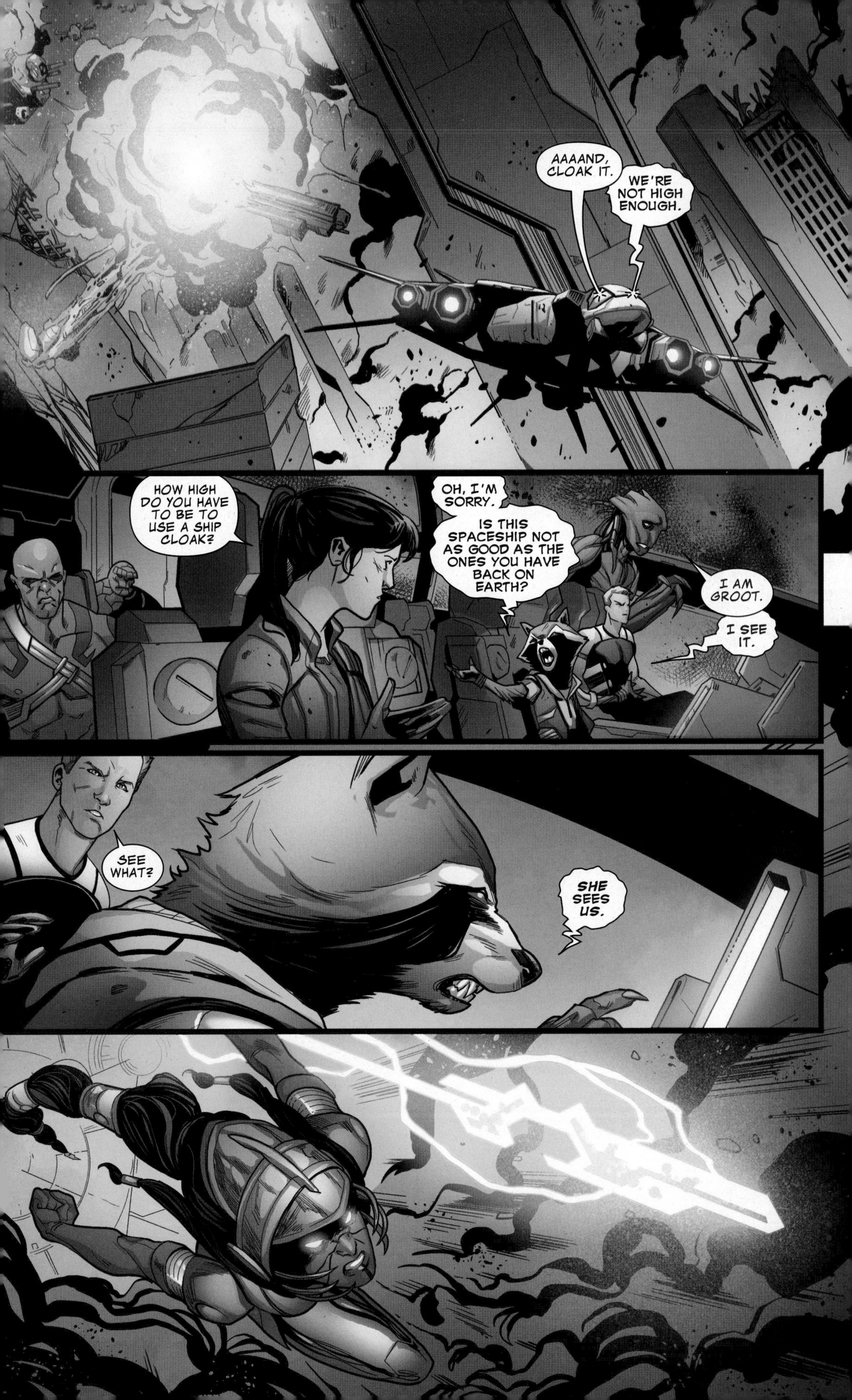
AAAAND, CLOAK IT.
WE'RE NOT HIGH ENOUGH.
HOW HIGH DO YOU HAVE TO BE TO USE A SHIP CLOAK?
OH, I'M SORRY.
IS THIS SPACESHIP NOT AS GOOD AS THE ONES YOU HAVE BACK ON EARTH?
I AM GROOT.
I SEE IT.
SEE WHAT?
SHE SEES US.

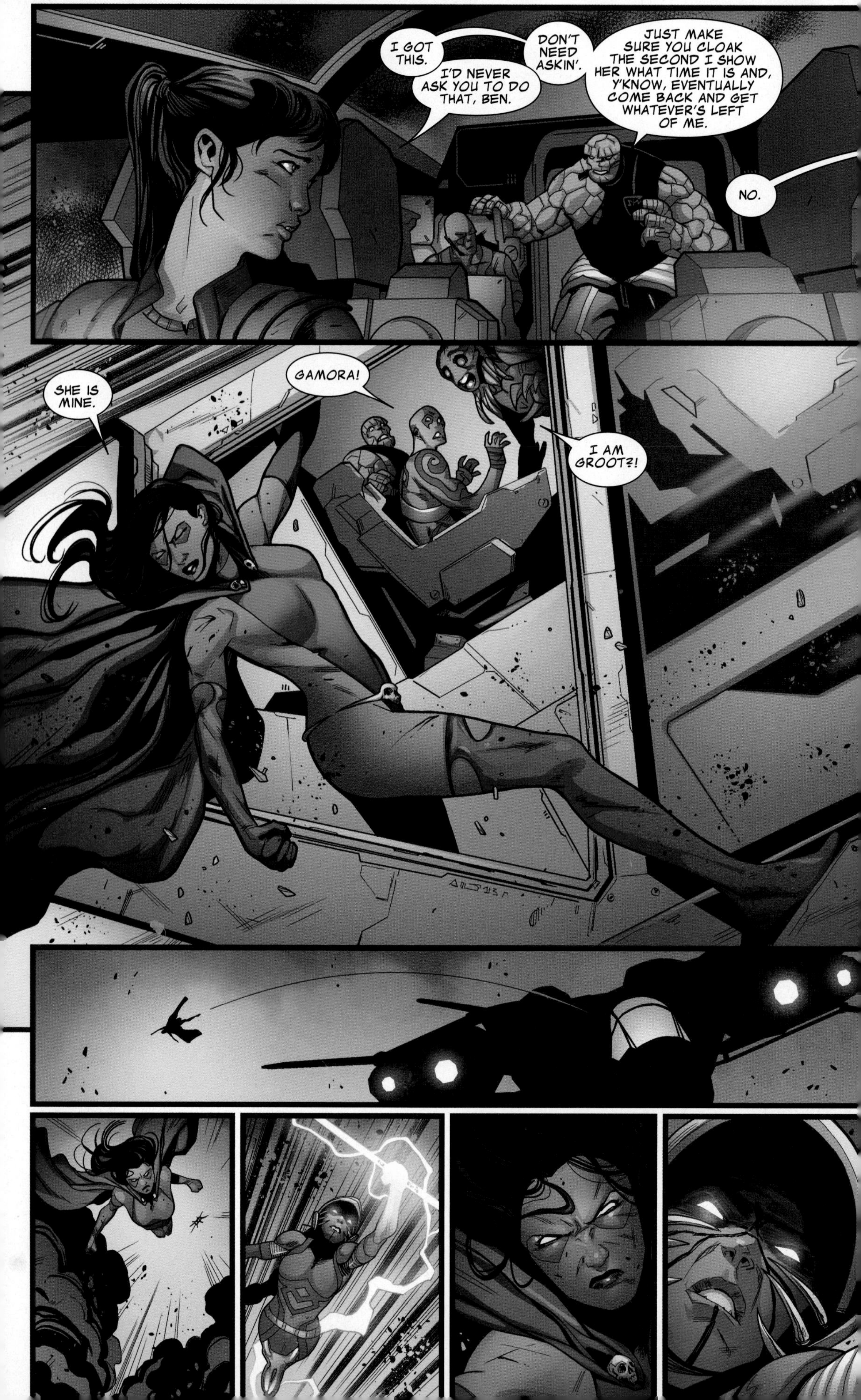
I GOT THIS.
DON'T NEED ASKIN'.
JUST MAKE SURE YOU CLOAK THE SECOND I SHOW HER WHAT TIME IT IS AND, Y'KNOW, EVENTUALLY COME BACK AND GET WHATEVER'S LEFT OF ME.
I'D NEVER ASK YOU TO DO THAT, BEN.
NO.
SHE IS MINE.
GAMORA!
I AM GROOT?!

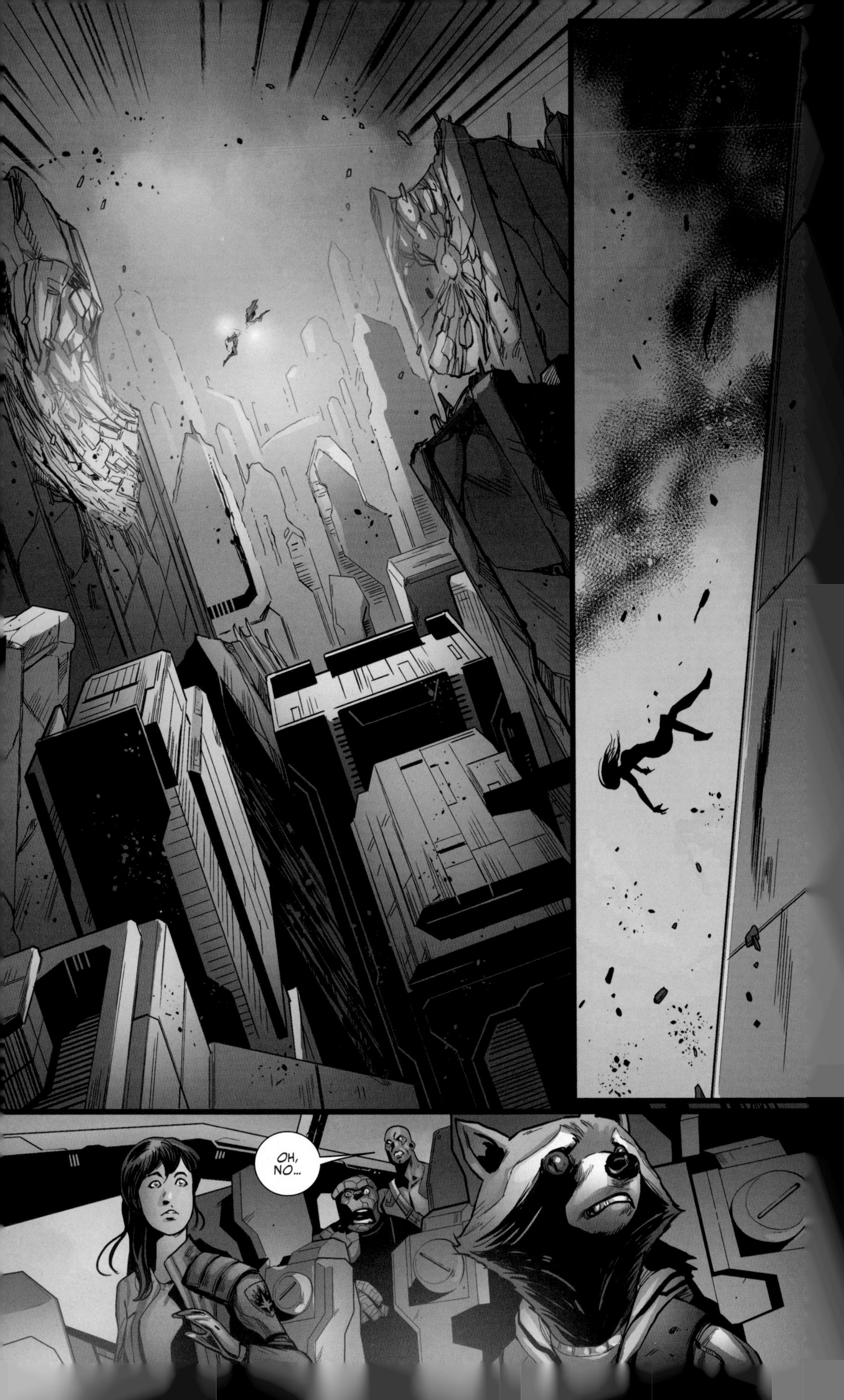
OH, NO...

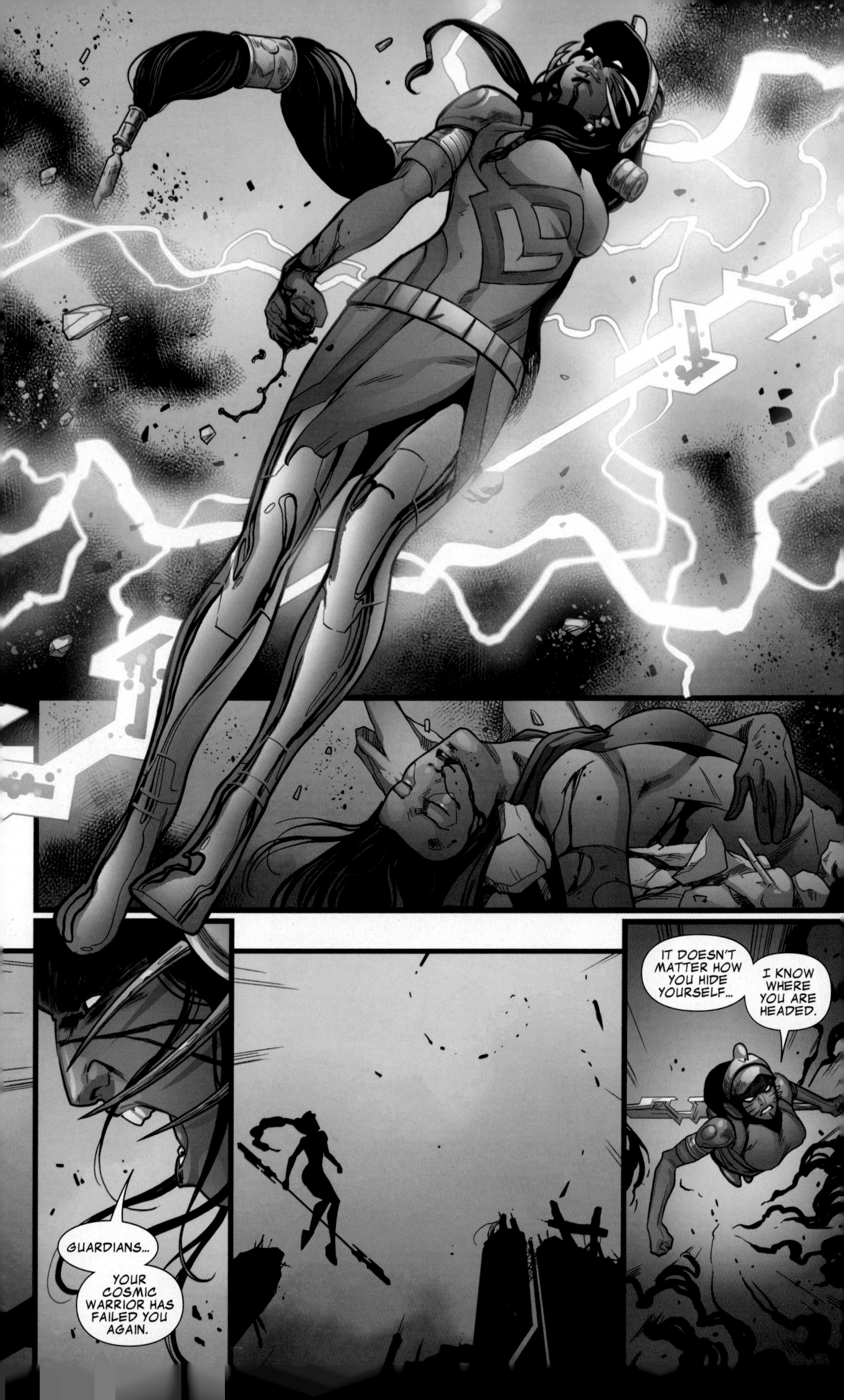
GUARDIANS...
YOUR COSMIC WARRIOR HAS FAILED YOU AGAIN.
IT DOESN'T MATTER HOW YOU HIDE YOURSELF...
I KNOW WHERE YOU ARE HEADED.

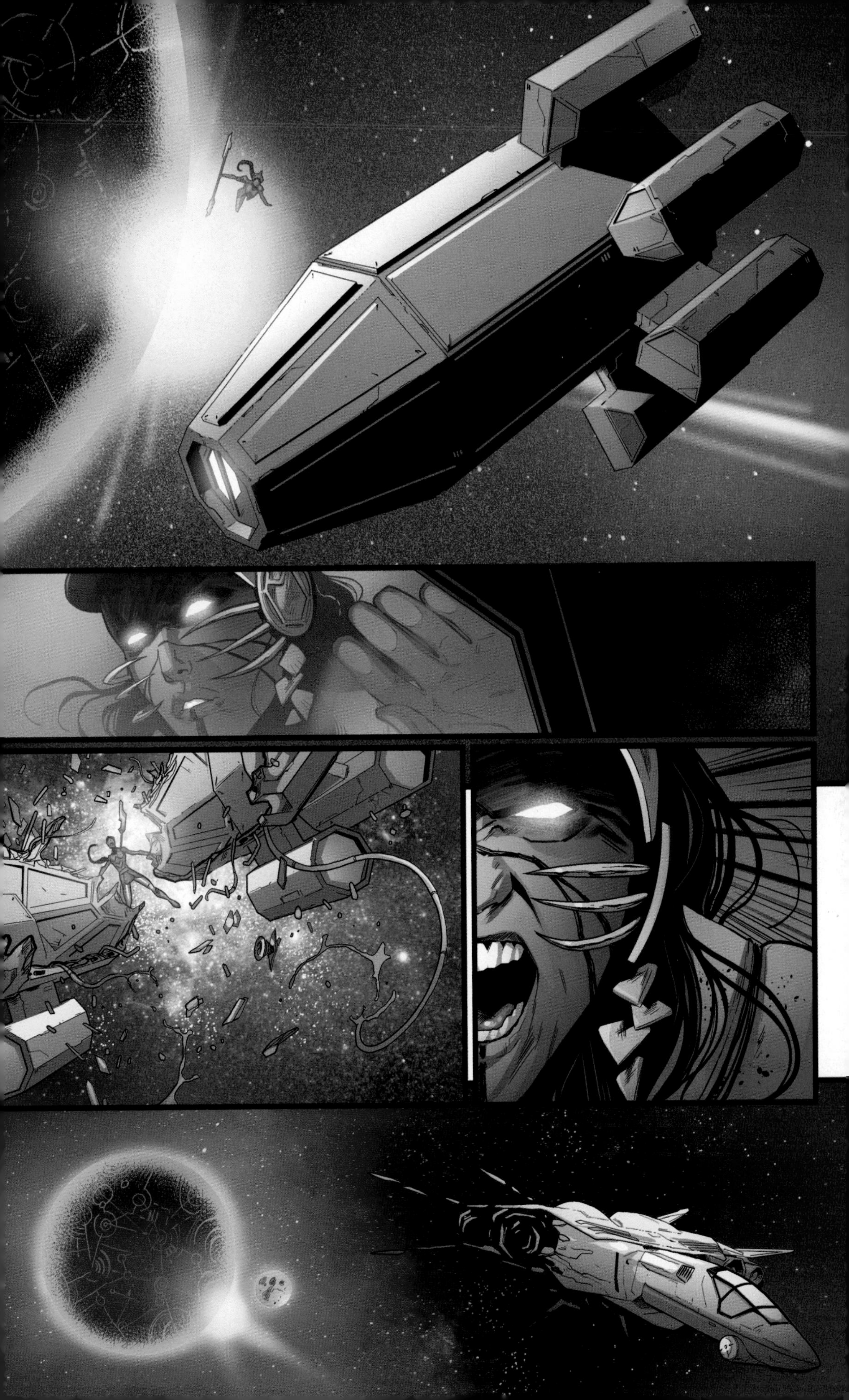

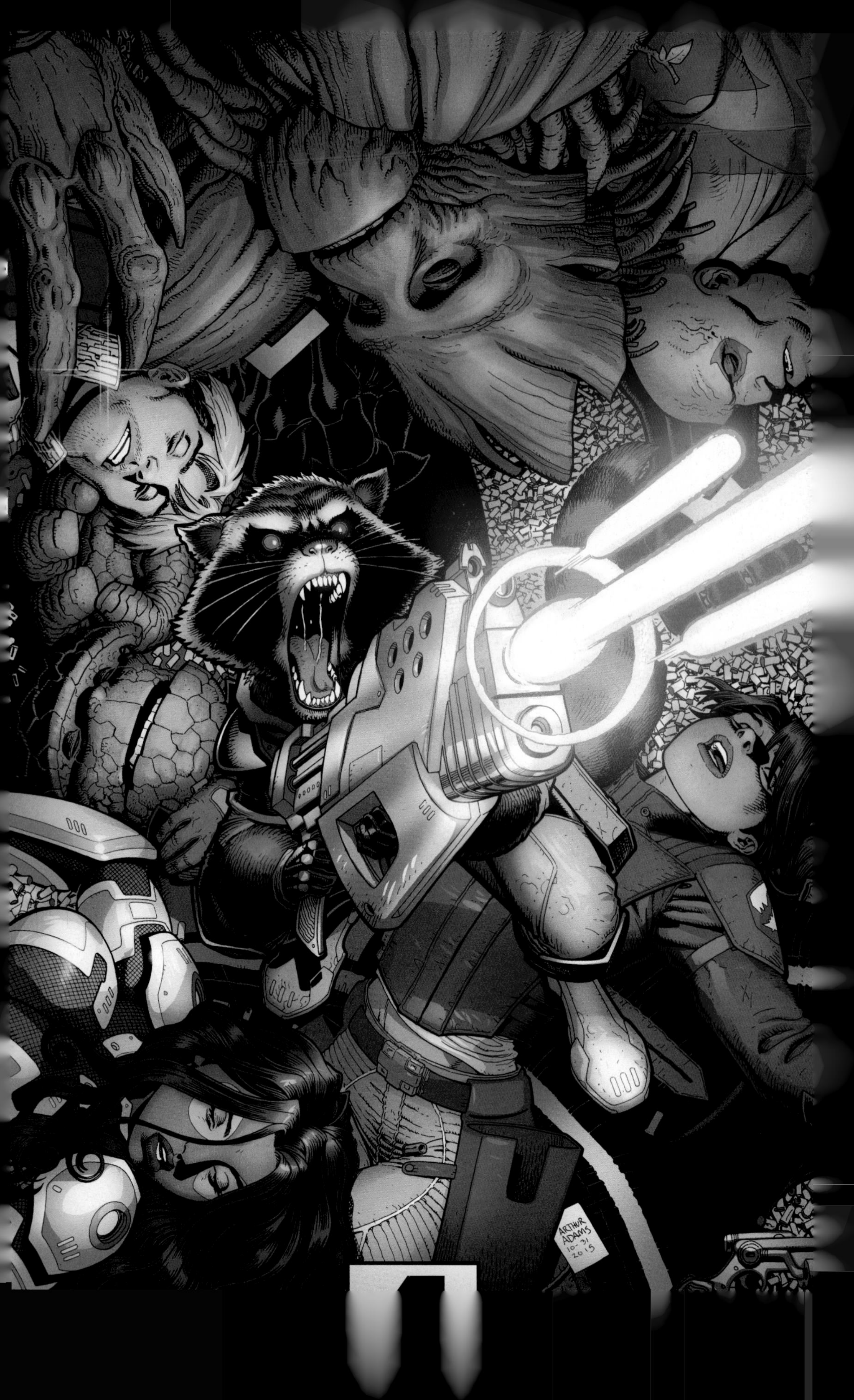
ARTHUR
ADAMS
10-31
2015

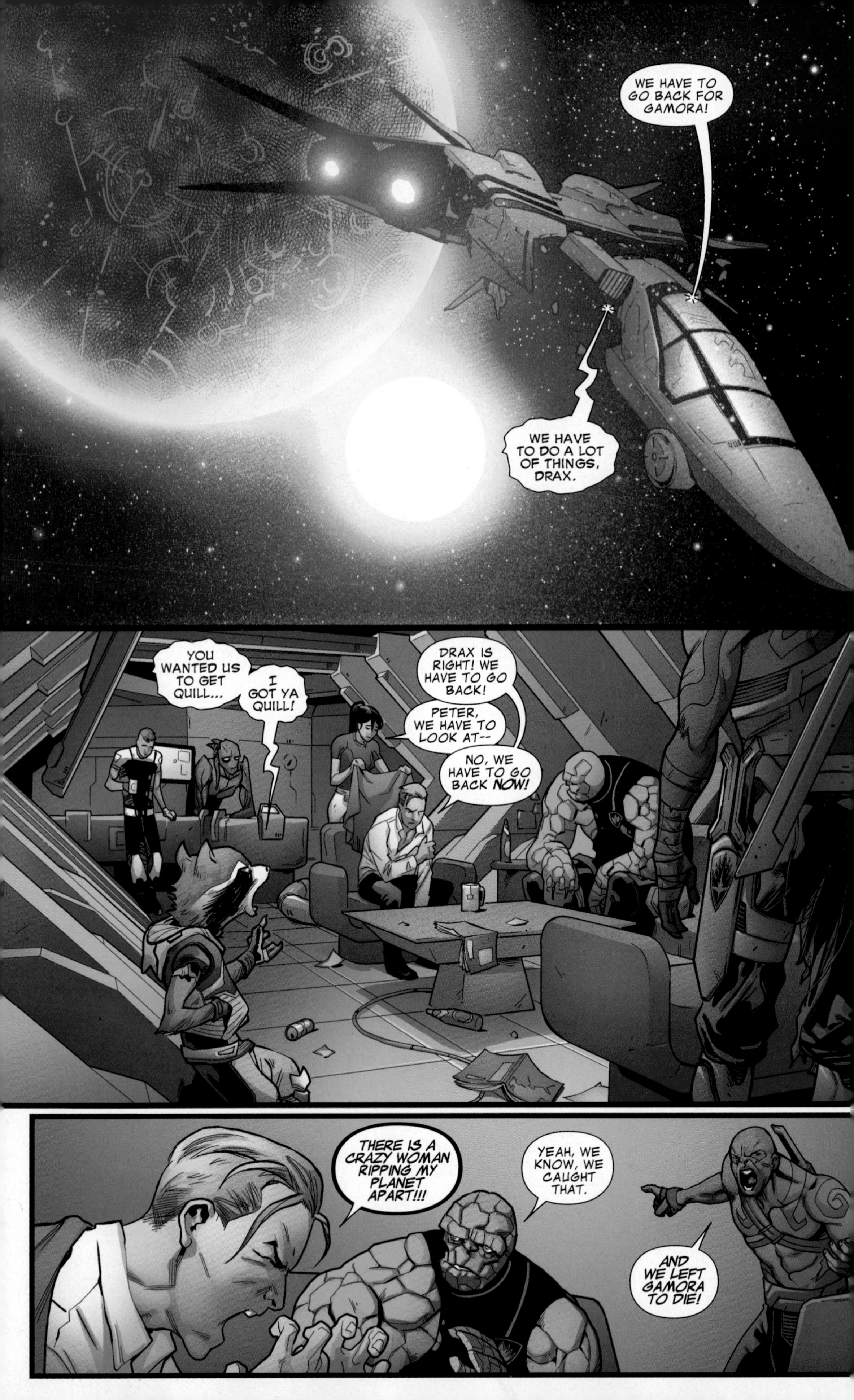
WE HAVE TO GO BACK FOR GAMORA!
WE HAVE TO DO A LOT OF THINGS, DRAX.
YOU WANTED US TO GET QUILL...
I GOT YA QUILL!
DRAX IS RIGHT! WE HAVE TO GO BACK!
PETER, WE HAVE TO LOOK AT--
NO, WE HAVE TO GO BACK NOW!
THERE IS A CRAZY WOMAN RIPPING MY PLANET APART!!!
YEAH, WE KNOW, WE CAUGHT THAT.
AND WE LEFT GAMORA TO DIE!

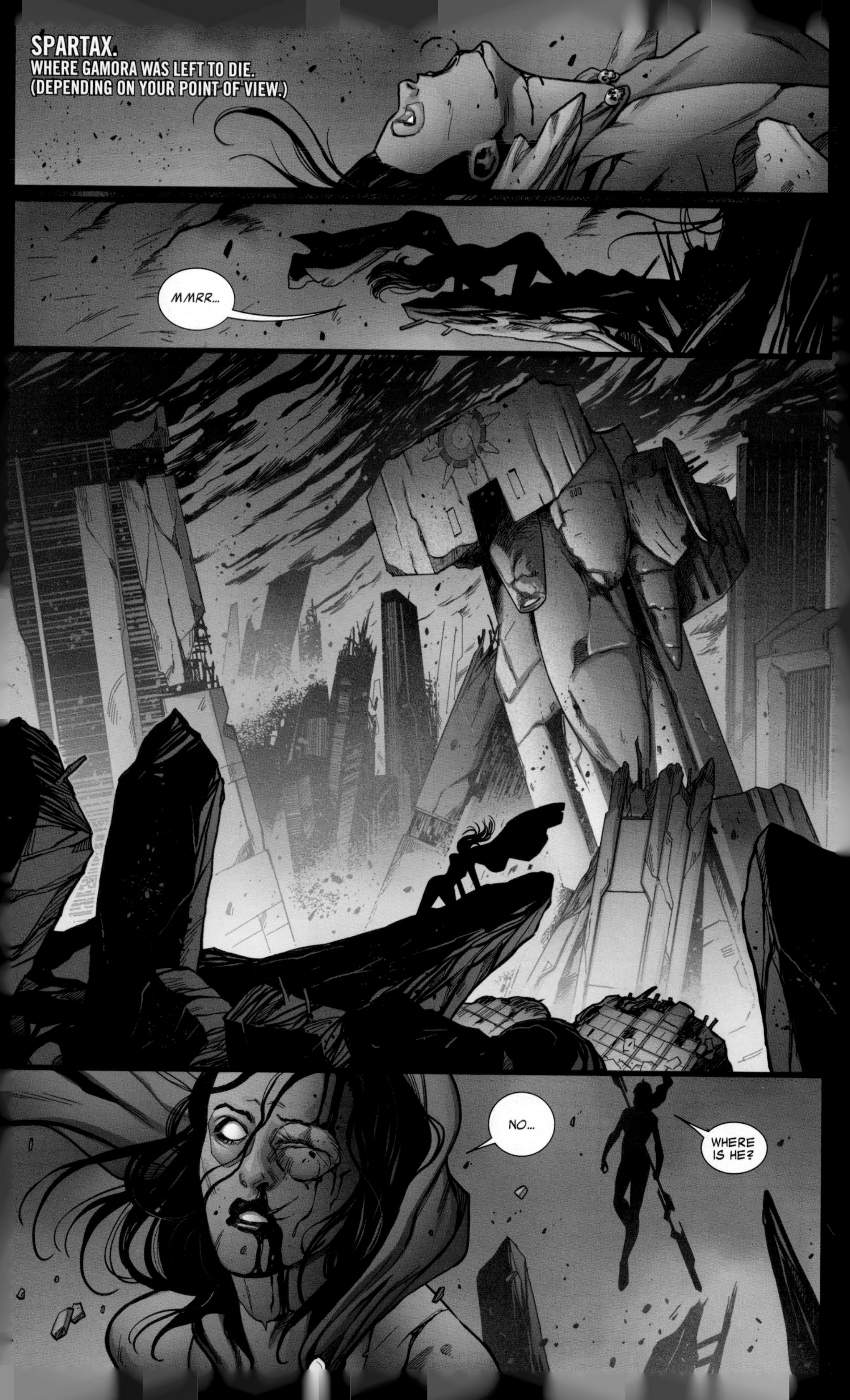
SPARTAX.
WHERE GAMORA WAS LEFT TO DIE.
(DEPENDING ON YOUR POINT OF VIEW.)
MMRR...
NO...
WHERE IS HE?

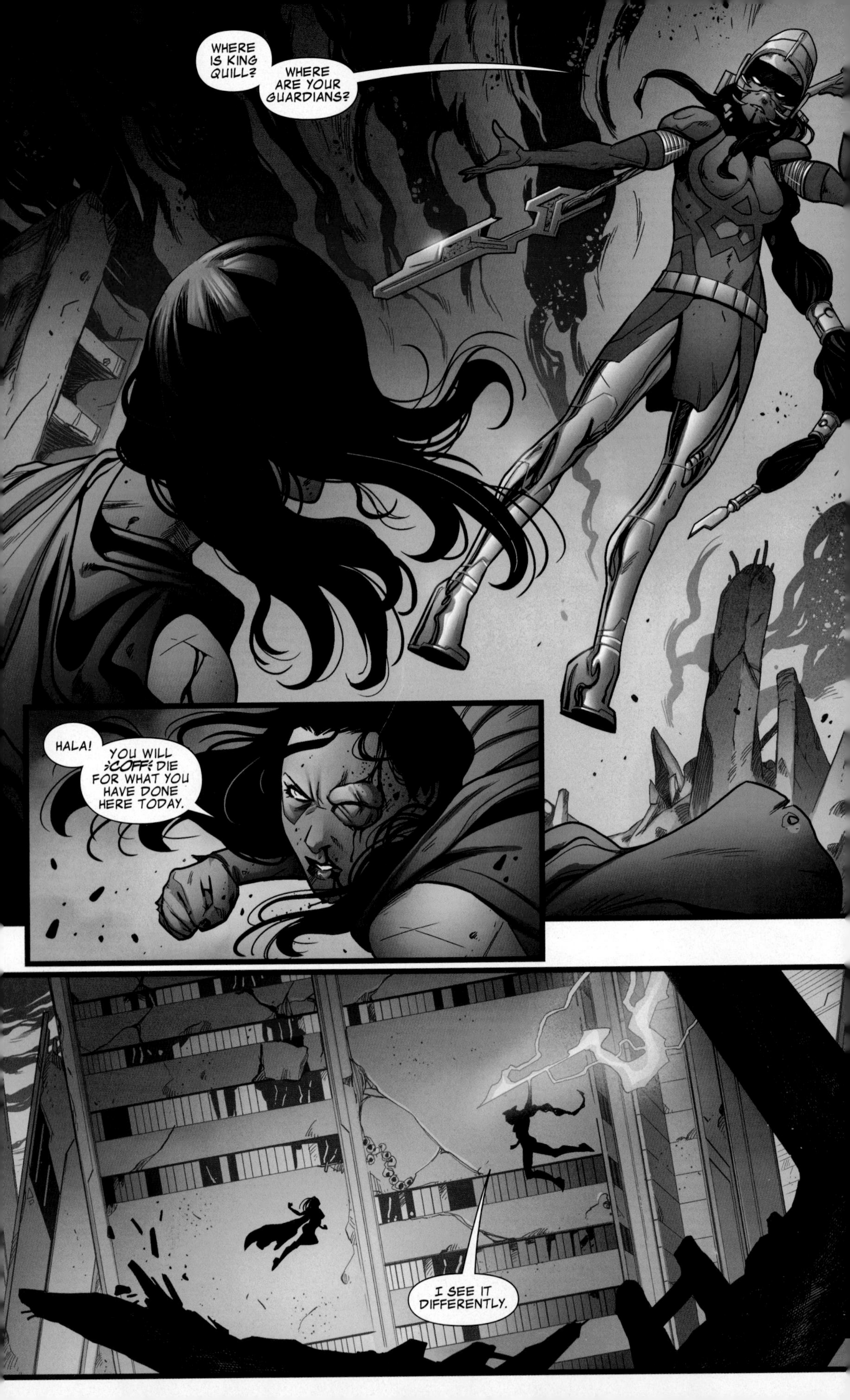
WHERE IS KING QUILL?
WHERE ARE YOUR GUARDIANS?
HALA!
YOU WILL *COFF* DIE FOR WHAT YOU HAVE DONE HERE TODAY.
I SEE IT DIFFERENTLY.

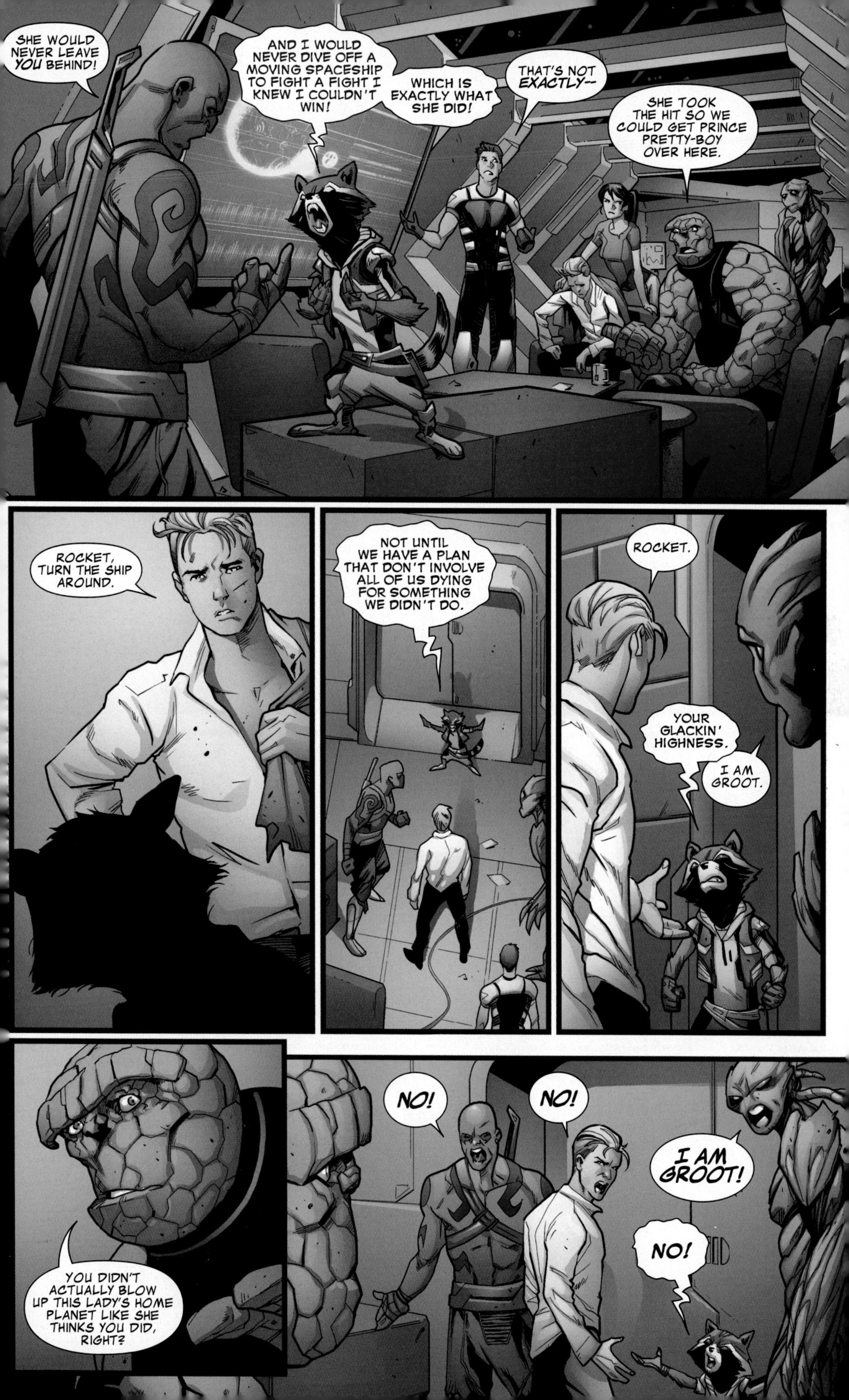
SHE WOULD NEVER LEAVE YOU BEHIND!
AND I WOULD NEVER DIVE OFF A MOVING SPACESHIP TO FIGHT A FIGHT I KNEW I COULDN'T WIN!
WHICH IS EXACTLY WHAT SHE DID!
THAT'S NOT EXACTLY--
SHE TOOK THE HIT SO WE COULD GET PRINCE PRETTY-BOY OVER HERE.
ROCKET, TURN THE SHIP AROUND.
NOT UNTIL WE HAVE A PLAN THAT DON'T INVOLVE ALL OF US DYING FOR SOMETHING WE DIDN'T DO.
ROCKET.
YOUR GLACKIN' HIGHNESS.
I AM GROOT.
YOU DIDN'T ACTUALLY BLOW UP THIS LADY'S HOME PLANET LIKE SHE THINKS YOU DID, RIGHT?
NO!
NO!
I AM GROOT!
NO!

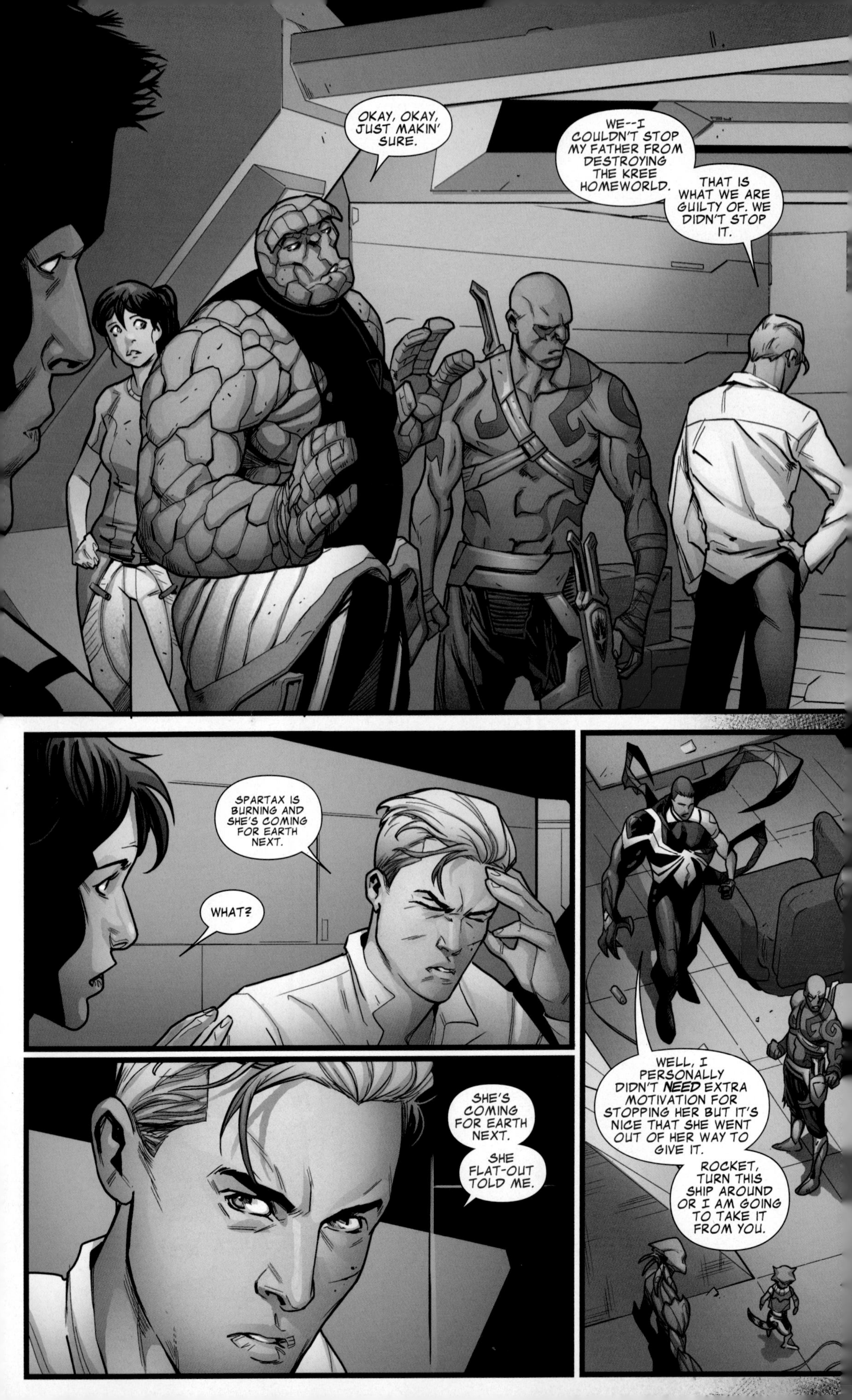
OKAY, OKAY, JUST MAKIN' SURE.
WE--I COULDN'T STOP MY FATHER FROM DESTROYING THE KREE HOMEWORLD.
THAT IS WHAT WE ARE GUILTY OF. WE DIDN'T STOP IT.
SPARTAX IS BURNING AND SHE'S COMING FOR EARTH NEXT.
WHAT?
SHE'S COMING FOR EARTH NEXT.
SHE FLAT-OUT TOLD ME.
WELL, I PERSONALLY DIDN'T NEED EXTRA MOTIVATION FOR STOPPING HER BUT IT'S NICE THAT SHE WENT OUT OF HER WAY TO GIVE IT.
ROCKET, TURN THIS SHIP AROUND OR I AM GOING TO TAKE IT FROM YOU.

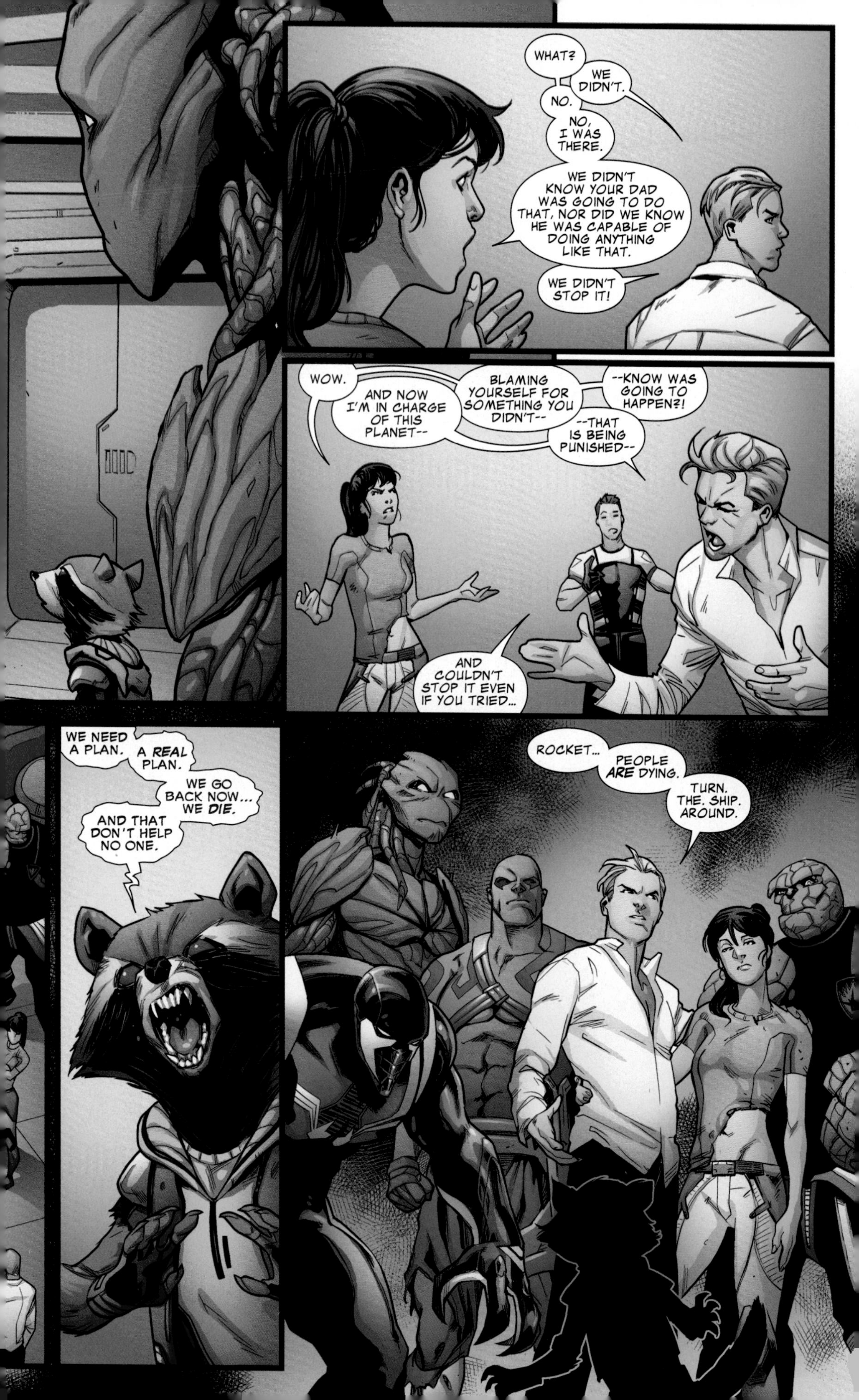

WHAT?
WE DIDN'T.
NO.
NO, I WAS THERE.
WE DIDN'T KNOW YOUR DAD WAS GOING TO DO THAT, NOR DID WE KNOW HE WAS CAPABLE OF DOING ANYTHING LIKE THAT.
WE DIDN'T STOP IT!
WOW.
AND NOW I'M IN CHARGE OF THIS PLANET--
BLAMING YOURSELF FOR SOMETHING YOU DIDN'T--
--KNOW WAS GOING TO HAPPEN?!
--THAT IS BEING PUNISHED--
AND COULDN'T STOP IT EVEN IF YOU TRIED...
WE NEED A PLAN.
A REAL PLAN.
WE GO BACK NOW... WE DIE.
AND THAT DON'T HELP NO ONE.
ROCKET...
PEOPLE ARE DYING.
TURN. THE. SHIP. AROUND.

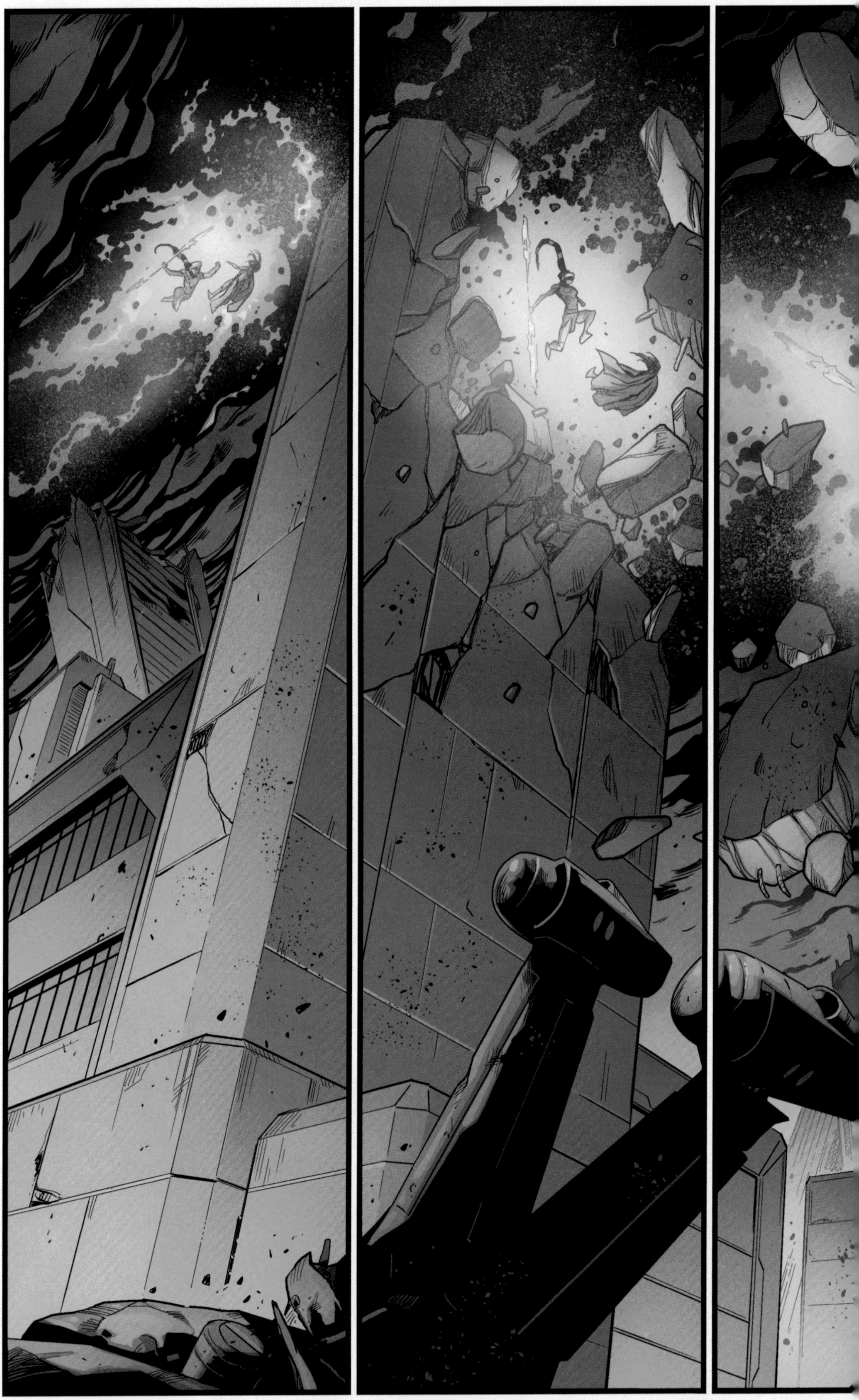

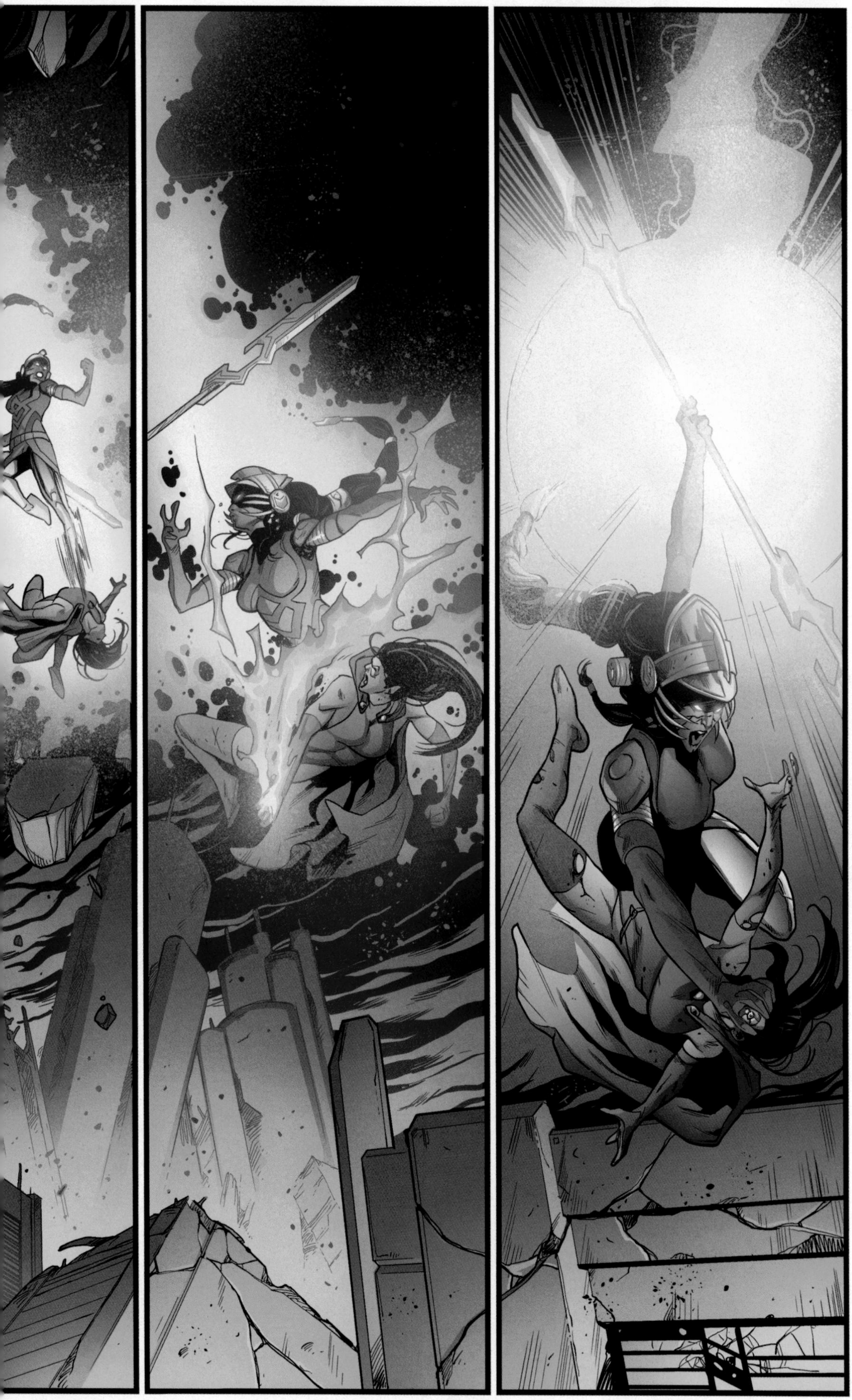

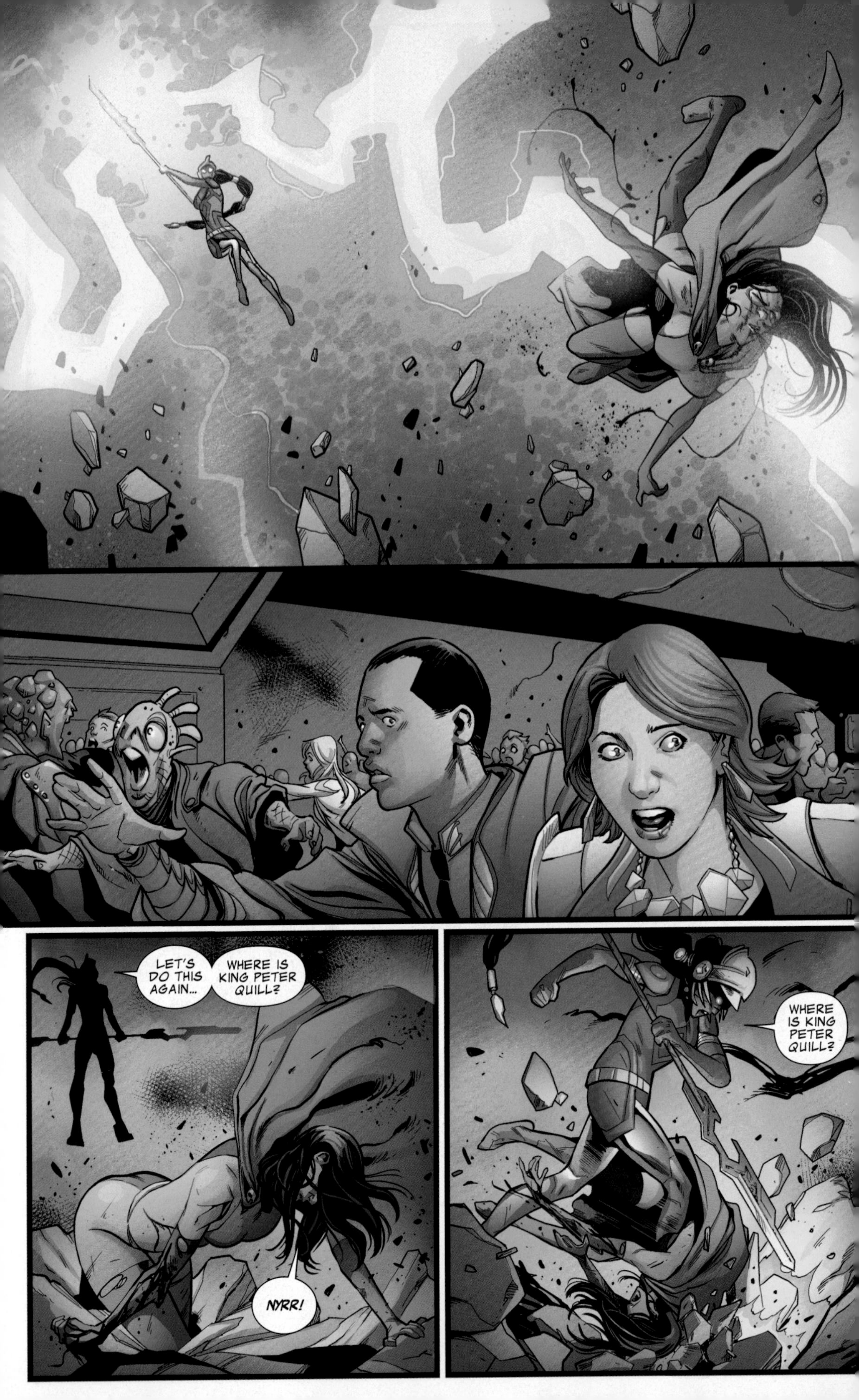
LET'S DO THIS AGAIN...
WHERE IS KING PETER QUILL?
NYRR!
WHERE IS KING PETER QUILL?

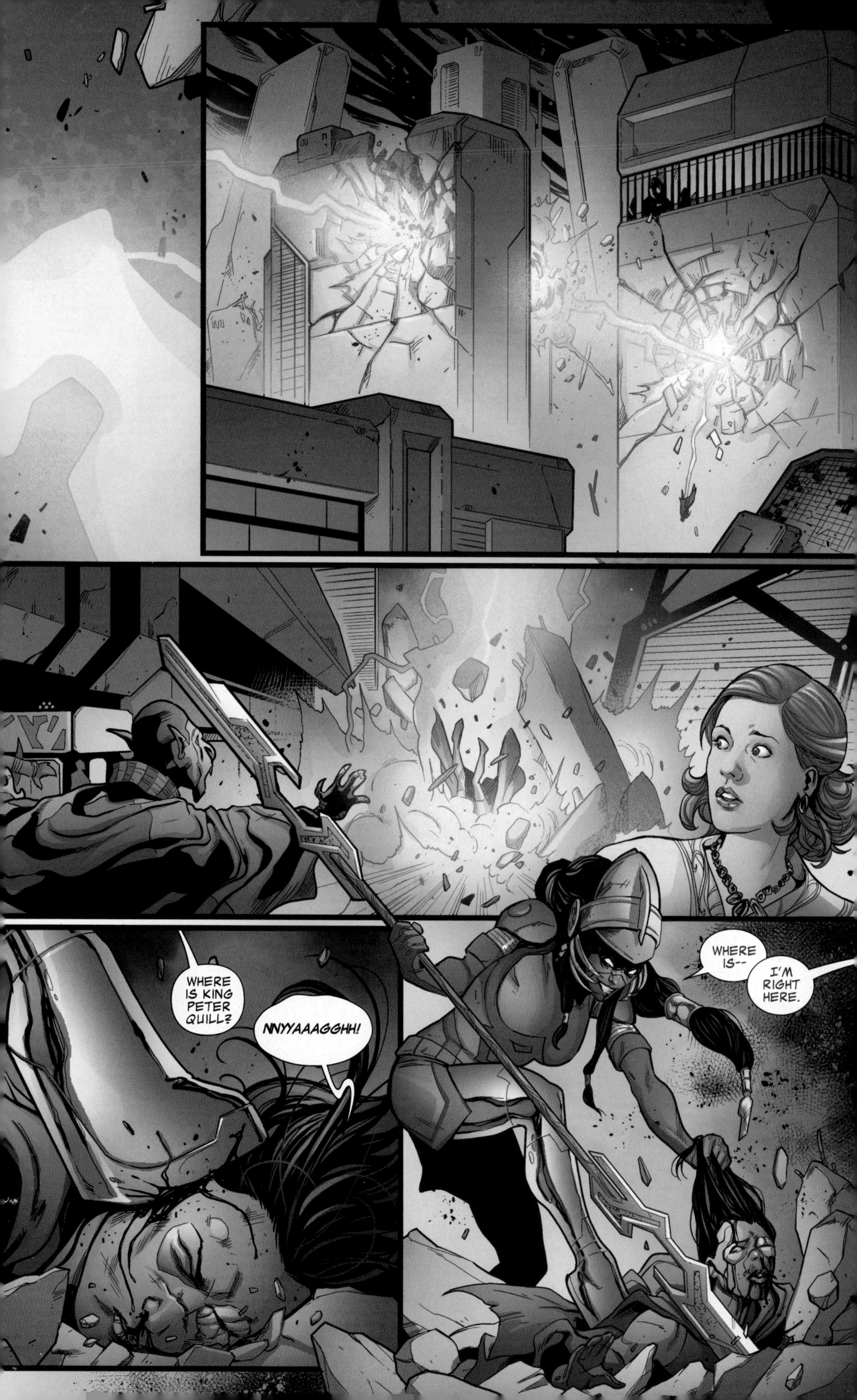
WHERE IS KING PETER QUILL?
NNYYAAAGGHH!
WHERE IS--
I'M RIGHT HERE.

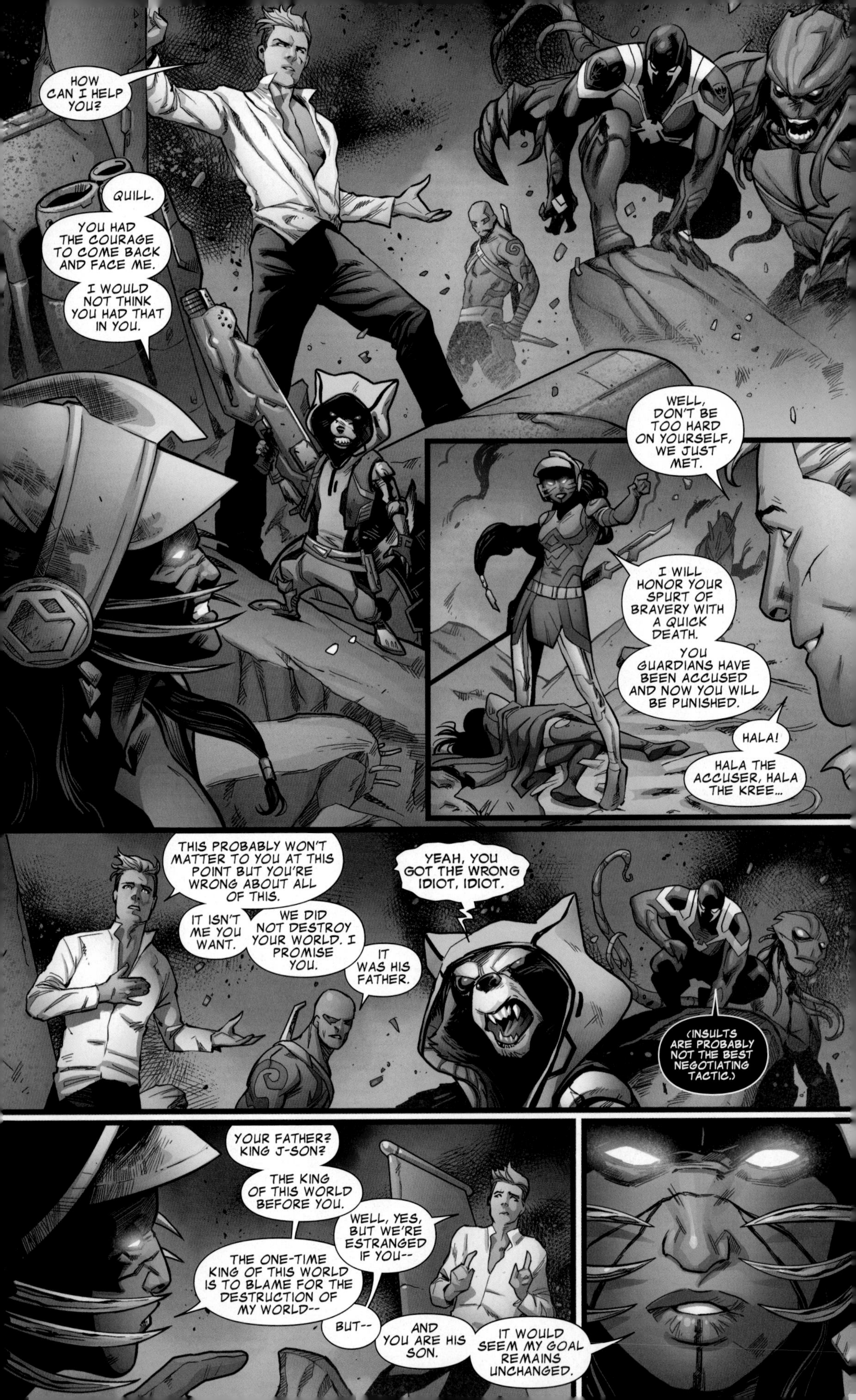
HOW CAN I HELP YOU?
QUILL.
YOU HAD THE COURAGE TO COME BACK AND FACE ME.
I WOULD NOT THINK YOU HAD THAT IN YOU.
WELL, DON'T BE TOO HARD ON YOURSELF, WE JUST MET.
I WILL HONOR YOUR SPURT OF BRAVERY WITH A QUICK DEATH.
YOU GUARDIANS HAVE BEEN ACCUSED AND NOW YOU WILL BE PUNISHED.
HALA!
HALA THE ACCUSER, HALA THE KREE...
THIS PROBABLY WON'T MATTER TO YOU AT THIS POINT BUT YOU'RE WRONG ABOUT ALL OF THIS.
IT ISN'T ME YOU WANT.
WE DID NOT DESTROY YOUR WORLD. I PROMISE YOU.
IT WAS HIS FATHER.
YEAH, YOU GOT THE WRONG IDIOT, IDIOT.
(INSULTS ARE PROBABLY NOT THE BEST NEGOTIATING TACTIC.)
YOUR FATHER? KING J-SON?
THE KING OF THIS WORLD BEFORE YOU.
WELL, YES, BUT WE'RE ESTRANGED IF YOU--
THE ONE-TIME KING OF THIS WORLD IS TO BLAME FOR THE DESTRUCTION OF MY WORLD--
BUT--
AND YOU ARE HIS SON.
IT WOULD SEEM MY GOAL REMAINS UNCHANGED.

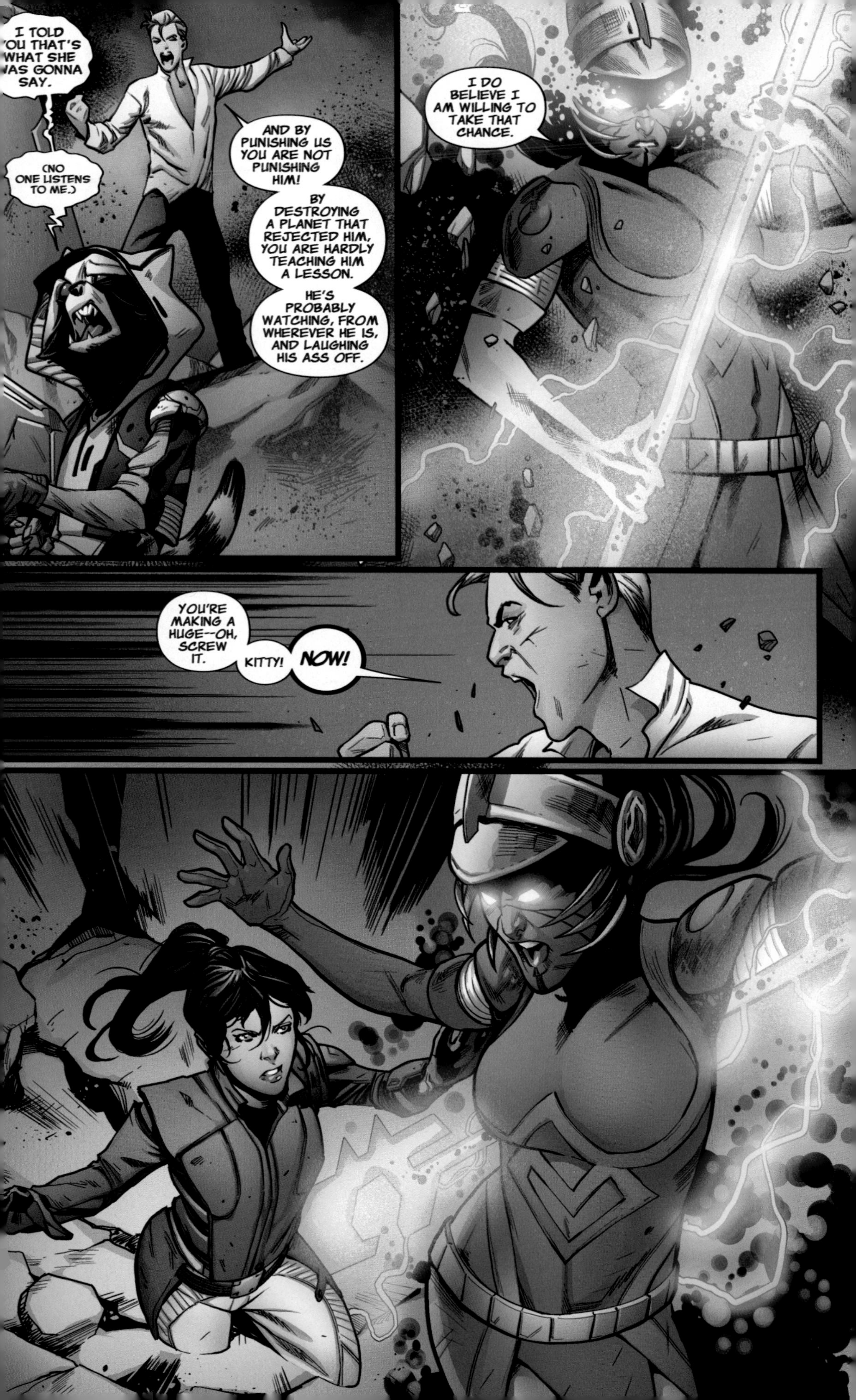
I TOLD YOU THAT'S WHAT SHE WAS GONNA SAY.
(NO ONE LISTENS TO ME.)
AND BY PUNISHING US YOU ARE NOT PUNISHING HIM!
BY DESTROYING A PLANET THAT REJECTED HIM, YOU ARE HARDLY TEACHING HIM A LESSON.
HE'S PROBABLY WATCHING, FROM WHEREVER HE IS, AND LAUGHING HIS ASS OFF.
I DO BELIEVE I AM WILLING TO TAKE THAT CHANCE.
YOU'RE MAKING A HUGE--OH, SCREW IT.
KITTY!
NOW!

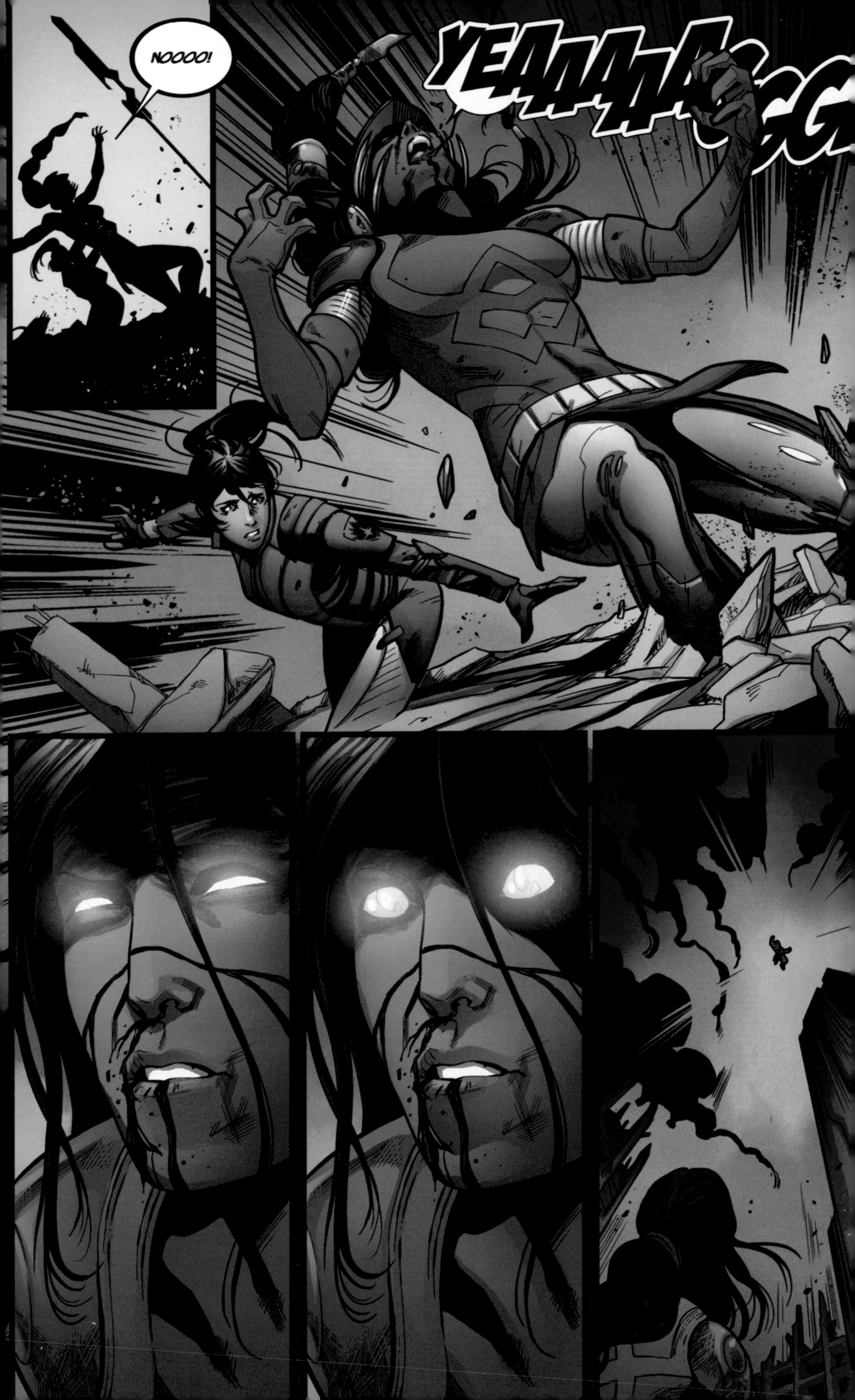
NOOOO!
YEAAAAAGGG

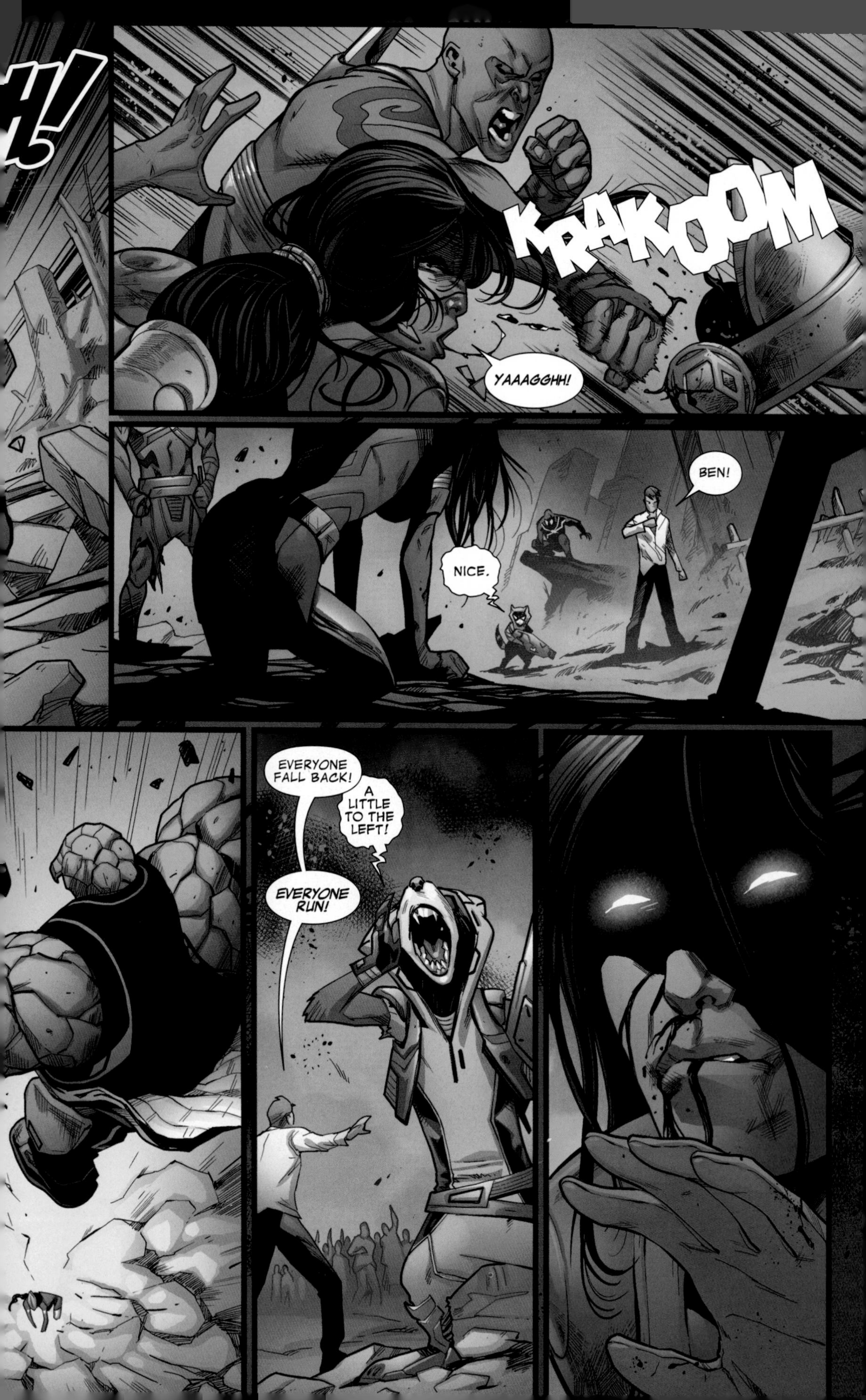
H!
KRAKOOM
YAAAGGHH!
BEN!
NICE.
EVERYONE FALL BACK!
A LITTLE TO THE LEFT!
EVERYONE RUN!

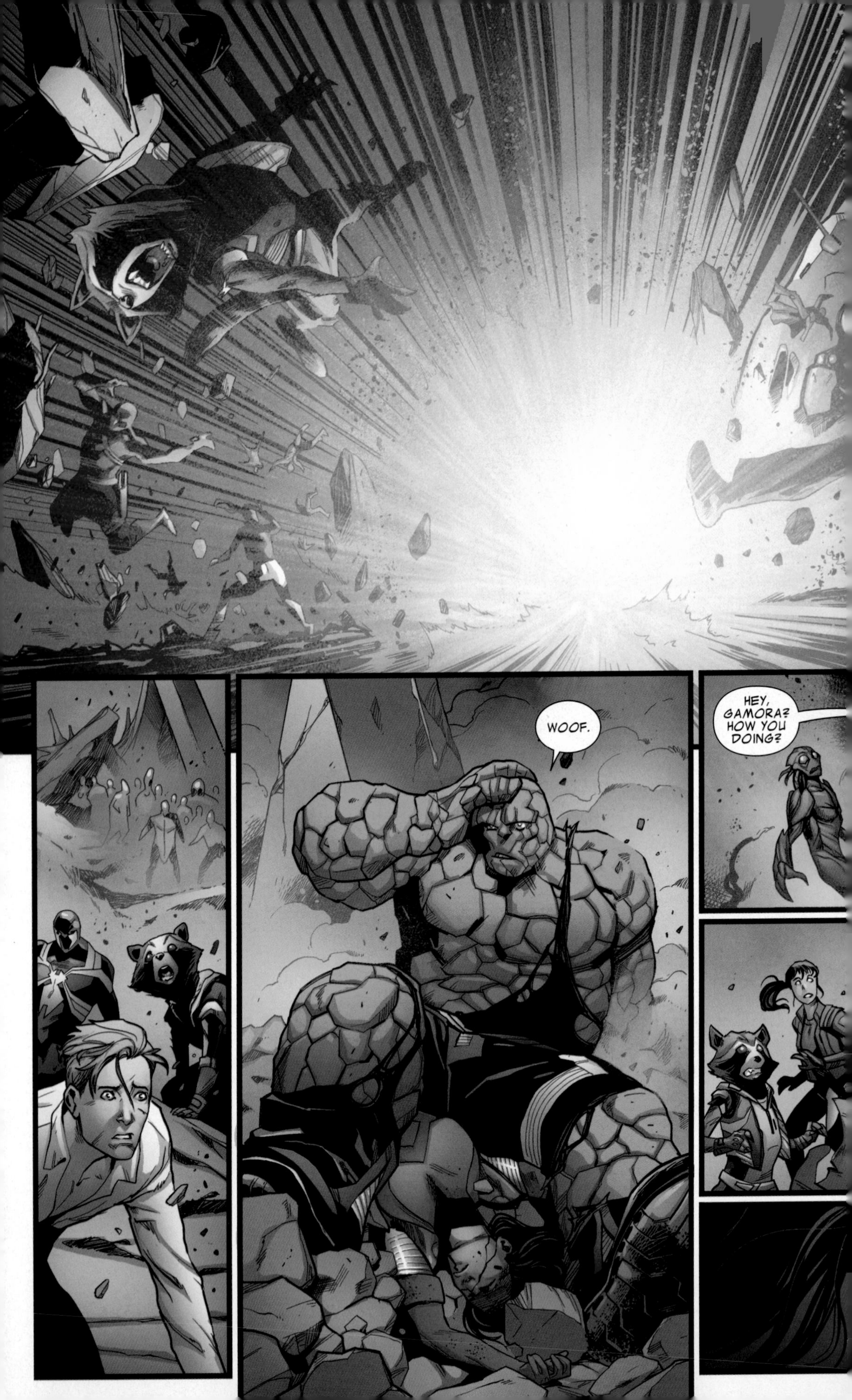
WOOF.
HEY, GAMORA? HOW YOU DOING?

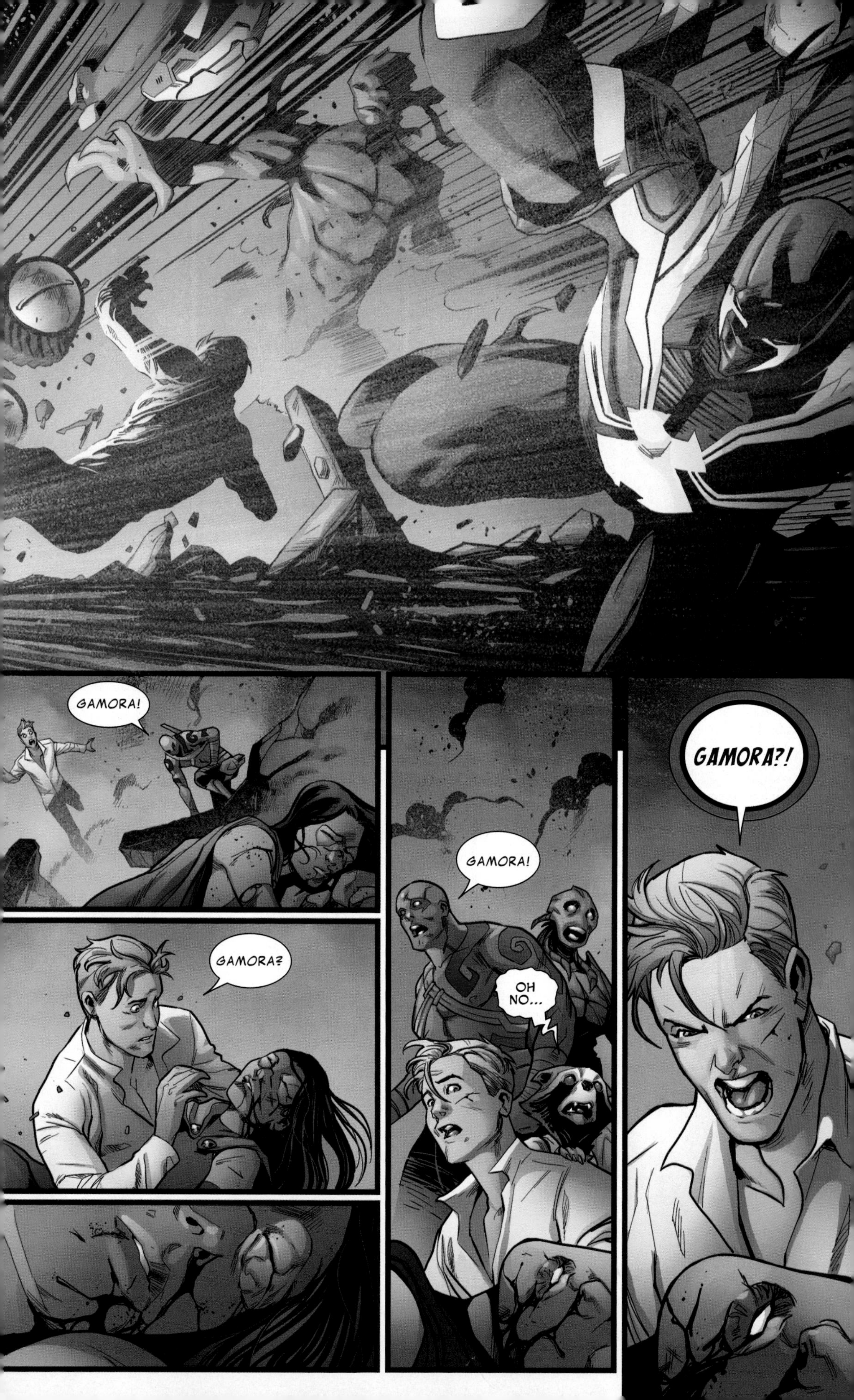
GAMORA!
GAMORA?
GAMORA!
OH NO...
GAMORA?!

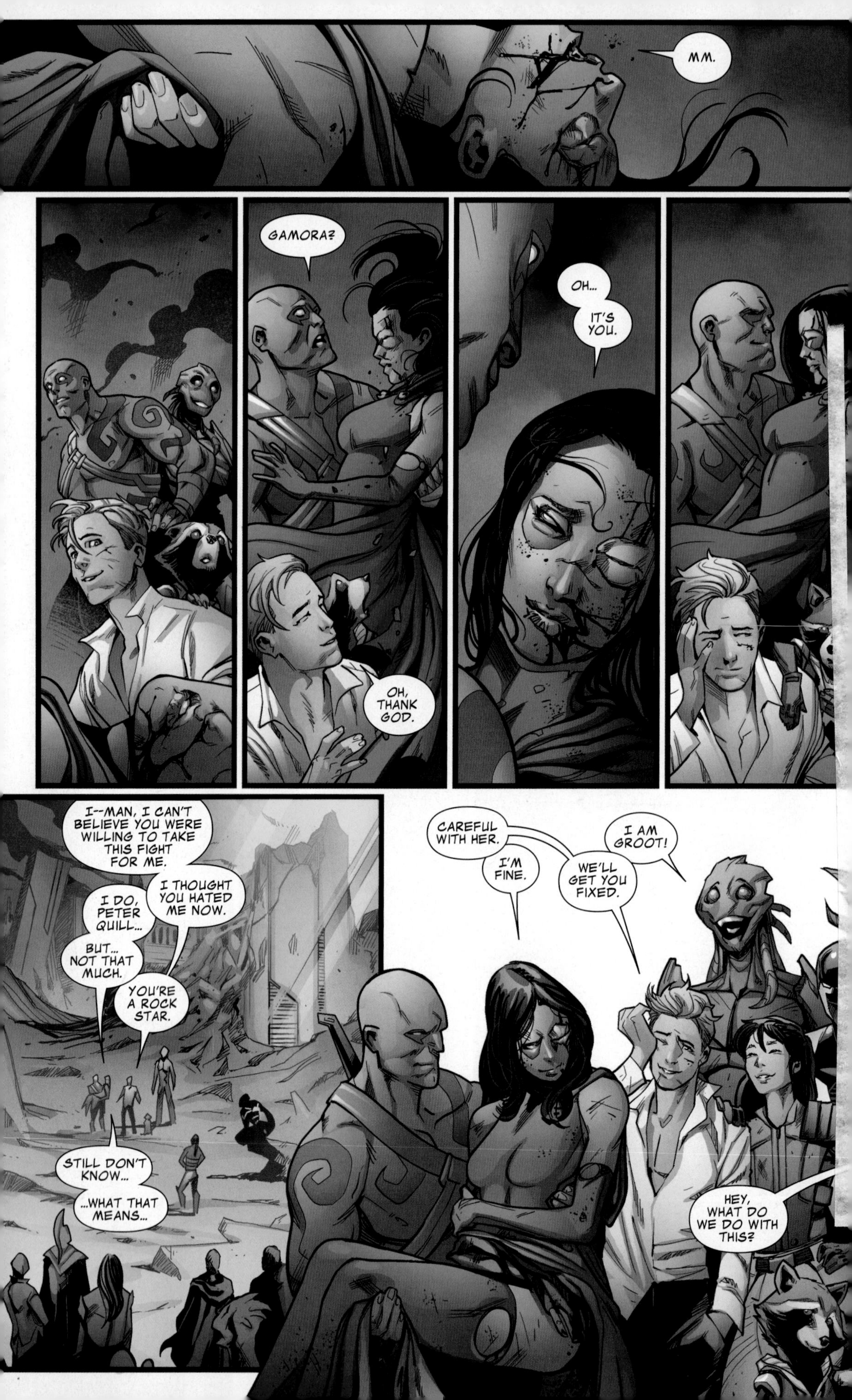
MM.
GAMORA?
OH, THANK GOD.
OH...
IT'S YOU.
I--MAN, I CAN'T BELIEVE YOU WERE WILLING TO TAKE THIS FIGHT FOR ME.
I THOUGHT YOU HATED ME NOW.
I DO, PETER QUILL...
BUT... NOT THAT MUCH.
YOU'RE A ROCK STAR.
STILL DON'T KNOW...
...WHAT THAT MEANS...
CAREFUL WITH HER.
I'M FINE.
WE'LL GET YOU FIXED.
I AM GROOT!
HEY, WHAT DO WE DO WITH THIS?

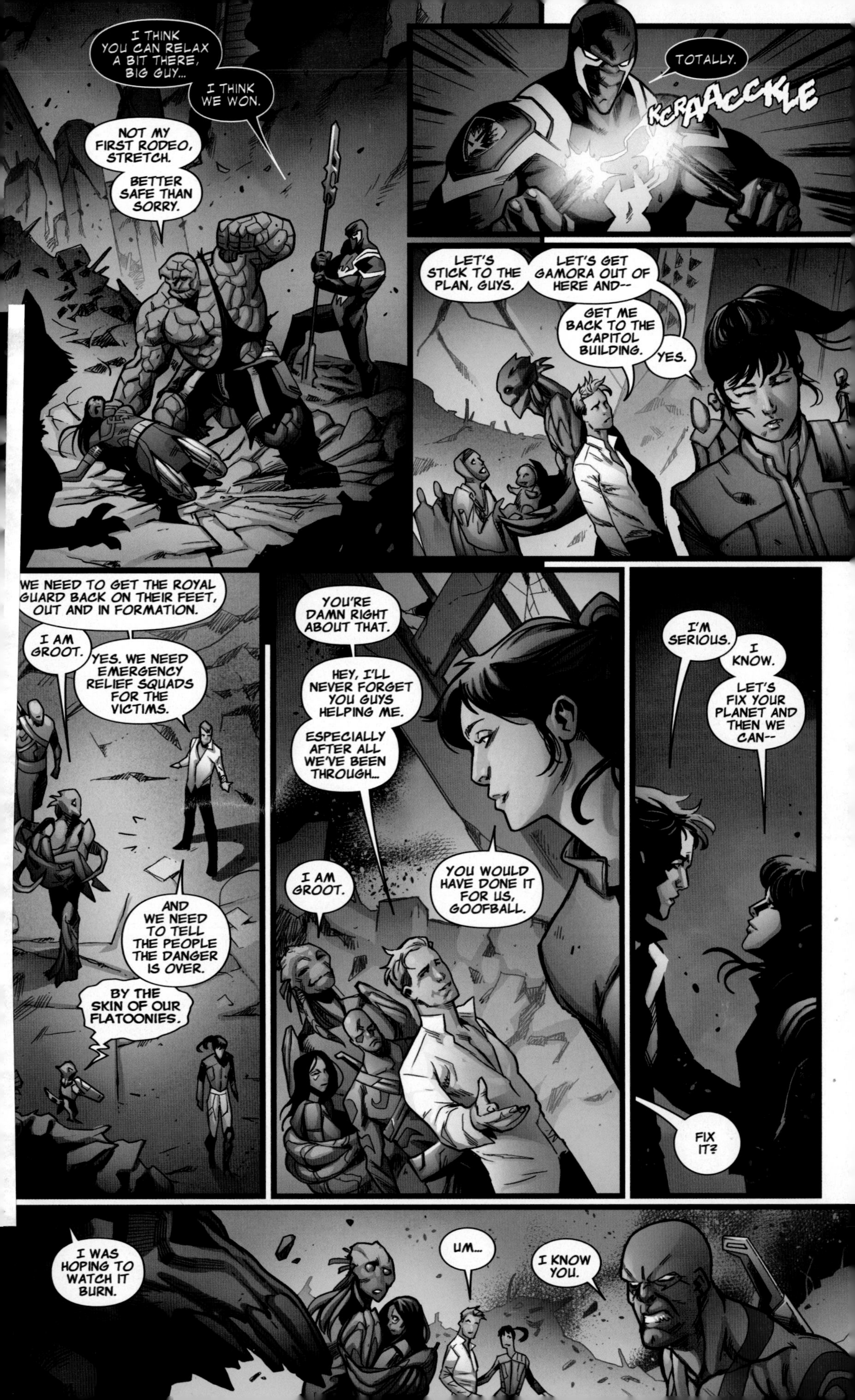
I THINK YOU CAN RELAX A BIT THERE, BIG GUY...
I THINK WE WON.
NOT MY FIRST RODEO, STRETCH.
BETTER SAFE THAN SORRY.
TOTALLY.
KCRAACCKLE
LET'S STICK TO THE PLAN, GUYS.
LET'S GET GAMORA OUT OF HERE AND--
GET ME BACK TO THE CAPITOL BUILDING.
YES.
WE NEED TO GET THE ROYAL GUARD BACK ON THEIR FEET, OUT AND IN FORMATION.
I AM GROOT.
YES. WE NEED EMERGENCY RELIEF SQUADS FOR THE VICTIMS.
AND WE NEED TO TELL THE PEOPLE THE DANGER IS OVER.
BY THE SKIN OF OUR FLATOONIES.
YOU'RE DAMN RIGHT ABOUT THAT.
HEY, I'LL NEVER FORGET YOU GUYS HELPING ME.
ESPECIALLY AFTER ALL WE'VE BEEN THROUGH...
I AM GROOT.
YOU WOULD HAVE DONE IT FOR US, GOOFBALL.
I'M SERIOUS.
I KNOW.
LET'S FIX YOUR PLANET AND THEN WE CAN--
FIX IT?
I WAS HOPING TO WATCH IT BURN.
UM...
I KNOW YOU.

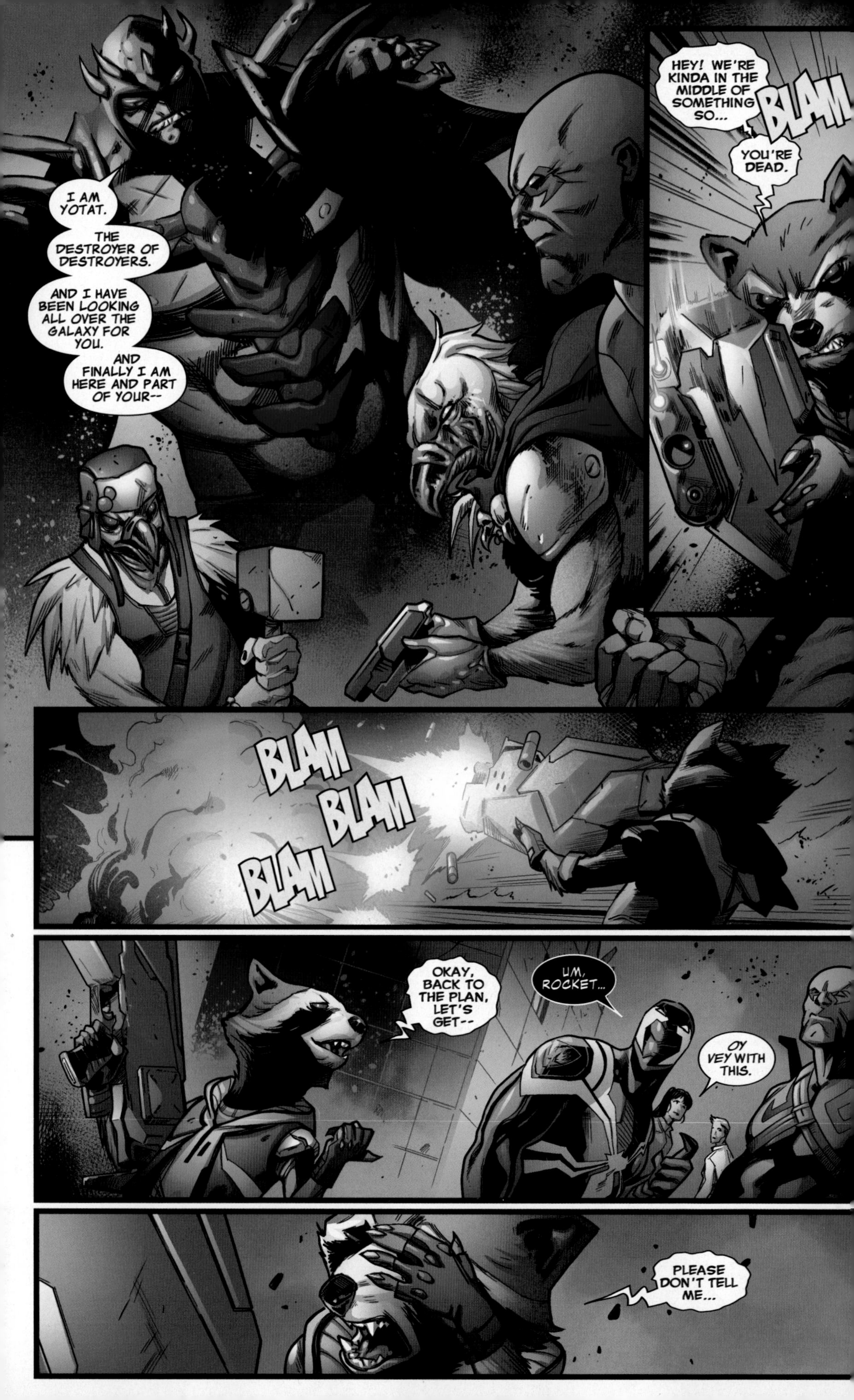
I AM YOTAT.
THE DESTROYER OF DESTROYERS.
AND I HAVE BEEN LOOKING ALL OVER THE GALAXY FOR YOU.
AND FINALLY I AM HERE AND PART OF YOUR--
HEY! WE'RE KINDA IN THE MIDDLE OF SOMETHING SO...
BLAM
YOU'RE DEAD.
BLAM
BLAM
BLAM
OKAY, BACK TO THE PLAN, LET'S GET--
UM, ROCKET...
OY VEY WITH THIS.
PLEASE DON'T TELL ME...

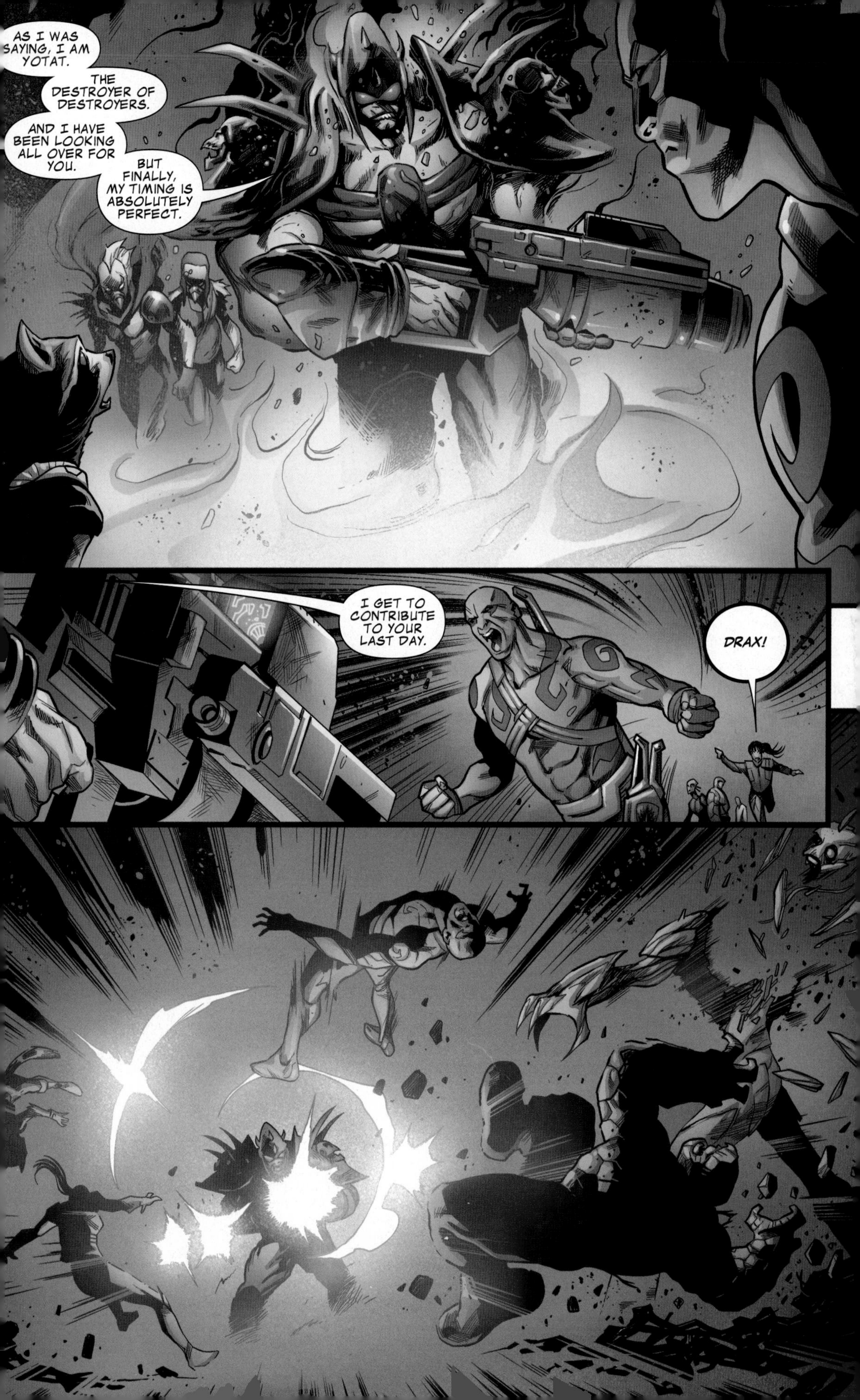
AS I WAS SAYING, I AM YOTAT.
THE DESTROYER OF DESTROYERS.
AND I HAVE BEEN LOOKING ALL OVER FOR YOU.
BUT FINALLY, MY TIMING IS ABSOLUTELY PERFECT.
I GET TO CONTRIBUTE TO YOUR LAST DAY.
DRAX!

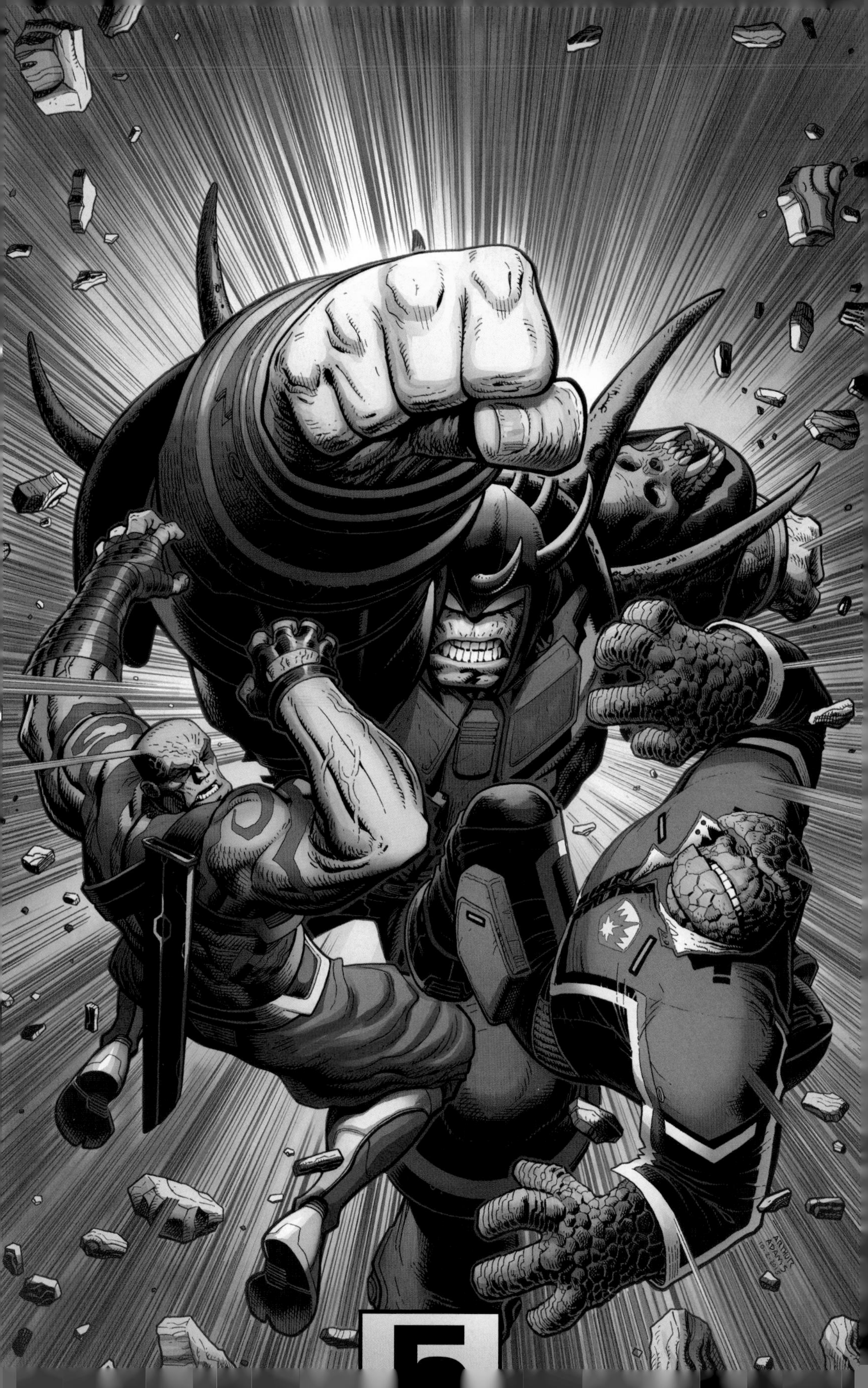

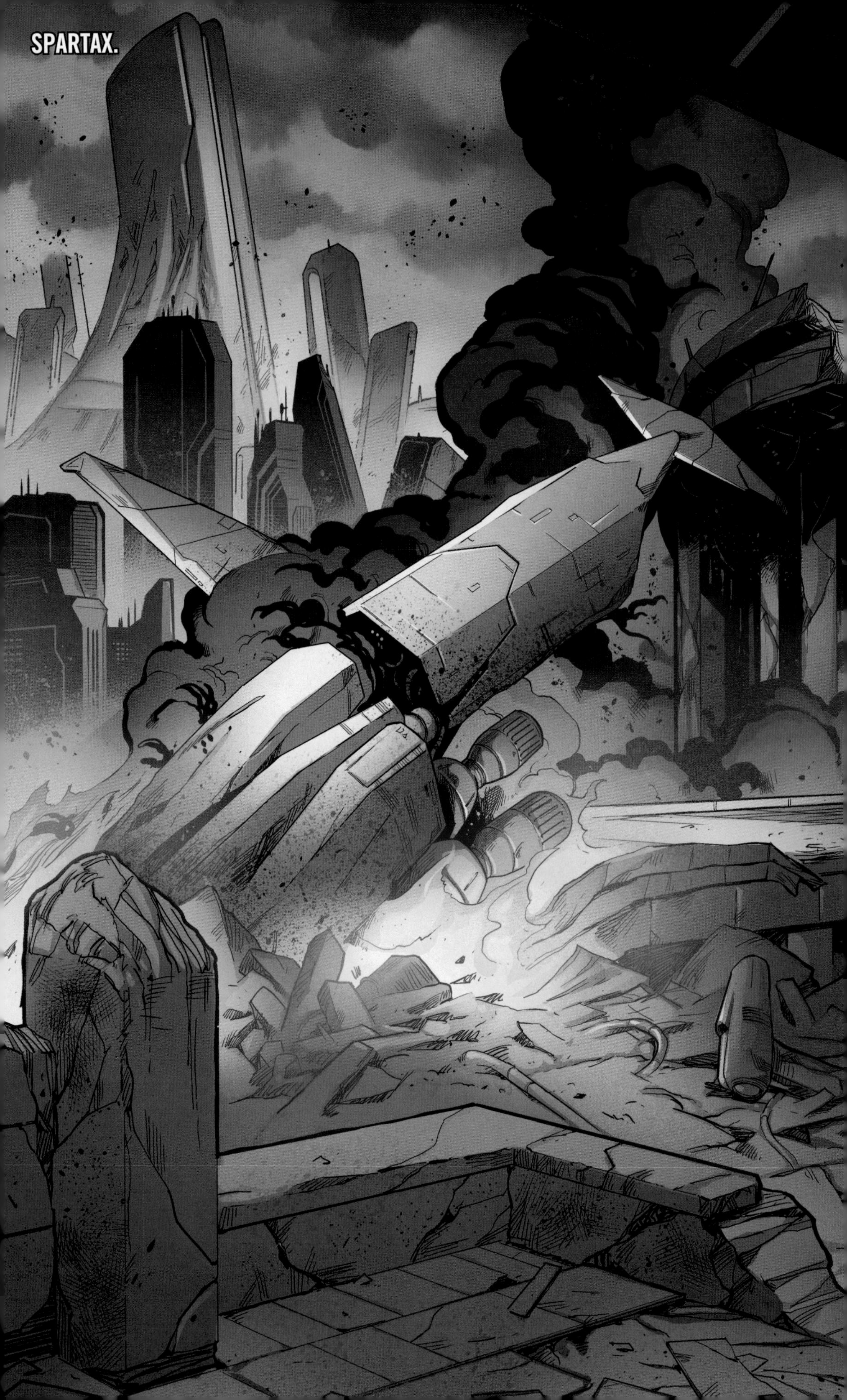
SPARTAX.

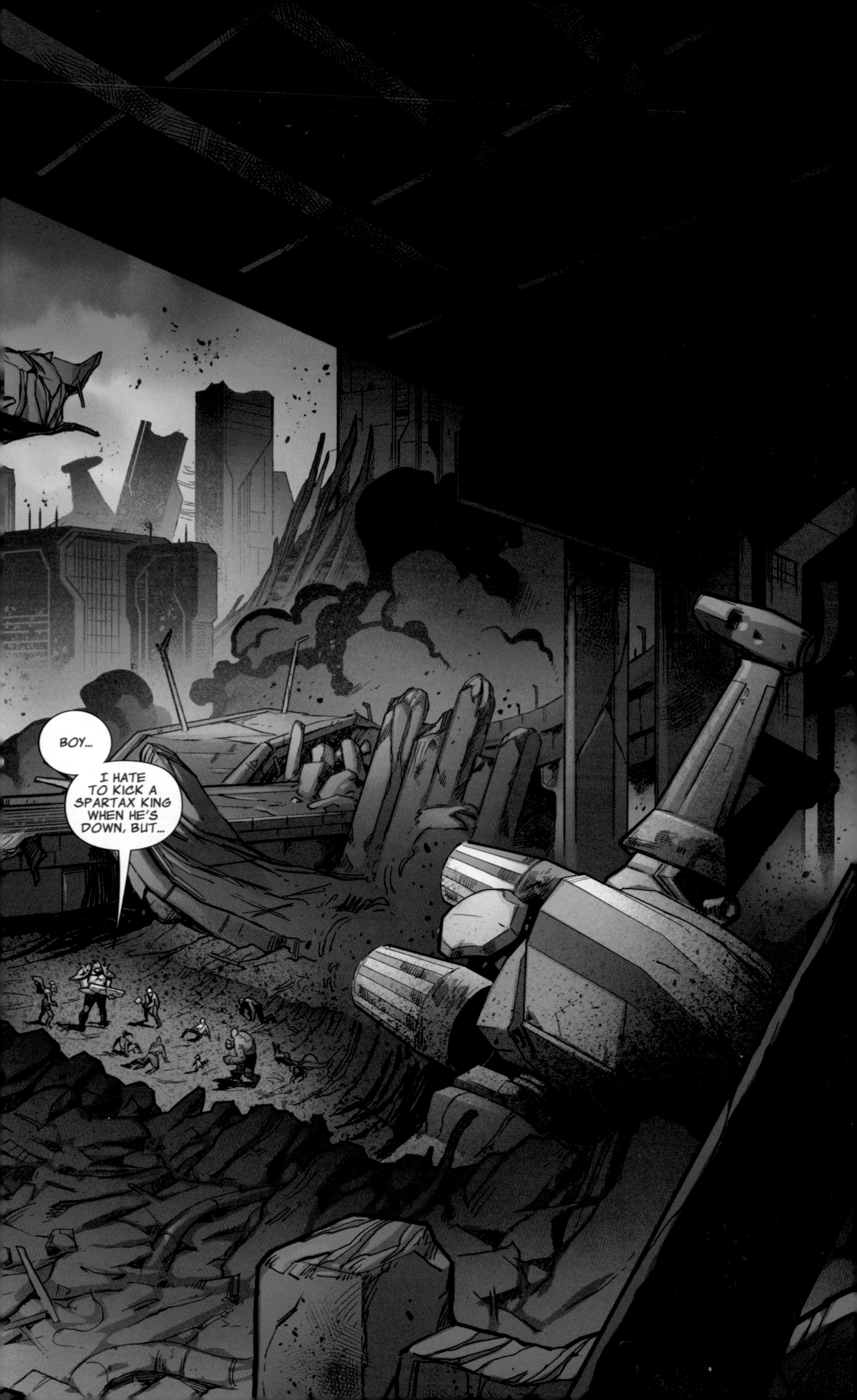
BOY...
I HATE TO KICK A SPARTAX KING WHEN HE'S DOWN, BUT...

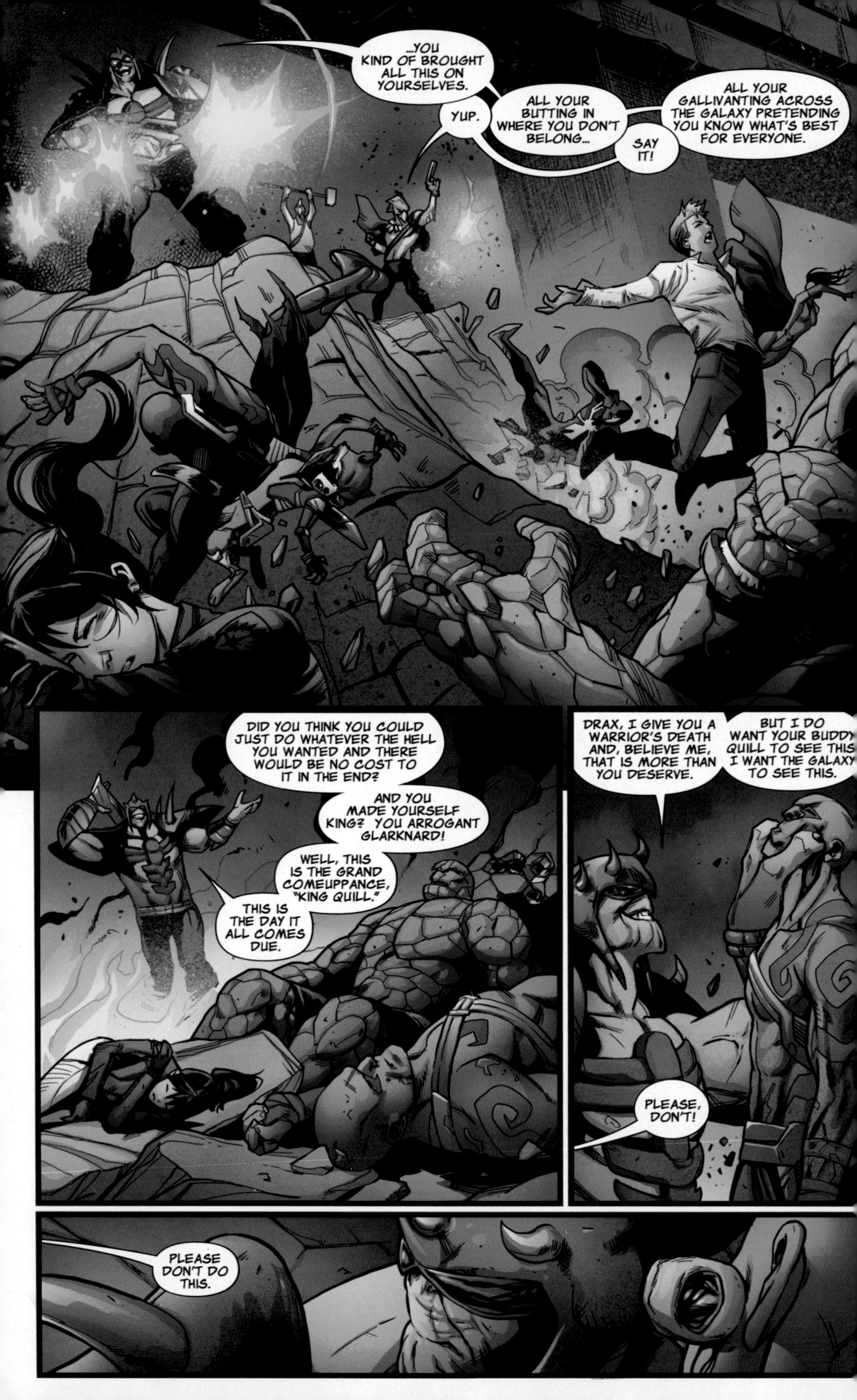
...YOU KIND OF BROUGHT ALL THIS ON YOURSELVES.
YUP.
ALL YOUR BUTTING IN WHERE YOU DON'T BELONG...
SAY IT!
ALL YOUR GALLIVANTING ACROSS THE GALAXY PRETENDING YOU KNOW WHAT'S BEST FOR EVERYONE.
DID YOU THINK YOU COULD JUST DO WHATEVER THE HELL YOU WANTED AND THERE WOULD BE NO COST TO IT IN THE END?
AND YOU MADE YOURSELF KING? YOU ARROGANT GLARKNARD!
WELL, THIS IS THE GRAND COMEUPPANCE, "KING QUILL."
THIS IS THE DAY IT ALL COMES DUE.
DRAX, I GIVE YOU A WARRIOR'S DEATH AND, BELIEVE ME, THAT IS MORE THAN YOU DESERVE.
BUT I DO WANT YOUR BUDDY QUILL TO SEE THIS I WANT THE GALAXY TO SEE THIS.
PLEASE, DON'T!
PLEASE DON'T DO THIS.

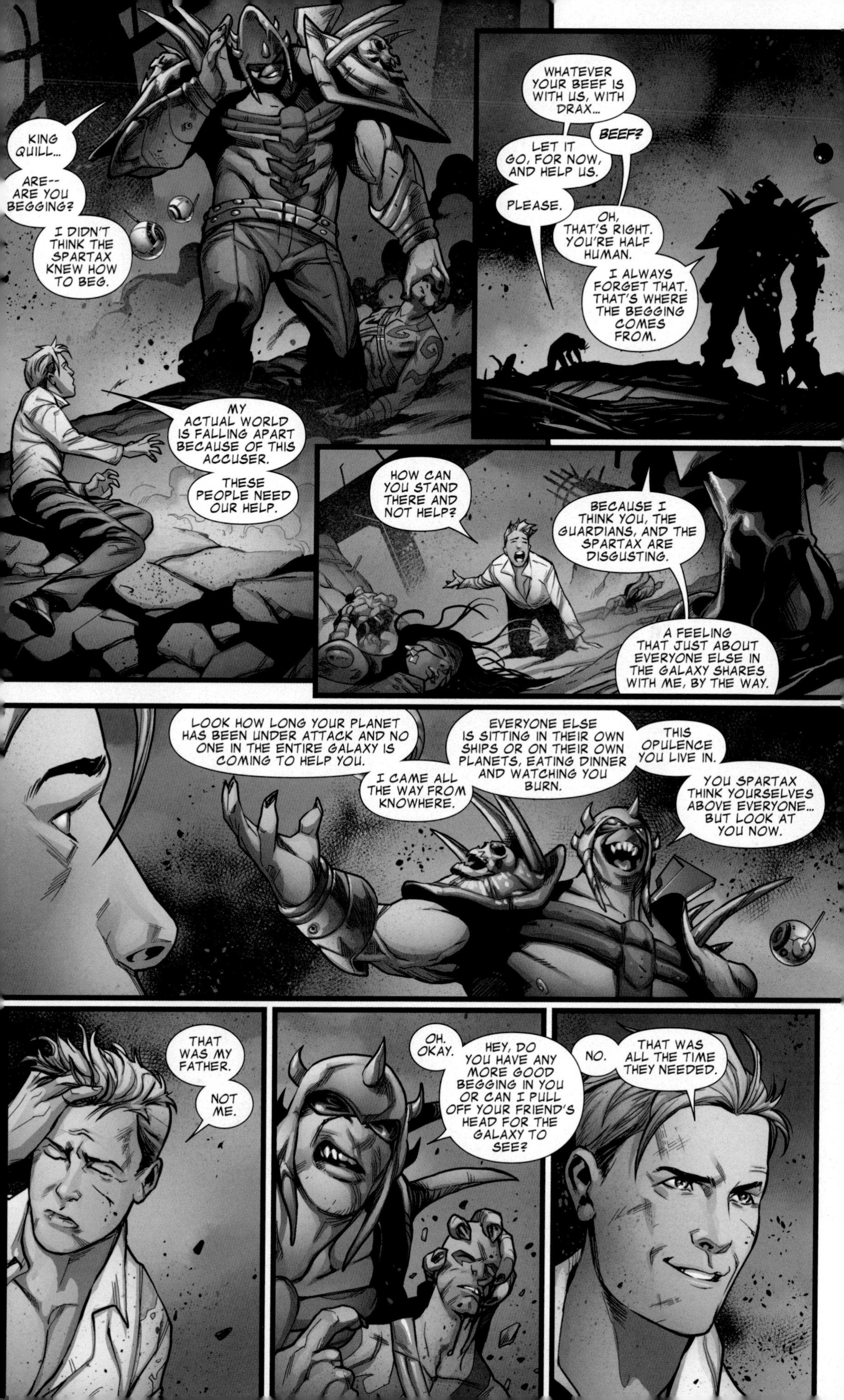
KING QUILL...
ARE-- ARE YOU BEGGING?
I DIDN'T THINK THE SPARTAX KNEW HOW TO BEG.
WHATEVER YOUR BEEF IS WITH US, WITH DRAX...
BEEF?
LET IT GO, FOR NOW, AND HELP US.
PLEASE.
OH, THAT'S RIGHT. YOU'RE HALF HUMAN.
I ALWAYS FORGET THAT. THAT'S WHERE THE BEGGING COMES FROM.
MY ACTUAL WORLD IS FALLING APART BECAUSE OF THIS ACCUSER.
THESE PEOPLE NEED OUR HELP.
HOW CAN YOU STAND THERE AND NOT HELP?
BECAUSE I THINK YOU, THE GUARDIANS, AND THE SPARTAX ARE DISGUSTING.
A FEELING THAT JUST ABOUT EVERYONE ELSE IN THE GALAXY SHARES WITH ME, BY THE WAY.
LOOK HOW LONG YOUR PLANET HAS BEEN UNDER ATTACK AND NO ONE IN THE ENTIRE GALAXY IS COMING TO HELP YOU.
I CAME ALL THE WAY FROM KNOWHERE.
EVERYONE ELSE IS SITTING IN THEIR OWN SHIPS OR ON THEIR OWN PLANETS, EATING DINNER AND WATCHING YOU BURN.
THIS OPULENCE YOU LIVE IN.
YOU SPARTAX THINK YOURSELVES ABOVE EVERYONE... BUT LOOK AT YOU NOW.
THAT WAS MY FATHER.
NOT ME.
OH. OKAY.
HEY, DO YOU HAVE ANY MORE GOOD BEGGING IN YOU OR CAN I PULL OFF YOUR FRIEND'S HEAD FOR THE GALAXY TO SEE?
NO.
THAT WAS ALL THE TIME THEY NEEDED.

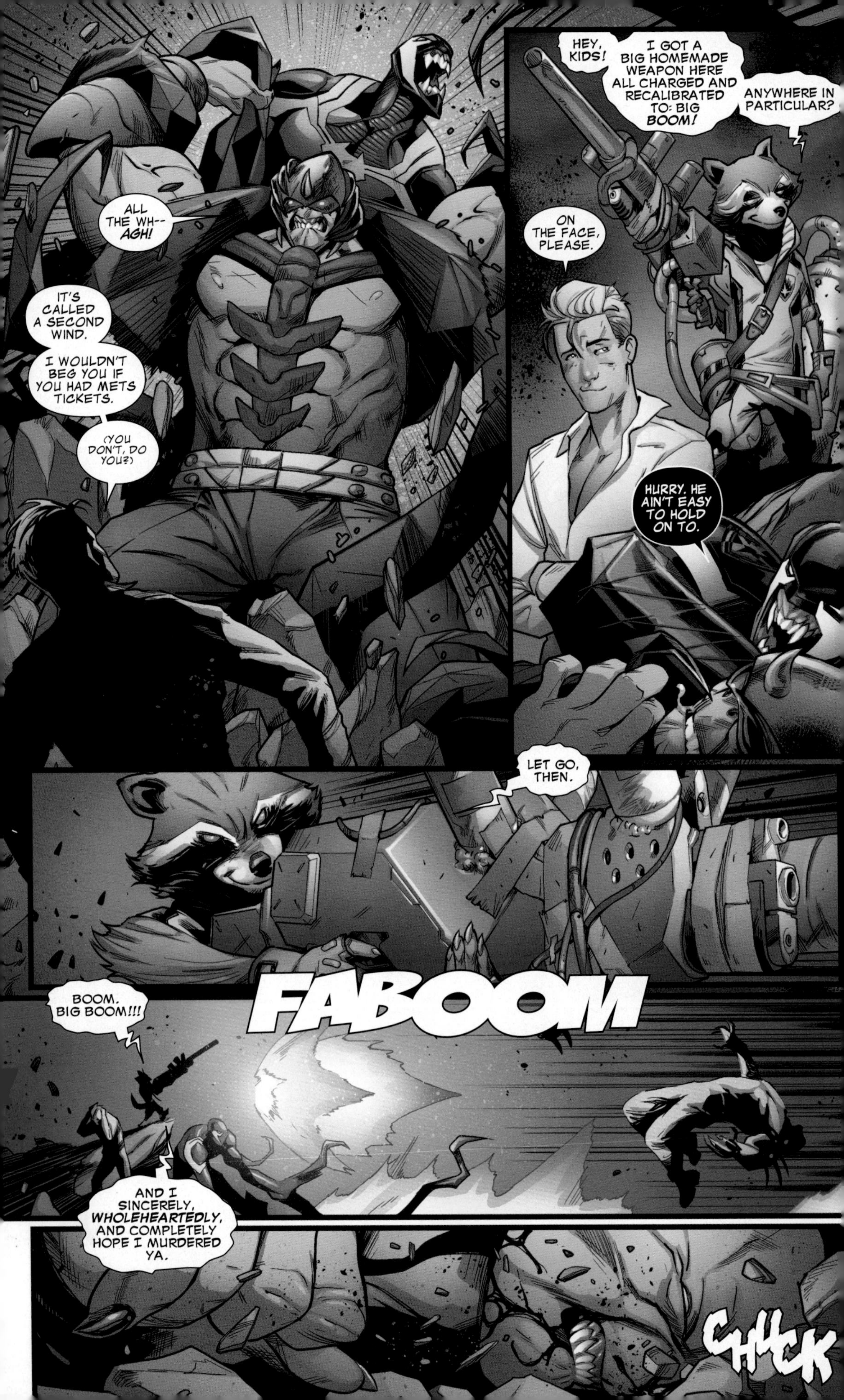
ALL THE WH-- AGH!
IT'S CALLED A SECOND WIND.
I WOULDN'T BEG YOU IF YOU HAD METS TICKETS.
(YOU DON'T, DO YOU?)
HEY, KIDS!
I GOT A BIG HOMEMADE WEAPON HERE ALL CHARGED AND RECALIBRATED TO: BIG BOOM!
ANYWHERE IN PARTICULAR?
ON THE FACE, PLEASE.
HURRY. HE AIN'T EASY TO HOLD ON TO.
LET GO, THEN.
FABOOM
BOOM. BIG BOOM!!!
AND I SINCERELY, WHOLEHEARTEDLY, AND COMPLETELY HOPE I MURDERED YA.
CHUCK

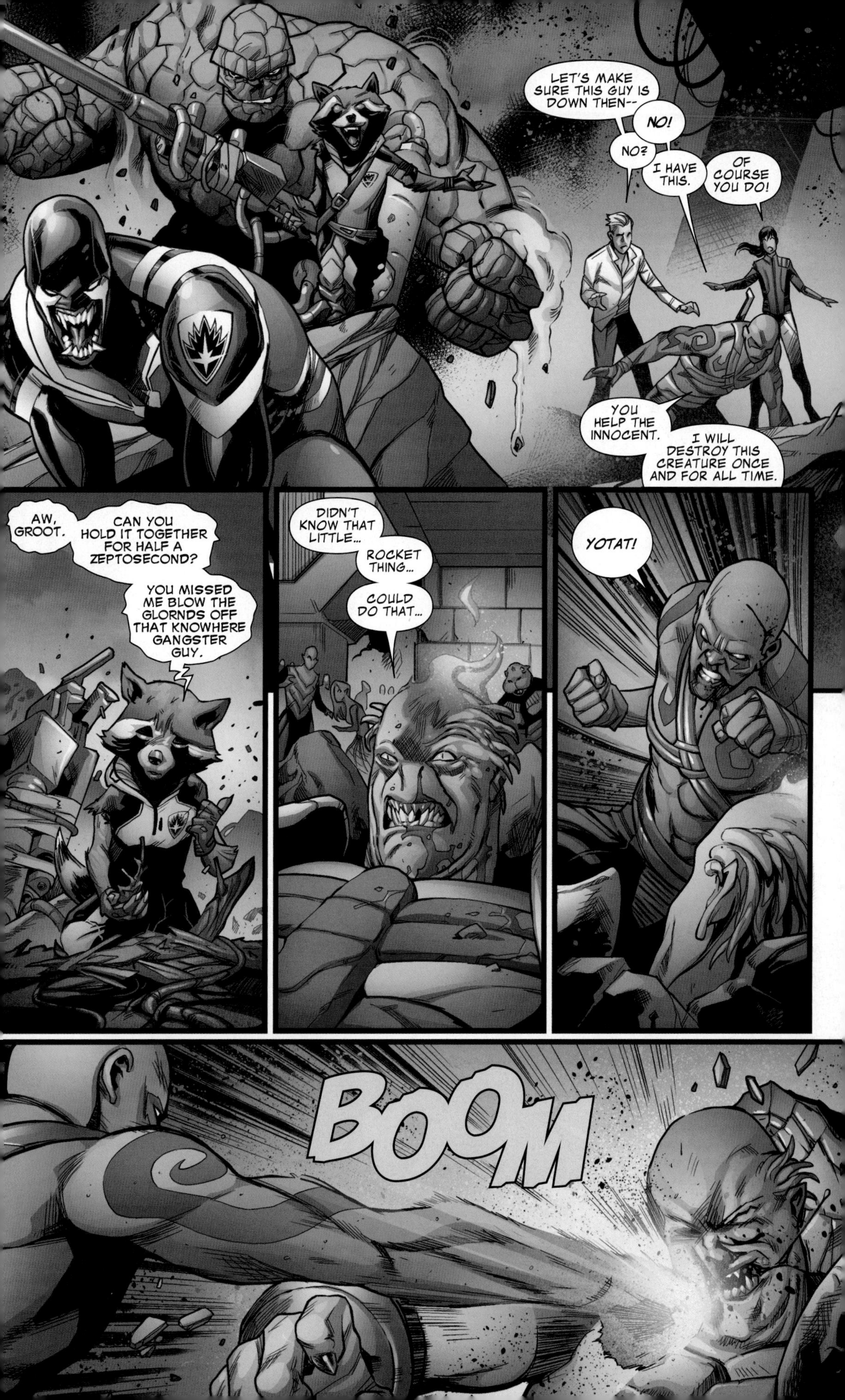
LET'S MAKE SURE THIS GUY IS DOWN THEN--
NO!
NO?
I HAVE THIS.
OF COURSE YOU DO!
YOU HELP THE INNOCENT.
I WILL DESTROY THIS CREATURE ONCE AND FOR ALL TIME.
AW, GROOT.
CAN YOU HOLD IT TOGETHER FOR HALF A ZEPTOSECOND?
YOU MISSED ME BLOW THE GLORNDS OFF THAT KNOWHERE GANGSTER GUY.
DIDN'T KNOW THAT LITTLE...
ROCKET THING...
COULD DO THAT...
YOTAT!
BOOM

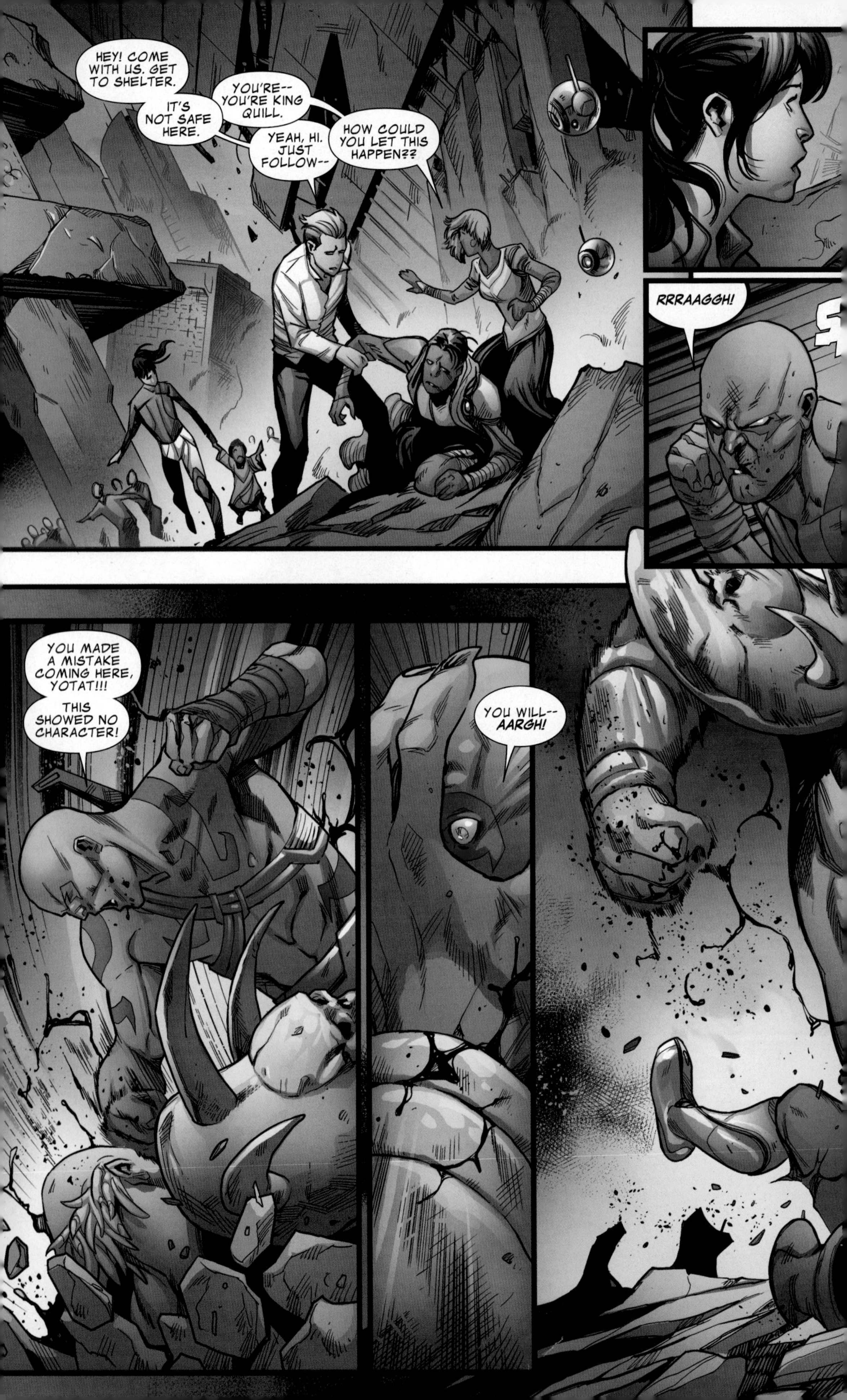
HEY! COME WITH US. GET TO SHELTER.
IT'S NOT SAFE HERE.
YOU'RE-- YOU'RE KING QUILL.
YEAH, HI. JUST FOLLOW--
HOW COULD YOU LET THIS HAPPEN??
RRRAAGGH!
YOU MADE A MISTAKE COMING HERE, YOTAT!!!
THIS SHOWED NO CHARACTER!
YOU WILL-- AARGH!

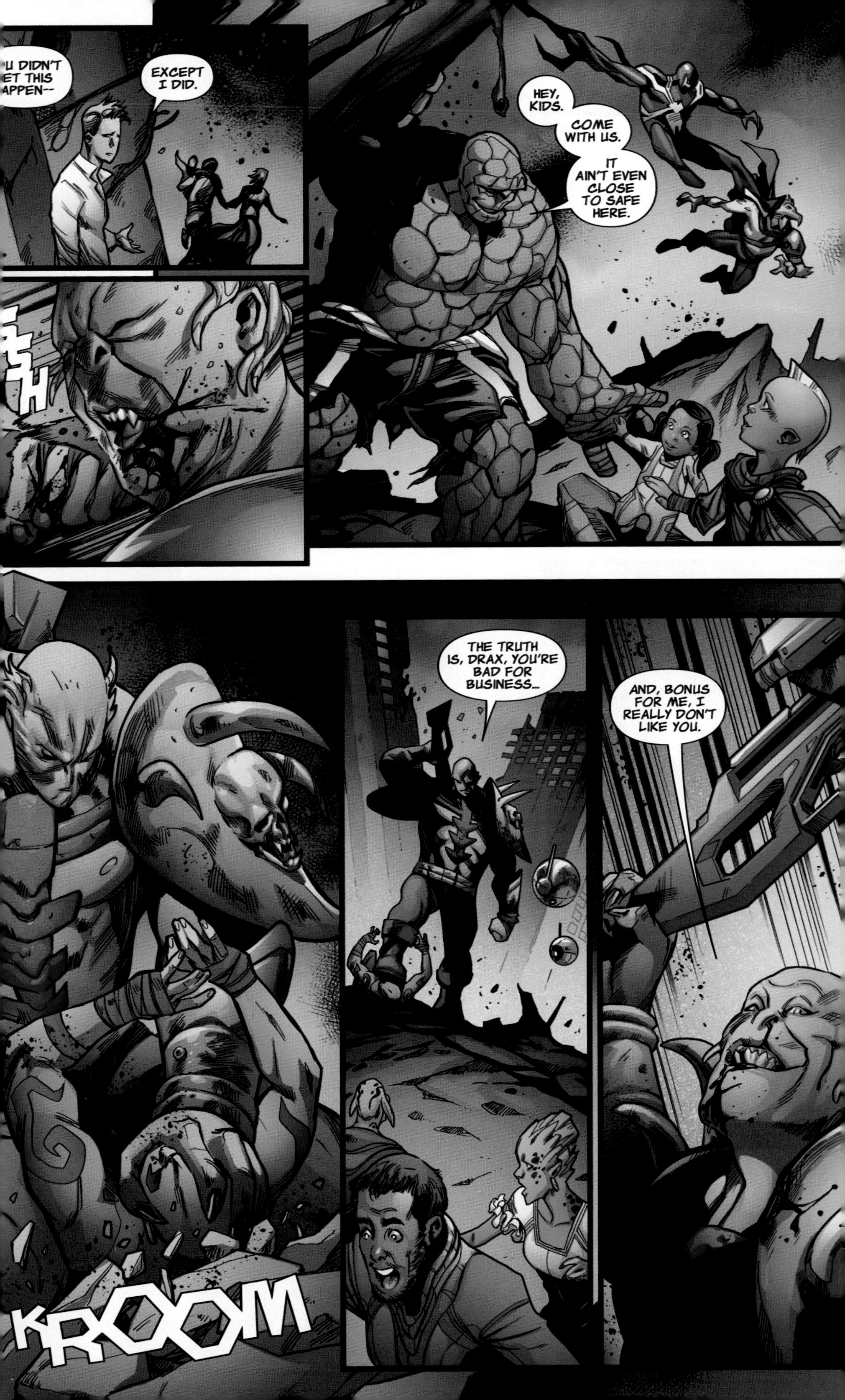
U DIDN'T
ET THIS
APPEN--
EXCEPT I DID.
HEY, KIDS.
COME WITH US.
IT AIN'T EVEN CLOSE TO SAFE HERE.
KROOOM
THE TRUTH IS, DRAX, YOU'RE BAD FOR BUSINESS...
AND, BONUS FOR ME, I REALLY DON'T LIKE YOU.

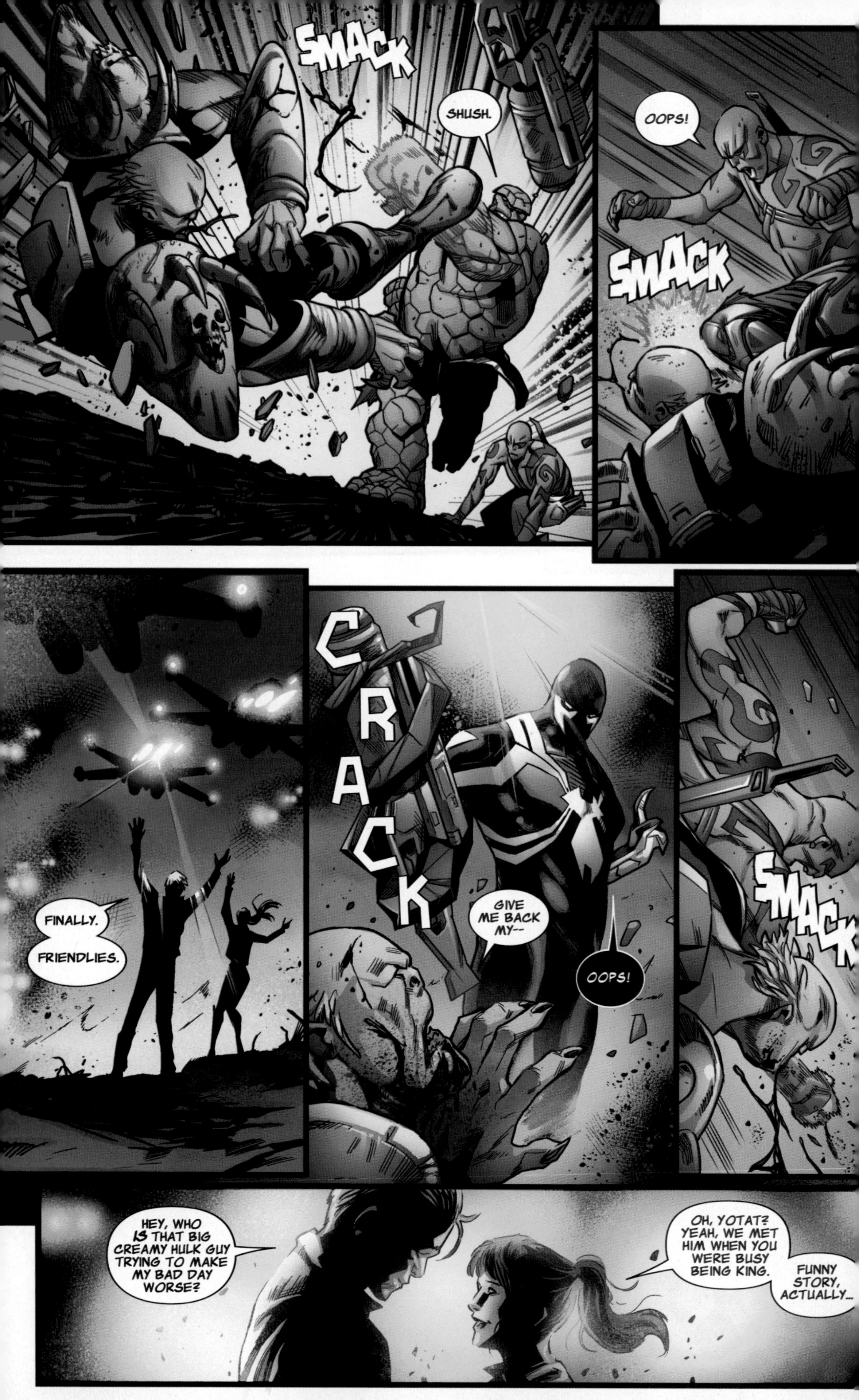
SMACK
SHUSH.
OOPS!
SMACK
FINALLY.
FRIENDLIES.
CRACK
GIVE ME BACK MY--
OOPS!
SMACK
HEY, WHO IS THAT BIG CREAMY HULK GUY TRYING TO MAKE MY BAD DAY WORSE?
OH, YOTAT? YEAH, WE MET HIM WHEN YOU WERE BUSY BEING KING.
FUNNY STORY, ACTUALLY...

KNOWHERE.
THE EDGE OF THE UNIVERSE.
LOCATED INSIDE THE DECAPITATED
HEAD OF A CELESTIAL.
THREE MONTHS AGO.
KITTY PRYDE-NARRATED FLASHBACK.

"KNOWHERE.

HISTORICALLY SHE IS AN UNRELIABLE
NARRATOR.

"ABOUT TWO
MONTHS AGO.

"WE WERE THERE TO STOCK
UP ON SUPPLIES AND TO
SHOW BEN GRIMM AROUND.

"TEACHING HIM THE DO'S
AND DON'TS OF THE
ARMPIT OF THE GALAXY."

AND NEVER
EAT THE
STREET VENDOR
GLARKIN.

MADNESS!
STREET VENDOR
GLARKIN IS PROOF
THERE IS A HIGHER
BEING.

I AM
GROOT.

I JUST
WANT TO
TAKE A SHOWER.
WITH WATER.

NOT THAT
WEIRD STEAM
STUFF WE USE
ON THE SHIP.

OH, I KIND
OF LIKE THE
STEAM SHOWER
THING.

WELL, YOU'RE
MADE OF ROCK.
YOU CAN CLEAN
YOURSELF
WITH A--

BOOM

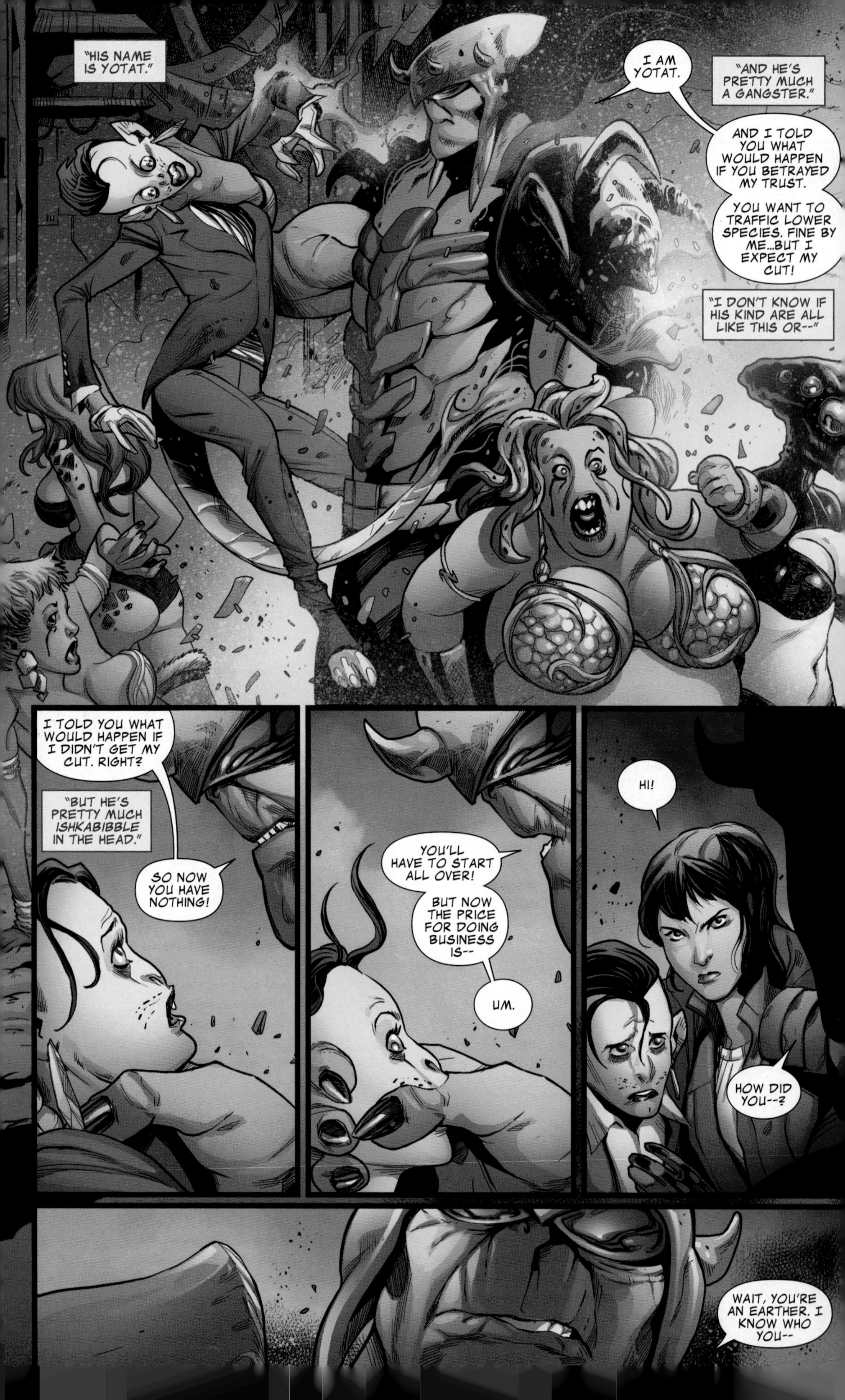
"HIS NAME IS YOTAT."
I AM YOTAT.
"AND HE'S PRETTY MUCH A GANGSTER."
AND I TOLD YOU WHAT WOULD HAPPEN IF YOU BETRAYED MY TRUST.
YOU WANT TO TRAFFIC LOWER SPECIES. FINE BY ME...BUT I EXPECT MY CUT!
"I DON'T KNOW IF HIS KIND ARE ALL LIKE THIS OR--"
I TOLD YOU WHAT WOULD HAPPEN IF I DIDN'T GET MY CUT. RIGHT?
"BUT HE'S PRETTY MUCH *ISHKABIBBLE* IN THE HEAD."
SO NOW YOU HAVE NOTHING!
YOU'LL HAVE TO START ALL OVER!
BUT NOW THE PRICE FOR DOING BUSINESS IS--
UM.
HI!
HOW DID YOU--?
WAIT, YOU'RE AN EARTHER. I KNOW WHO YOU--

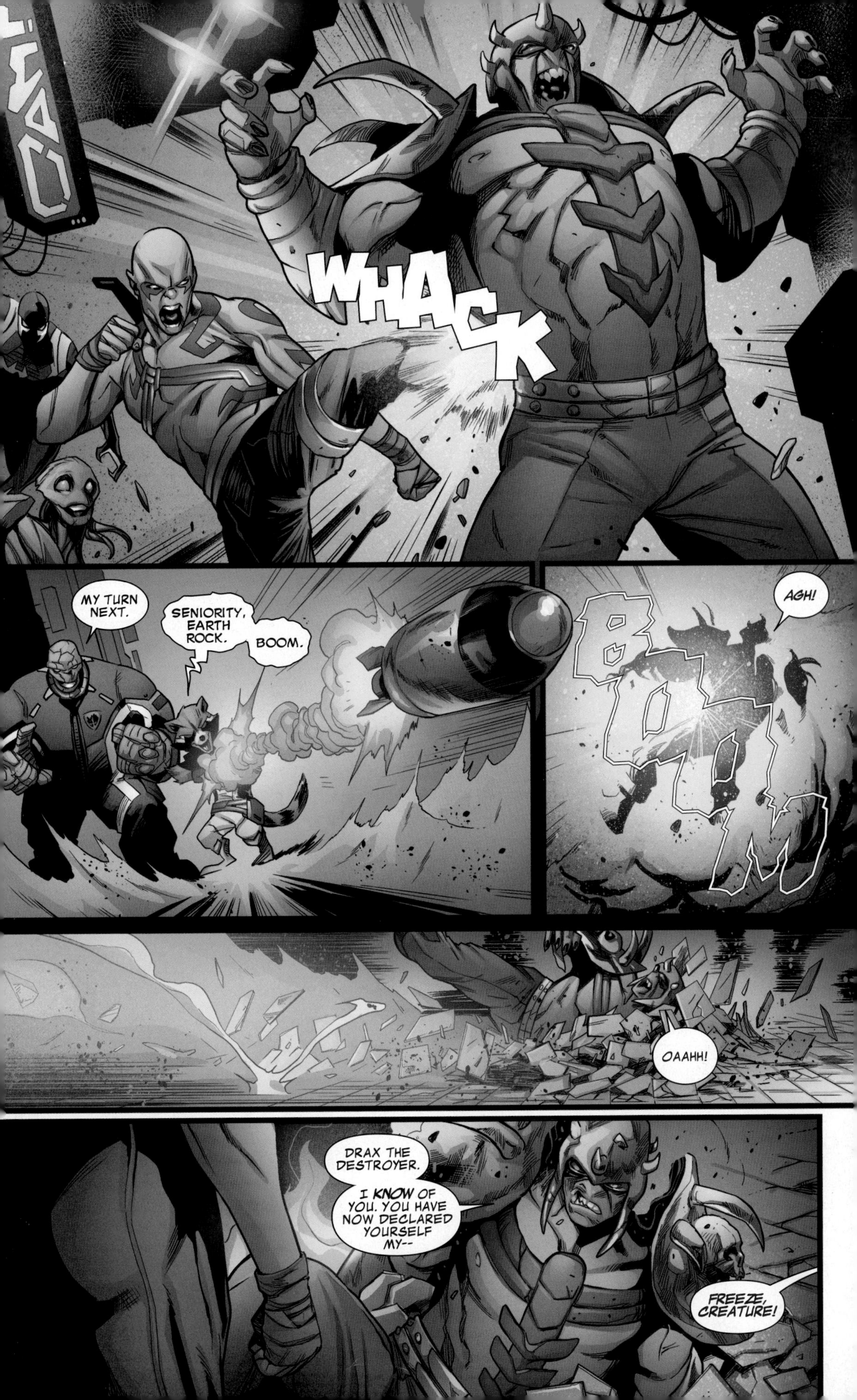
WHACK
MY TURN NEXT.
SENIORITY, EARTH ROCK.
BOOM.
BOOM
AGH!
OAAHH!
DRAX THE DESTROYER.
I KNOW OF YOU. YOU HAVE NOW DECLARED YOURSELF MY--
FREEZE, CREATURE!

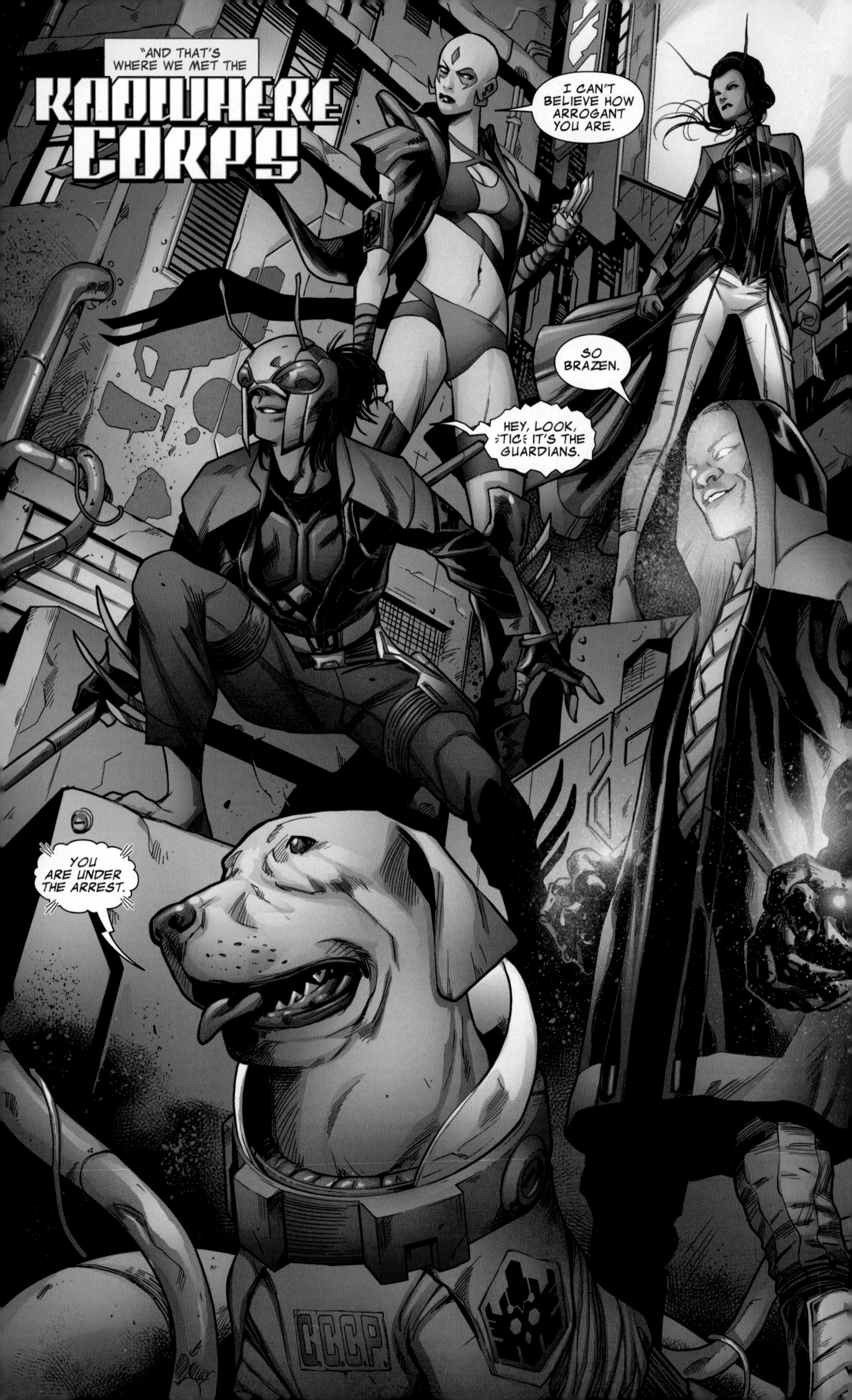

"AND THAT'S WHERE WE MET THE
KNOWHERE CORPS
I CAN'T BELIEVE HOW ARROGANT YOU ARE.
SO BRAZEN.
HEY, LOOK, TIC: IT'S THE GUARDIANS.
YOU ARE UNDER THE ARREST.
C.C.C.P.

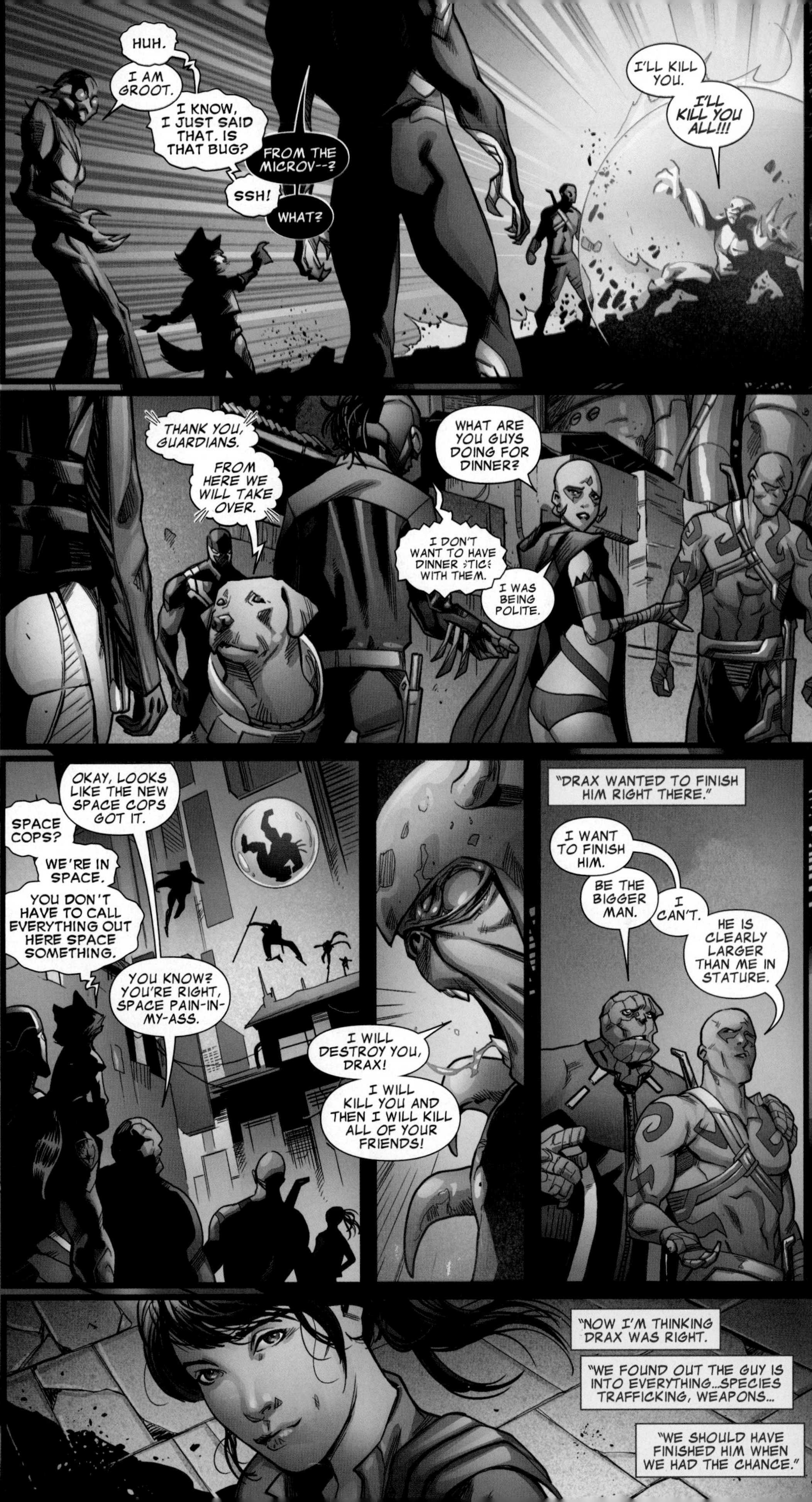
HUH.
I AM GROOT.
I KNOW, I JUST SAID THAT. IS THAT BUG?
FROM THE MICROV--?
SSH!
WHAT?
I'LL KILL YOU. I'LL KILL YOU ALL!!!
THANK YOU, GUARDIANS.
FROM HERE WE WILL TAKE OVER.
WHAT ARE YOU GUYS DOING FOR DINNER?
I DON'T WANT TO HAVE DINNER TIC WITH THEM.
I WAS BEING POLITE.
OKAY, LOOKS LIKE THE NEW SPACE COPS GOT IT.
SPACE COPS?
WE'RE IN SPACE.
YOU DON'T HAVE TO CALL EVERYTHING OUT HERE SPACE SOMETHING.
YOU KNOW? YOU'RE RIGHT, SPACE PAIN-IN-MY-ASS.
I WILL DESTROY YOU, DRAX!
I WILL KILL YOU AND THEN I WILL KILL ALL OF YOUR FRIENDS!
"DRAX WANTED TO FINISH HIM RIGHT THERE."
I WANT TO FINISH HIM.
BE THE BIGGER MAN.
I CAN'T.
HE IS CLEARLY LARGER THAN ME IN STATURE.
"NOW I'M THINKING DRAX WAS RIGHT.
"WE FOUND OUT THE GUY IS INTO EVERYTHING...SPECIES TRAFFICKING, WEAPONS...
"WE SHOULD HAVE FINISHED HIM WHEN WE HAD THE CHANCE."

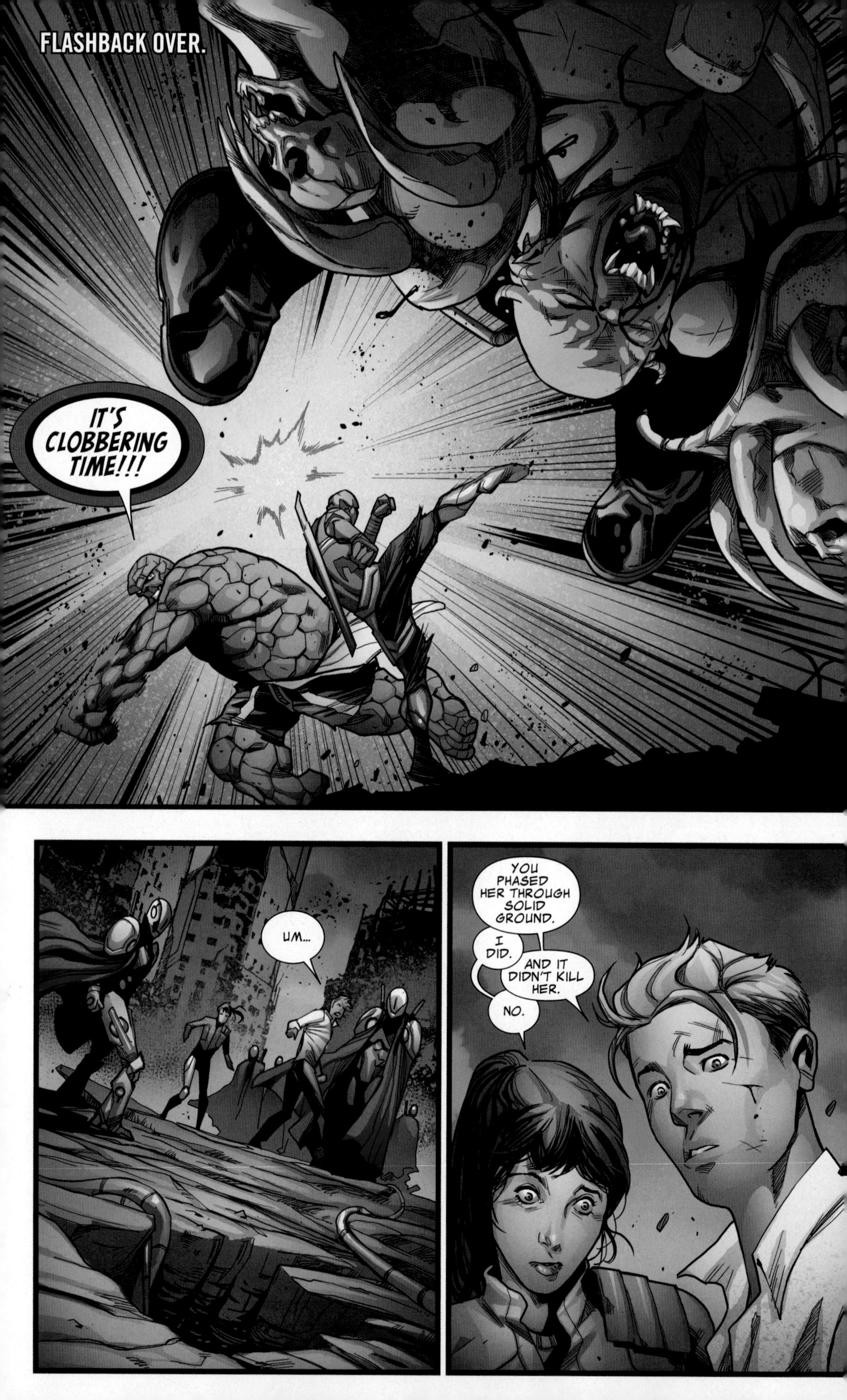
FLASHBACK OVER.
IT'S CLOBBERING TIME!!!
UM...
YOU PHASED HER THROUGH SOLID GROUND.
I DID.
AND IT DIDN'T KILL HER.
NO.

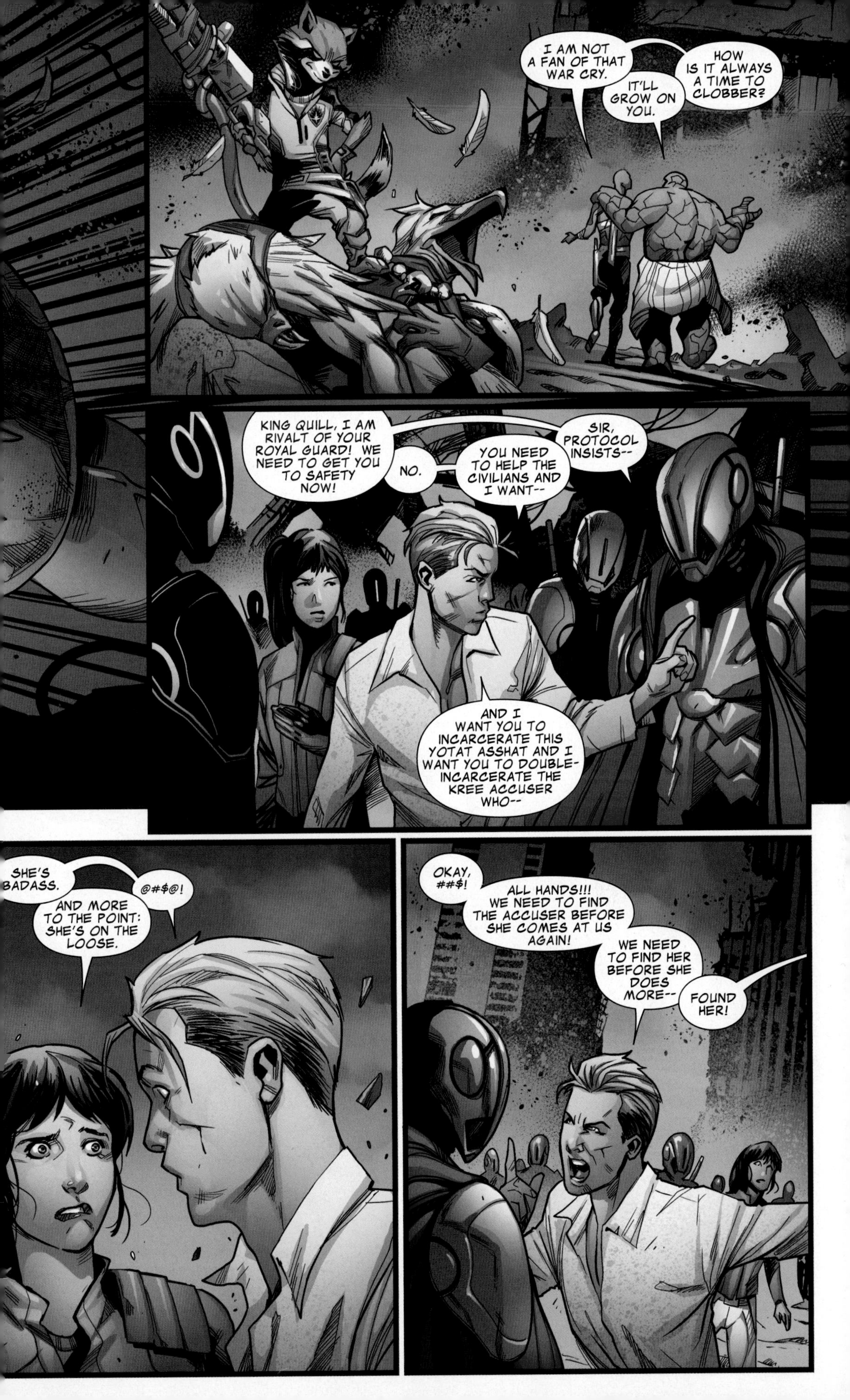
I AM NOT A FAN OF THAT WAR CRY.
HOW IS IT ALWAYS A TIME TO CLOBBER?
IT'LL GROW ON YOU.
KING QUILL, I AM RIVALT OF YOUR ROYAL GUARD! WE NEED TO GET YOU TO SAFETY NOW!
NO.
YOU NEED TO HELP THE CIVILIANS AND I WANT--
SIR, PROTOCOL INSISTS--
AND I WANT YOU TO INCARCERATE THIS YOTAT ASSHAT AND I WANT YOU TO DOUBLE-INCARCERATE THE KREE ACCUSER WHO--
SHE'S BADASS.
@#$@!
AND MORE TO THE POINT: SHE'S ON THE LOOSE.
OKAY, ##$!
ALL HANDS!!! WE NEED TO FIND THE ACCUSER BEFORE SHE COMES AT US AGAIN!
WE NEED TO FIND HER BEFORE SHE DOES MORE--
FOUND HER!

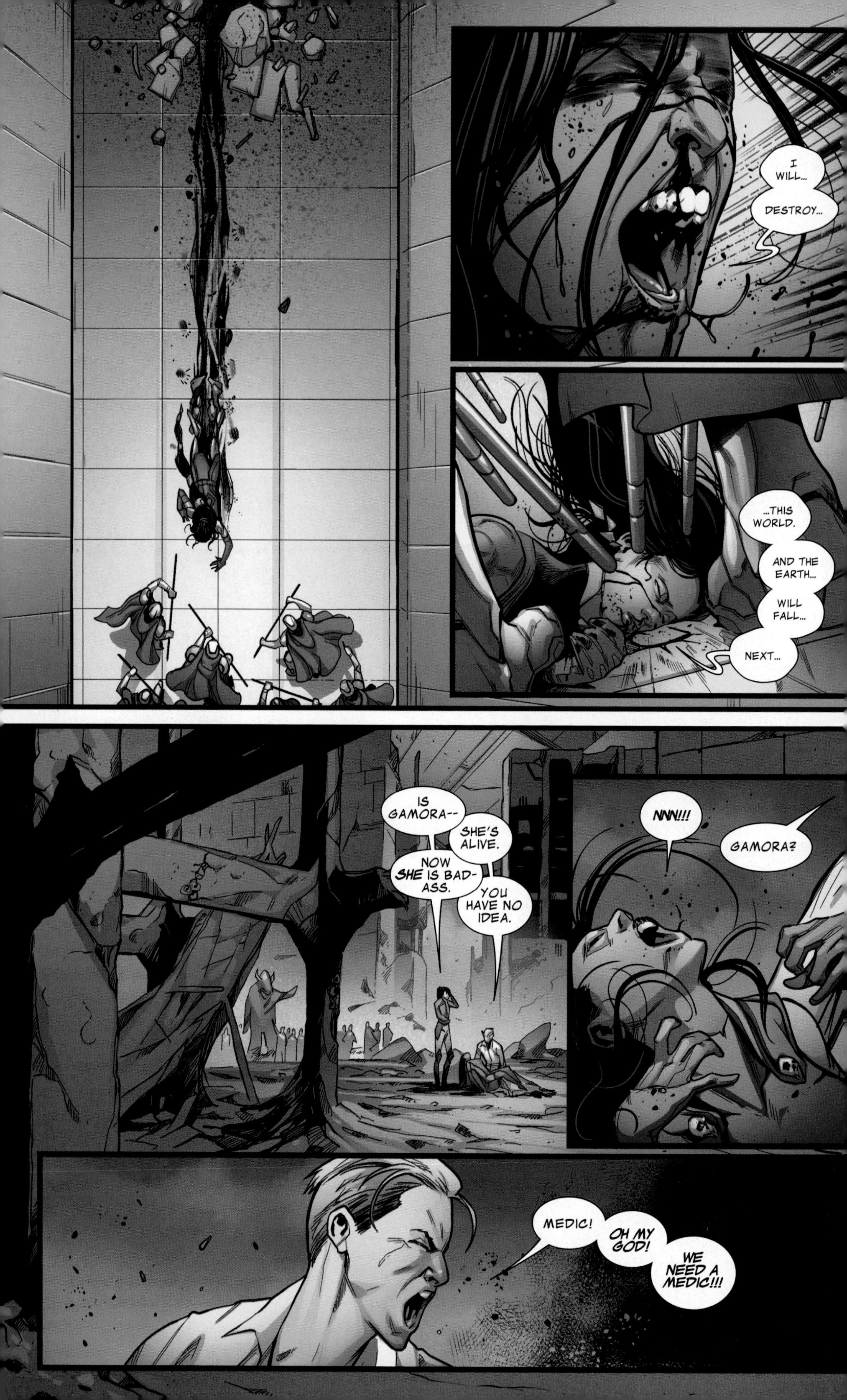
I WILL...
DESTROY...
...THIS WORLD.
AND THE EARTH...
WILL FALL...
NEXT...
IS GAMORA--
SHE'S ALIVE.
NOW SHE IS BAD-ASS.
YOU HAVE NO IDEA.
NNN!!!
GAMORA?
MEDIC!
OH MY GOD!
WE NEED A MEDIC!!!

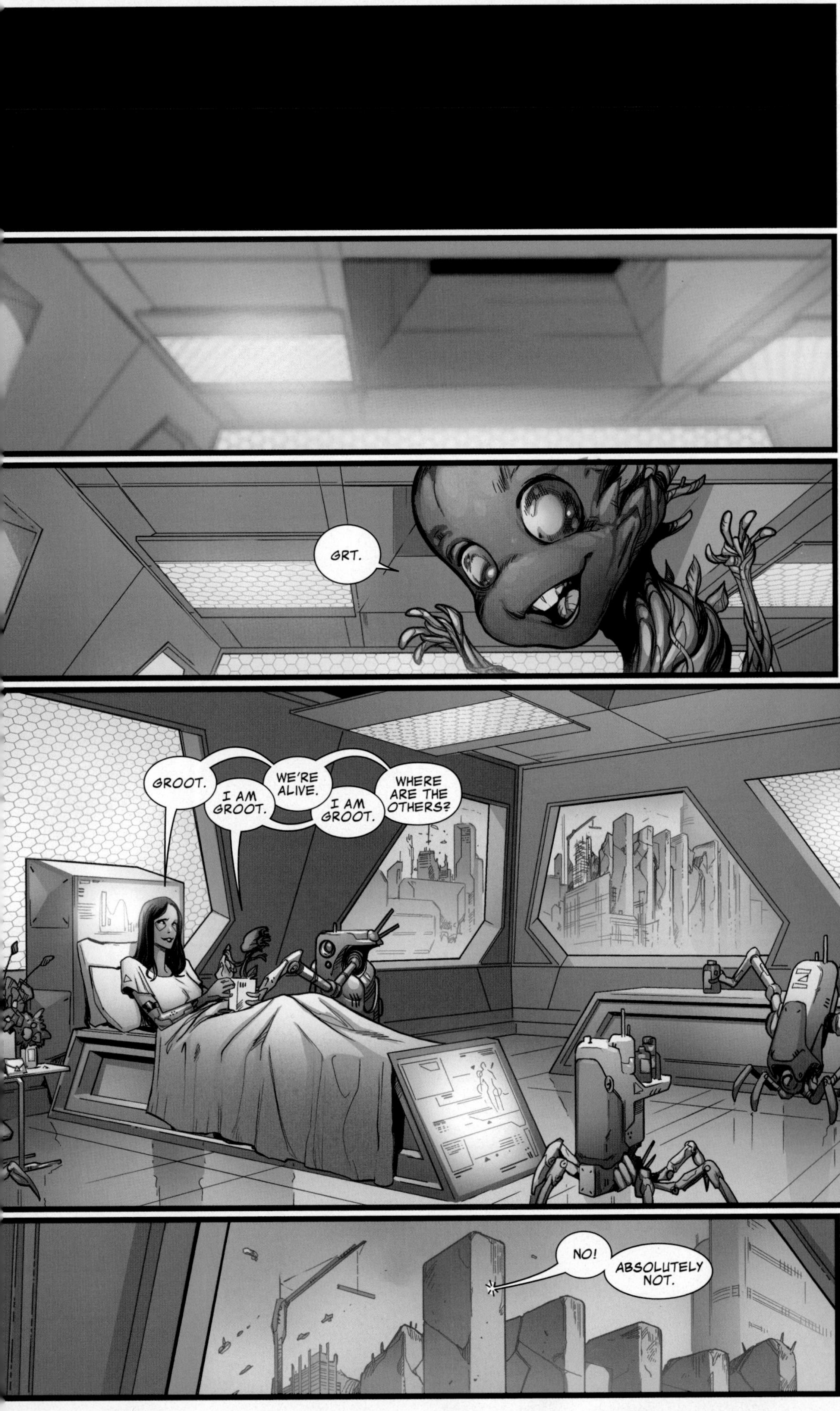
GRT.
GROOT.
I AM GROOT.
WE'RE ALIVE.
I AM GROOT.
WHERE ARE THE OTHERS?
NO!
ABSOLUTELY NOT.

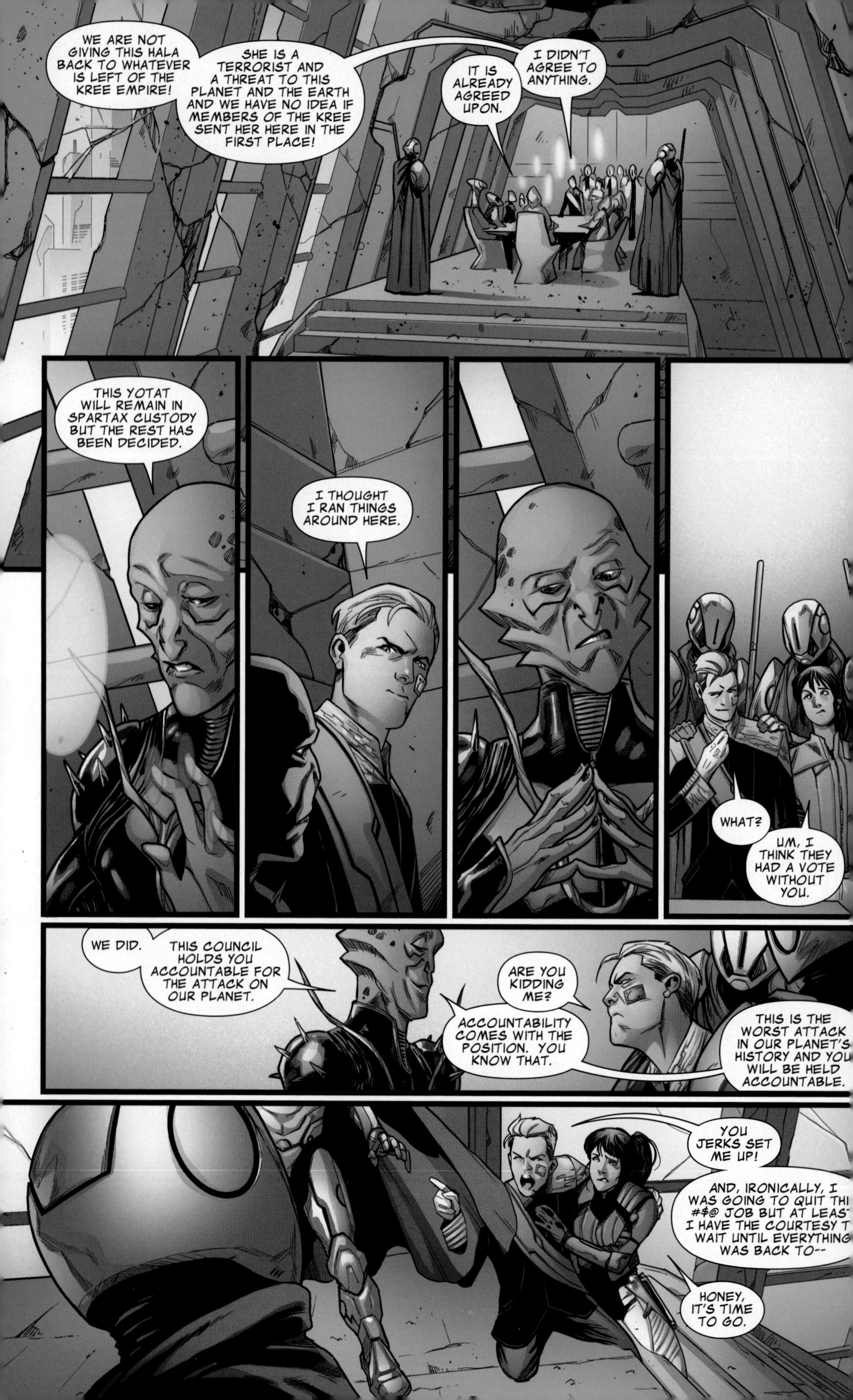
WE ARE NOT GIVING THIS HALA BACK TO WHATEVER IS LEFT OF THE KREE EMPIRE!
SHE IS A TERRORIST AND A THREAT TO THIS PLANET AND THE EARTH AND WE HAVE NO IDEA IF MEMBERS OF THE KREE SENT HER HERE IN THE FIRST PLACE!
IT IS ALREADY AGREED UPON.
I DIDN'T AGREE TO ANYTHING.
THIS YOTAT WILL REMAIN IN SPARTAX CUSTODY BUT THE REST HAS BEEN DECIDED.
I THOUGHT I RAN THINGS AROUND HERE.
WHAT?
UM, I THINK THEY HAD A VOTE WITHOUT YOU.
WE DID.
THIS COUNCIL HOLDS YOU ACCOUNTABLE FOR THE ATTACK ON OUR PLANET.
ARE YOU KIDDING ME?
ACCOUNTABILITY COMES WITH THE POSITION. YOU KNOW THAT.
THIS IS THE WORST ATTACK IN OUR PLANET'S HISTORY AND YOU WILL BE HELD ACCOUNTABLE.
YOU JERKS SET ME UP!
AND, IRONICALLY, I WAS GOING TO QUIT THI #$@ JOB BUT AT LEAS I HAVE THE COURTESY T WAIT UNTIL EVERYTHING WAS BACK TO--
HONEY, IT'S TIME TO GO.

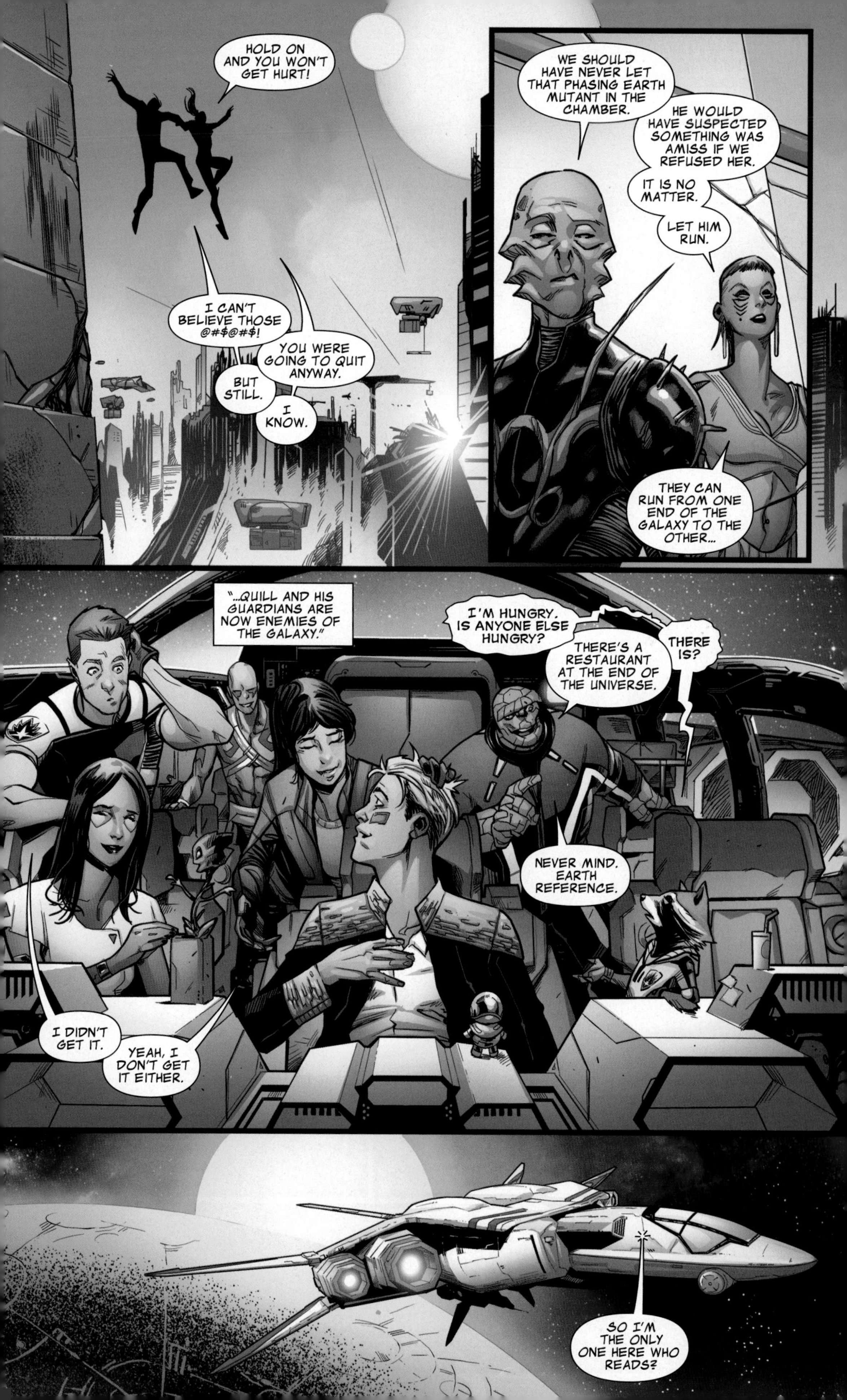
HOLD ON AND YOU WON'T GET HURT!
I CAN'T BELIEVE THOSE @#$@#$!
YOU WERE GOING TO QUIT ANYWAY.
BUT STILL.
I KNOW.
WE SHOULD HAVE NEVER LET THAT PHASING EARTH MUTANT IN THE CHAMBER.
HE WOULD HAVE SUSPECTED SOMETHING WAS AMISS IF WE REFUSED HER.
IT IS NO MATTER.
LET HIM RUN.
THEY CAN RUN FROM ONE END OF THE GALAXY TO THE OTHER...
"...QUILL AND HIS GUARDIANS ARE NOW ENEMIES OF THE GALAXY."
I'M HUNGRY. IS ANYONE ELSE HUNGRY?
THERE'S A RESTAURANT AT THE END OF THE UNIVERSE.
THERE IS?
NEVER MIND. EARTH REFERENCE.
I DIDN'T GET IT.
YEAH, I DON'T GET IT EITHER.
SO I'M THE ONLY ONE HERE WHO READS?

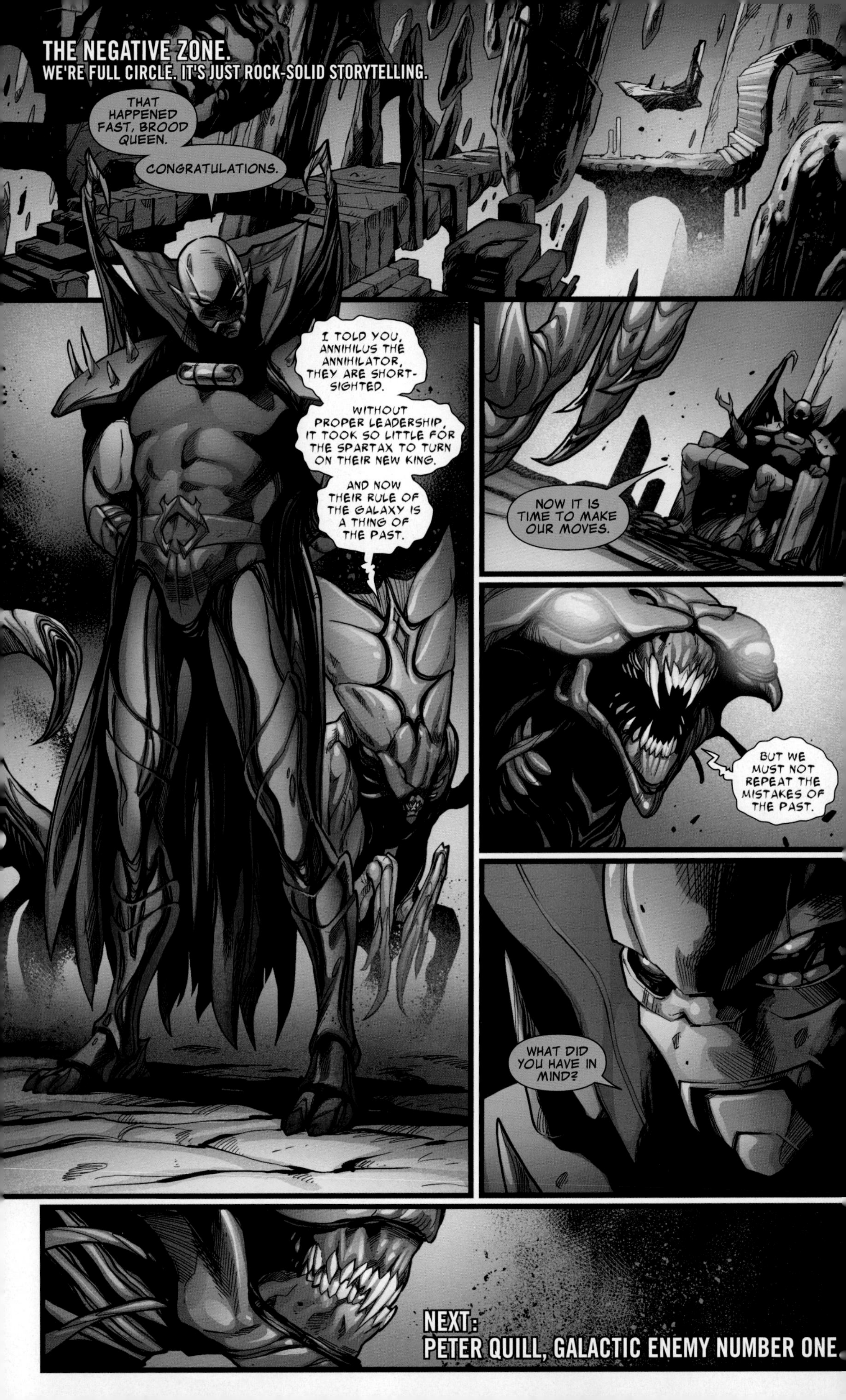
THE NEGATIVE ZONE.
WE'RE FULL CIRCLE. IT'S JUST ROCK-SOLID STORYTELLING.
THAT HAPPENED FAST, BROOD QUEEN.
CONGRATULATIONS.
I TOLD YOU, ANNIHILUS THE ANNIHILATOR, THEY ARE SHORT-SIGHTED.
WITHOUT PROPER LEADERSHIP, IT TOOK SO LITTLE FOR THE SPARTAX TO TURN ON THEIR NEW KING.
AND NOW THEIR RULE OF THE GALAXY IS A THING OF THE PAST.
NOW IT IS TIME TO MAKE OUR MOVES.
BUT WE MUST NOT REPEAT THE MISTAKES OF THE PAST.
WHAT DID YOU HAVE IN MIND?
NEXT:
PETER QUILL, GALACTIC ENEMY NUMBER ONE.

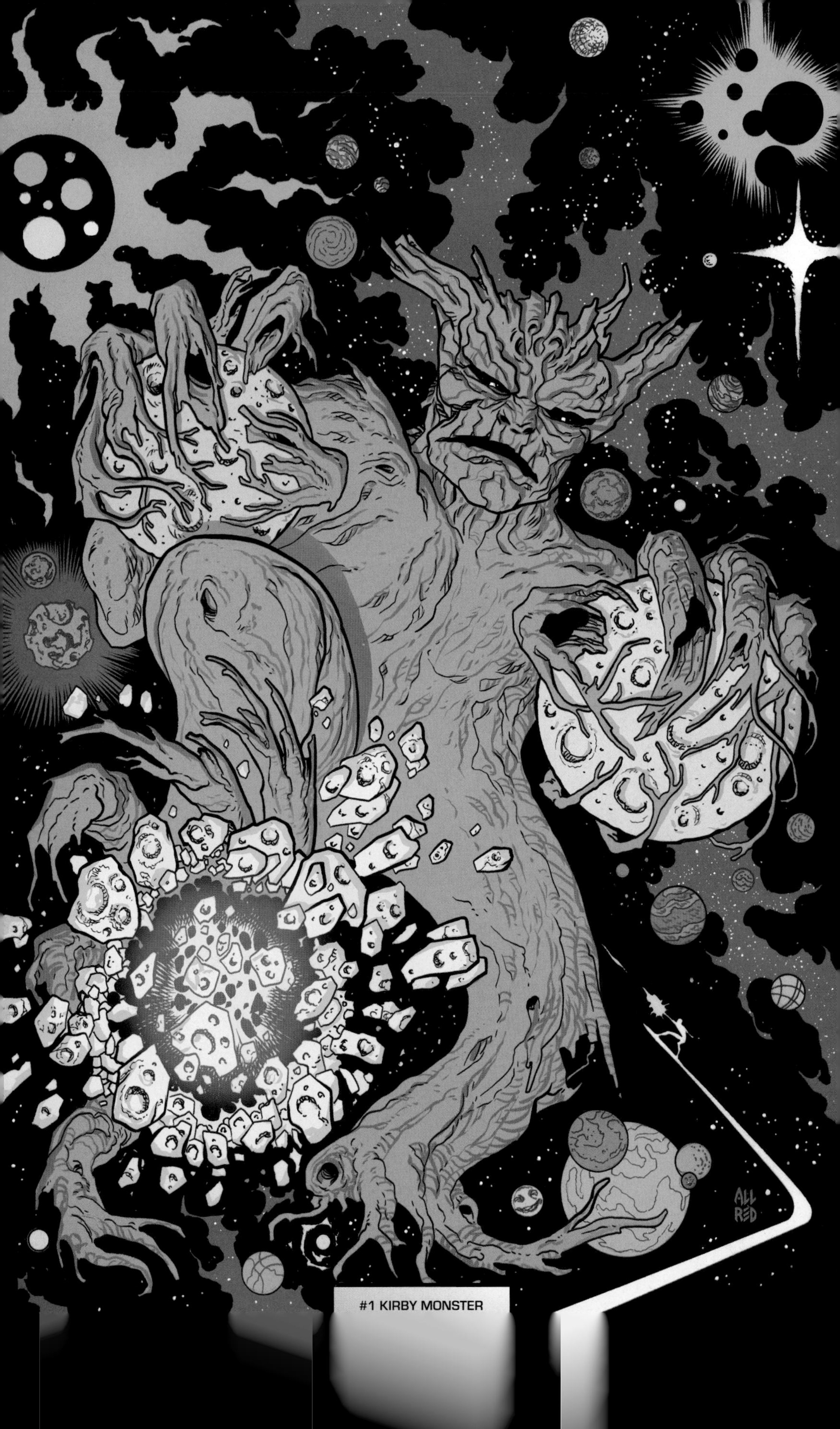
ALL
RED

#1 KIRBY MONSTER

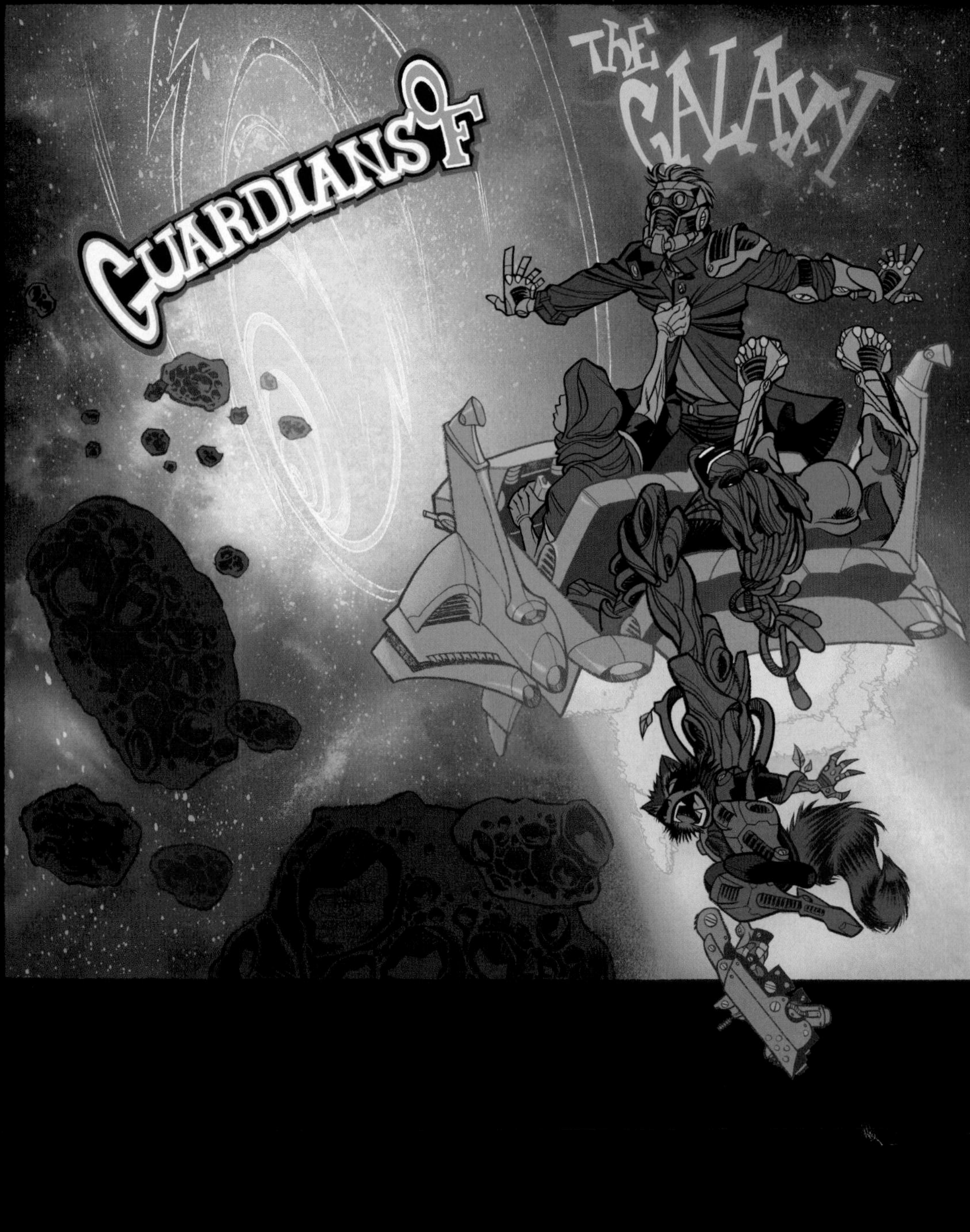
GUARDIANS OF
THE GALAXY

#1 HIP-HOP VARIANT BY
SHAWN CRYSTAL &
CHRISTOPHER BRUNNER

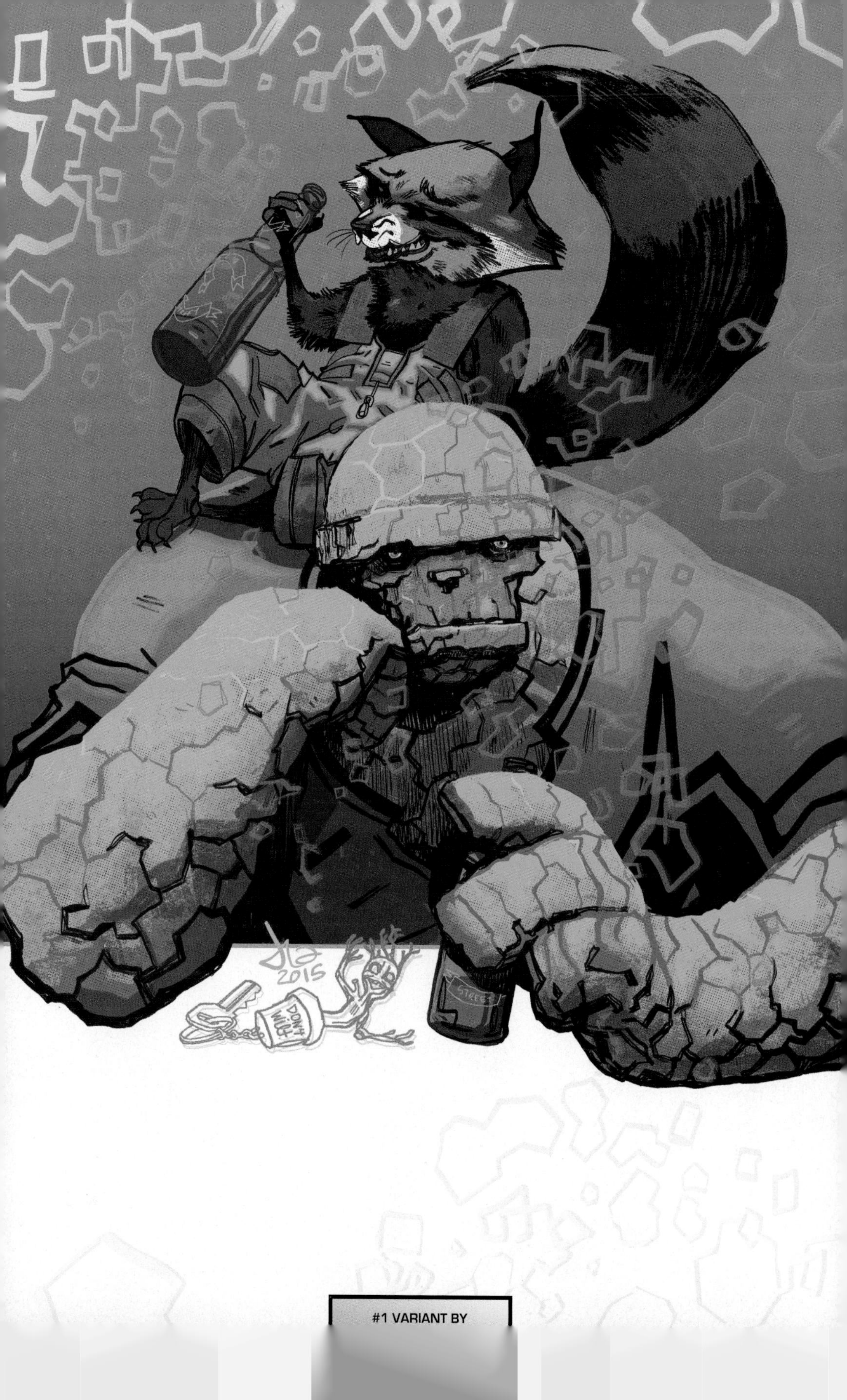
2015
DON'T WILT

#1 VARIANT BY

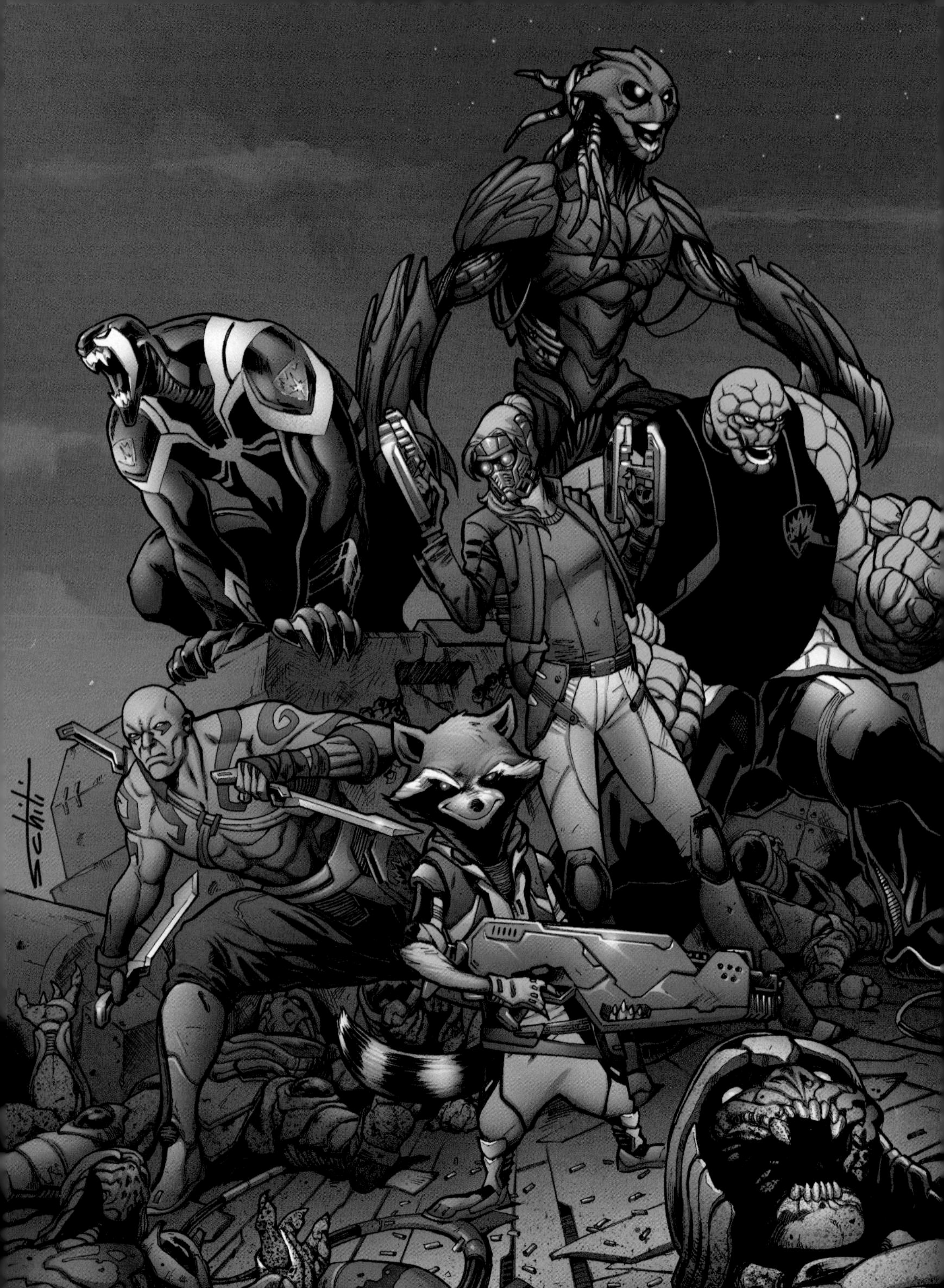
Schiti

#1 VARIANT BY

[redacted]

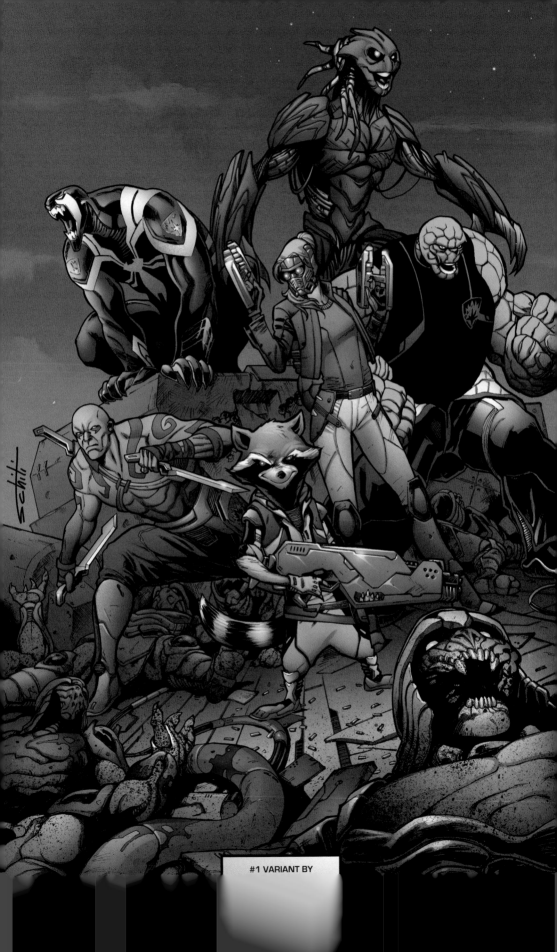

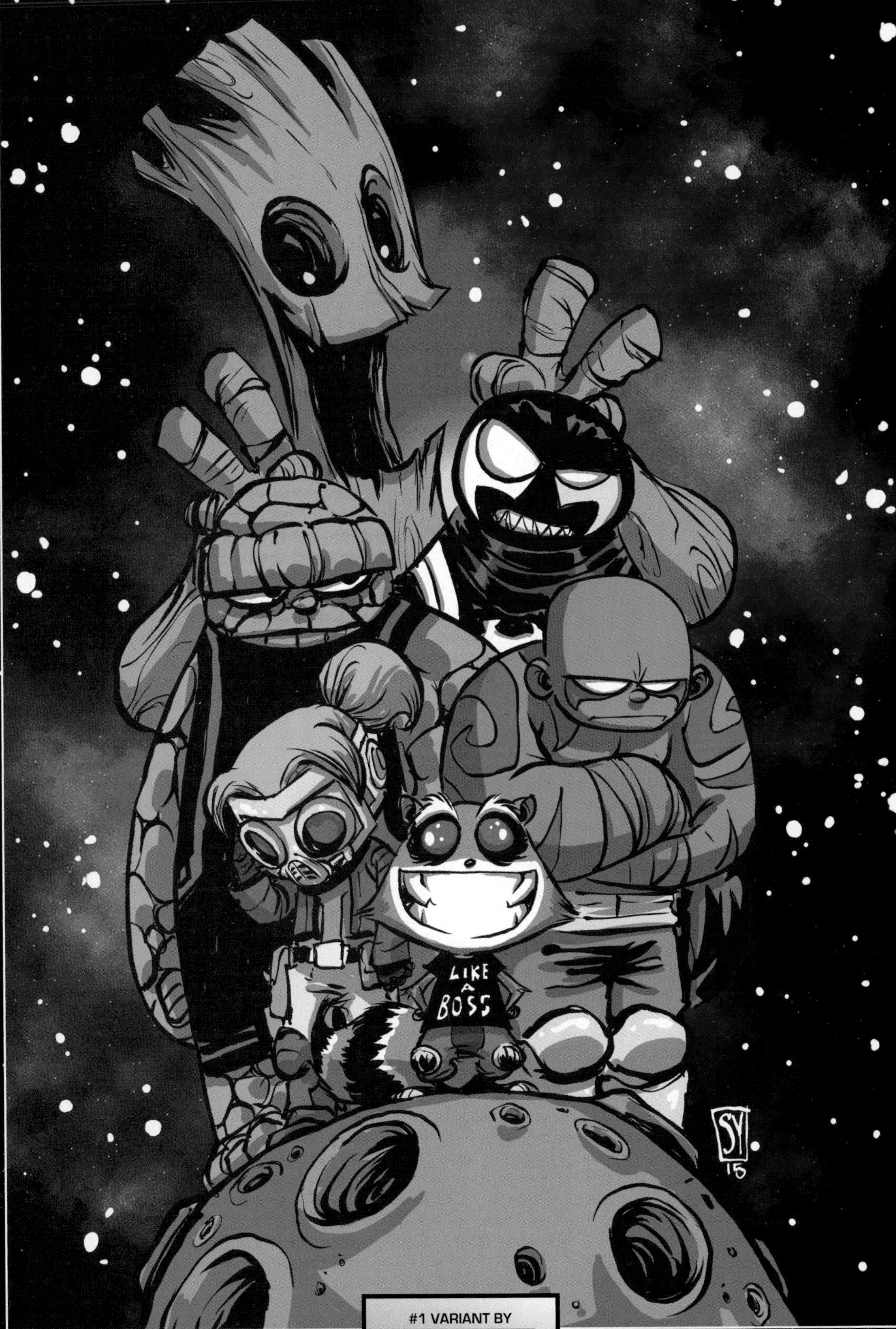
LIKE
A
BOSS

#1 VARIANT BY
SKOTTIE YOUNG

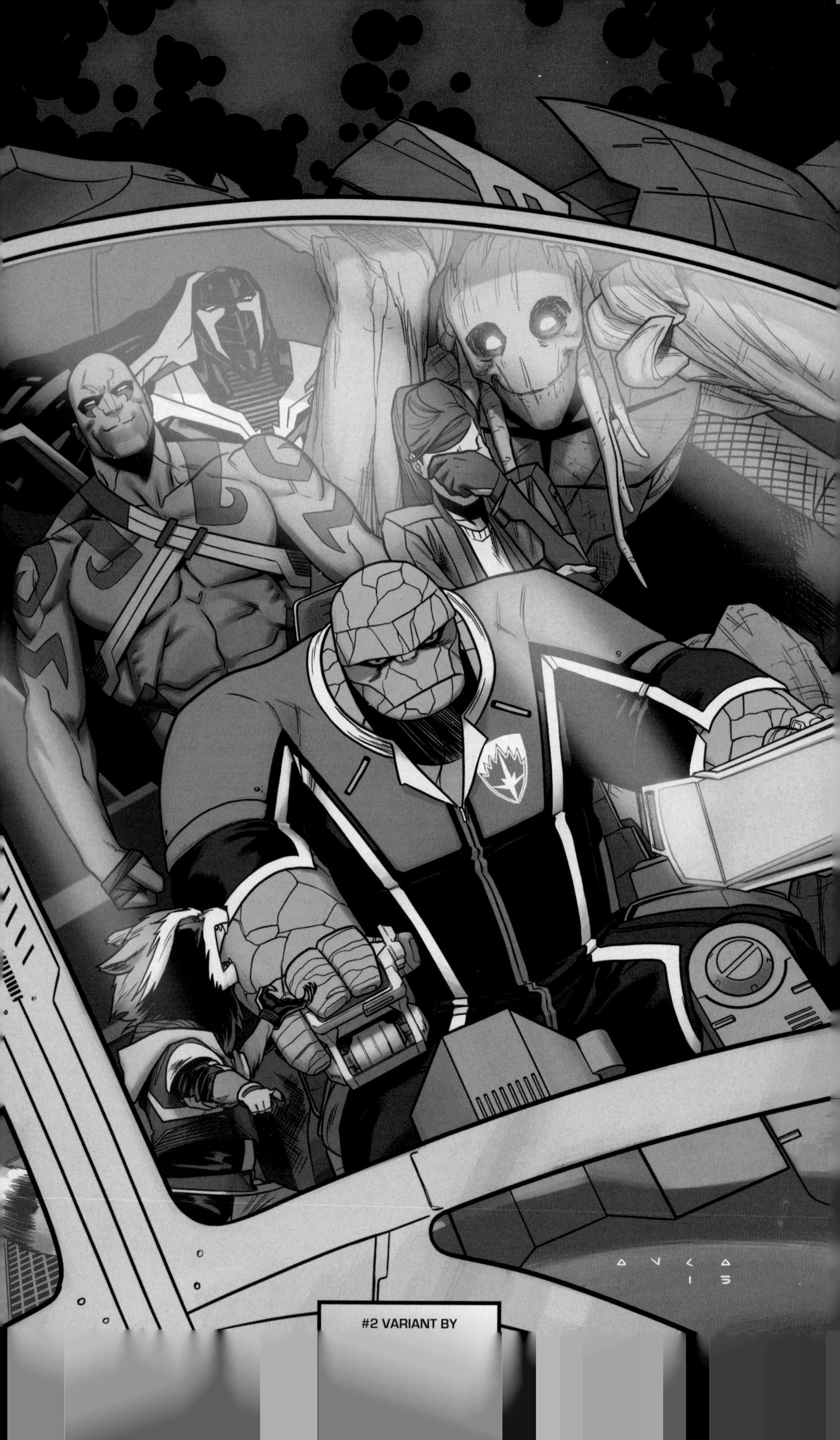

#2 VARIANT BY

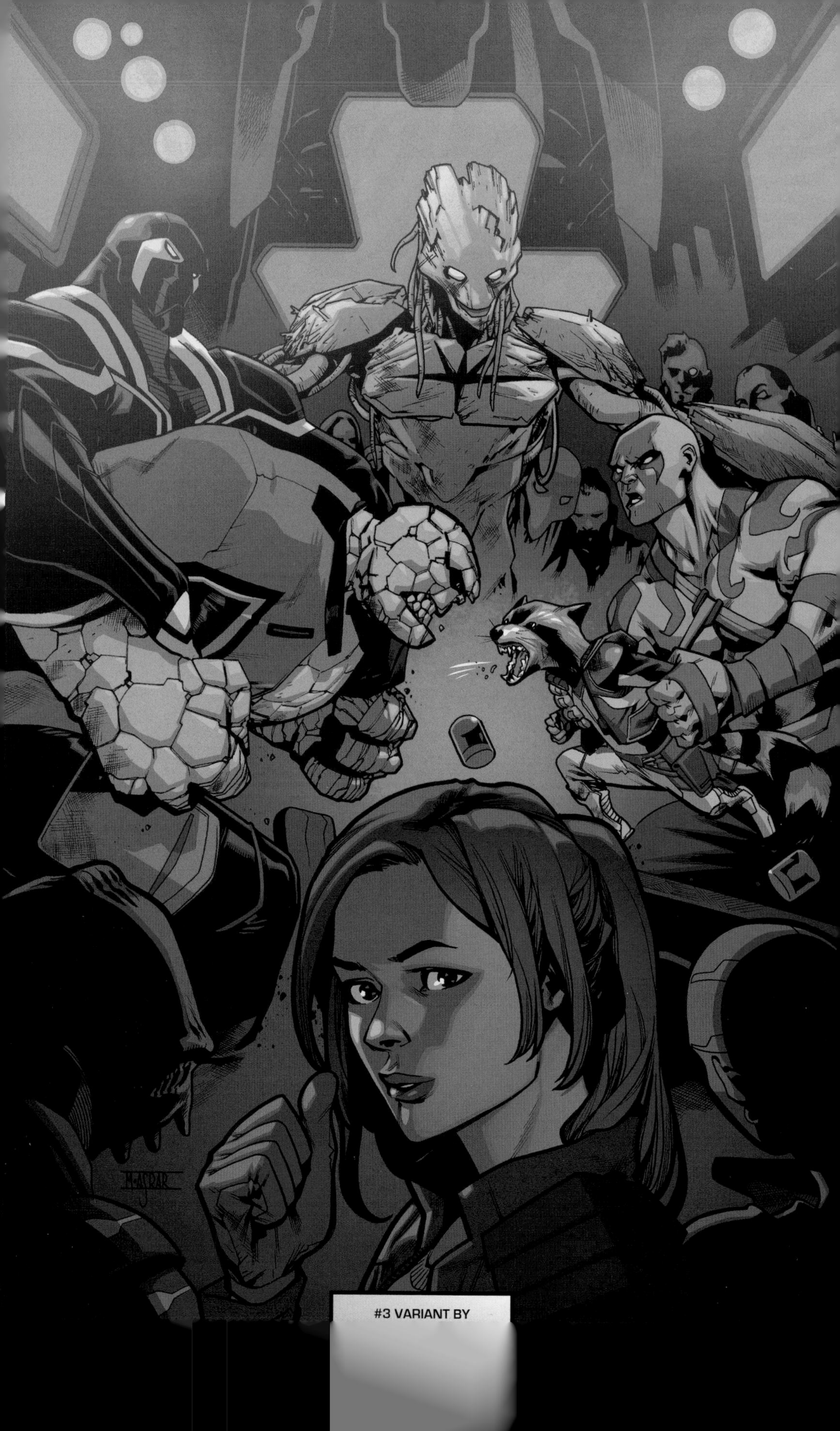

#3 VARIANT BY

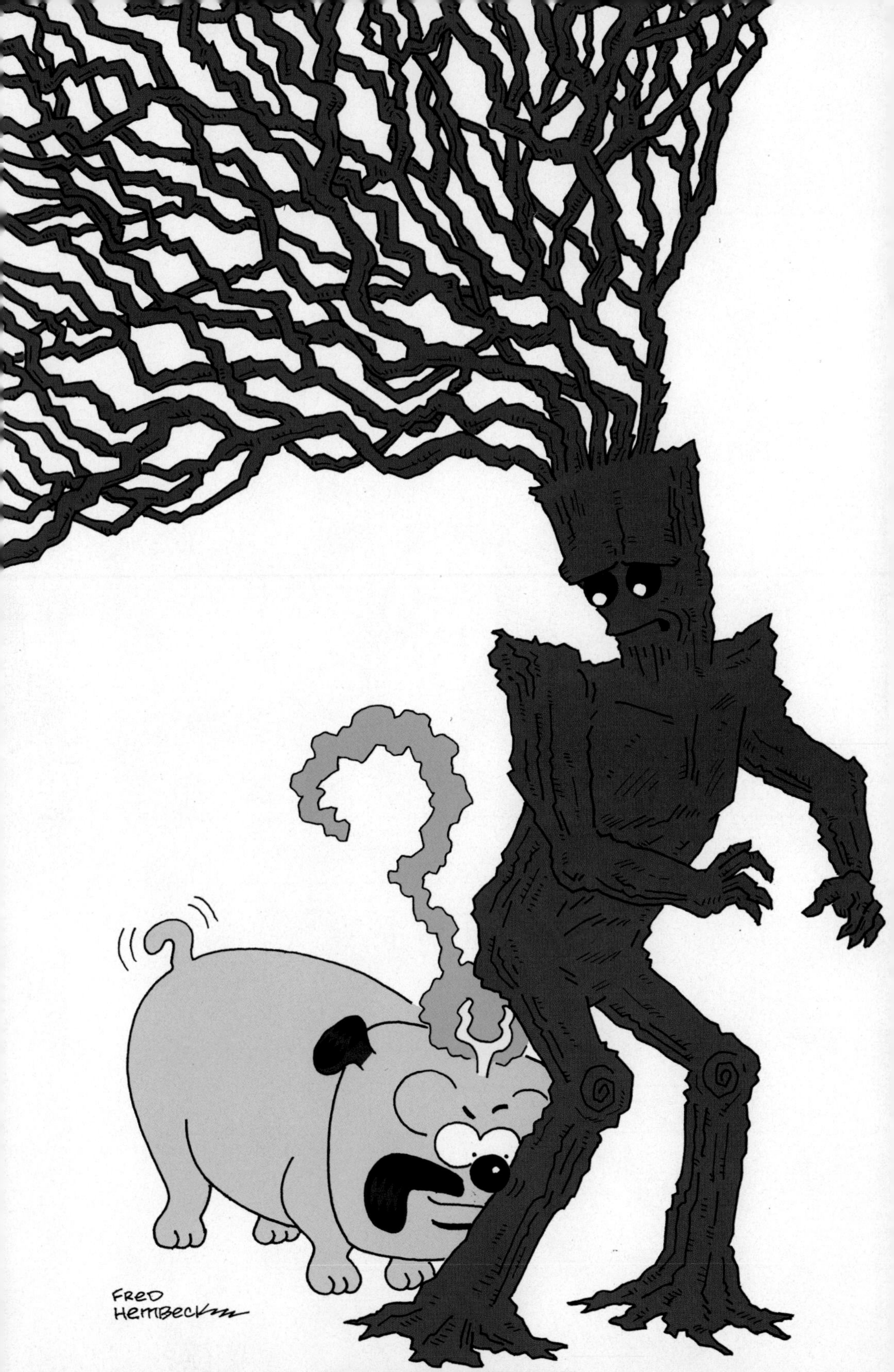
FRED
HEMBECK

#3 VARIANT BY

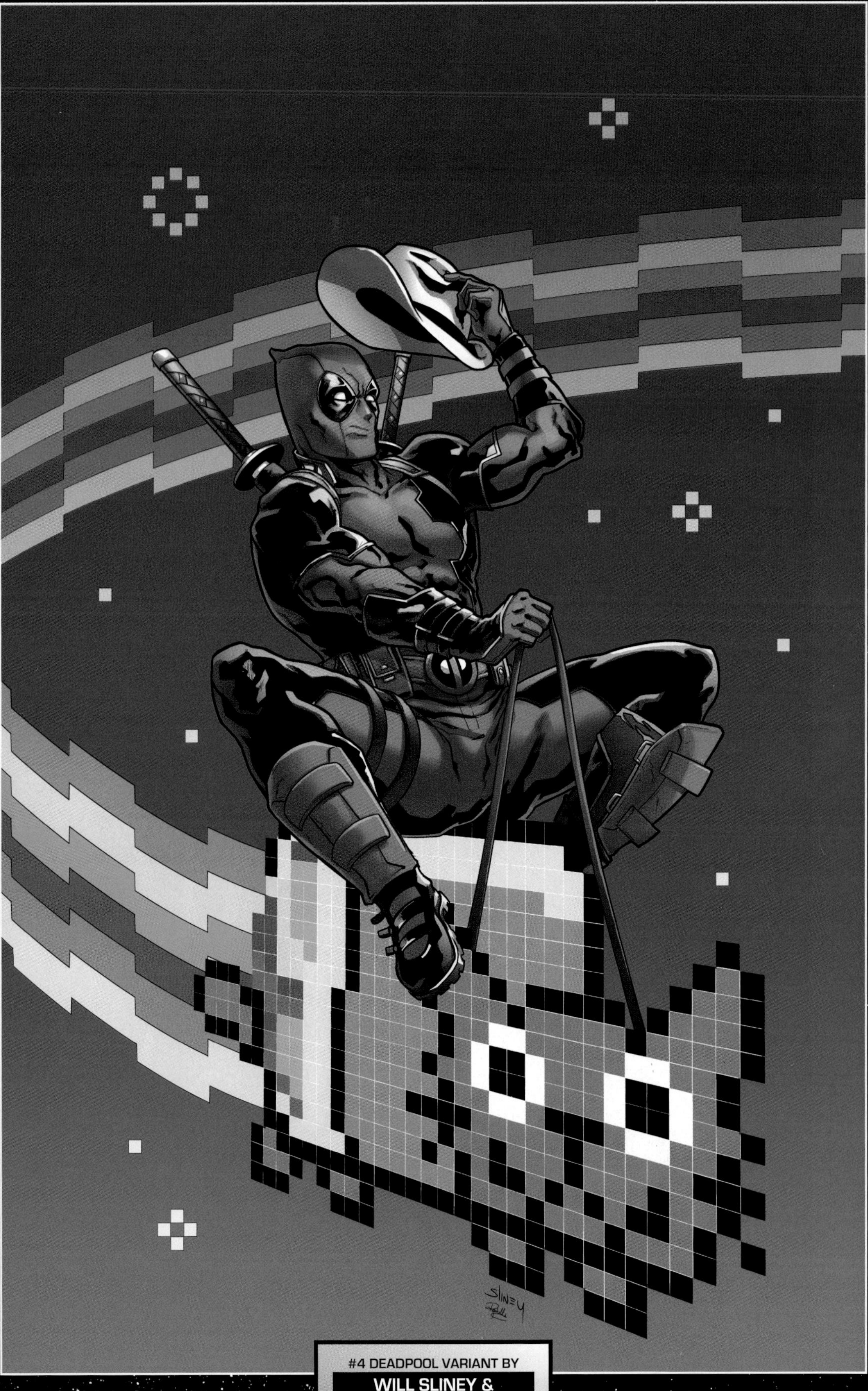

#4 DEADPOOL VARIANT BY
WILL SLINEY &
RACHELLE ROSENBERG

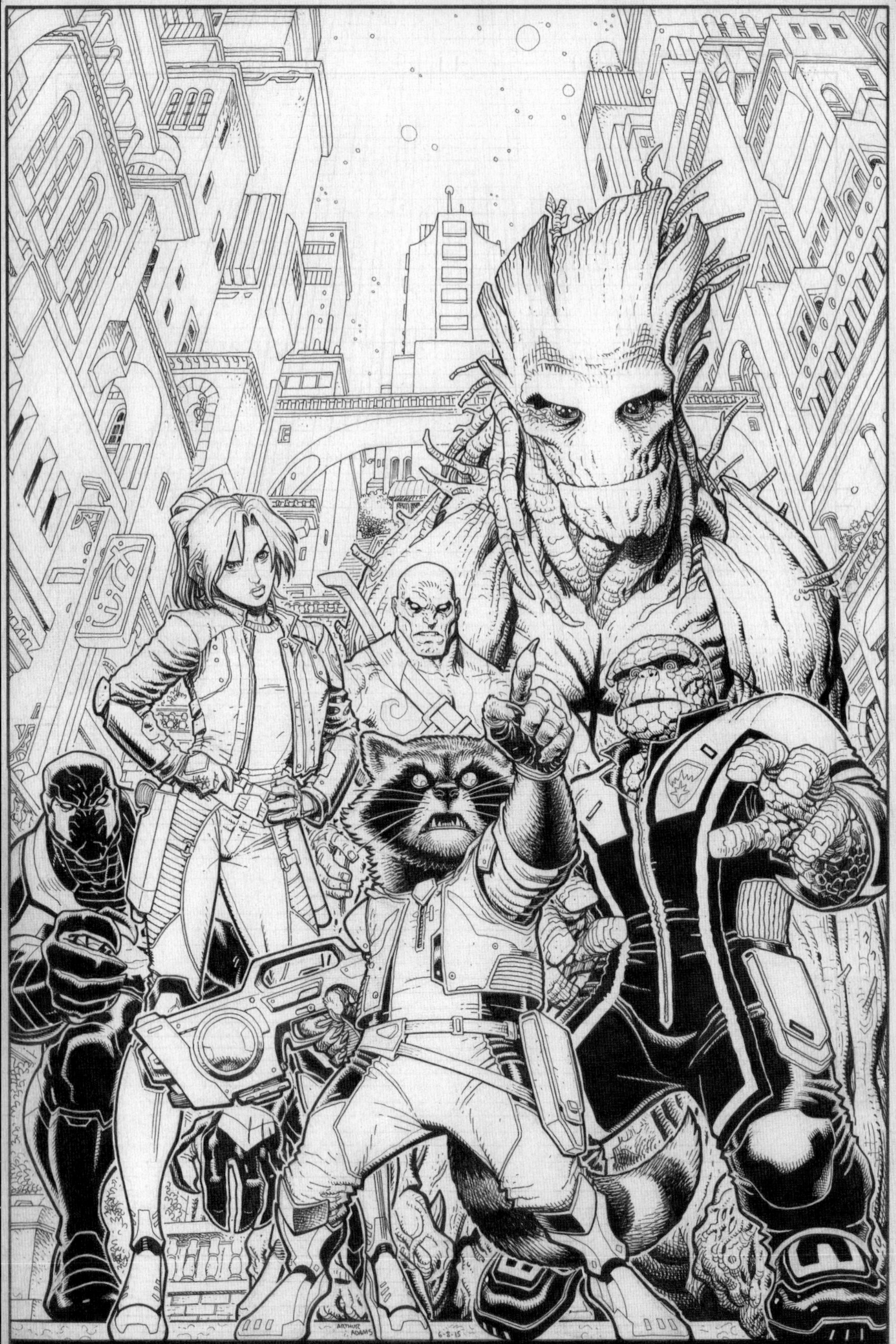

ARTHUR ADAMS 6-8-15
GUARDIANS of the GALAXY #1
ARTHUR ADAMS 6-8-2015

#1 FINAL COVER BY
ARTHUR ADAMS

COVER PENCILS BY
ARTHUR ADAMS

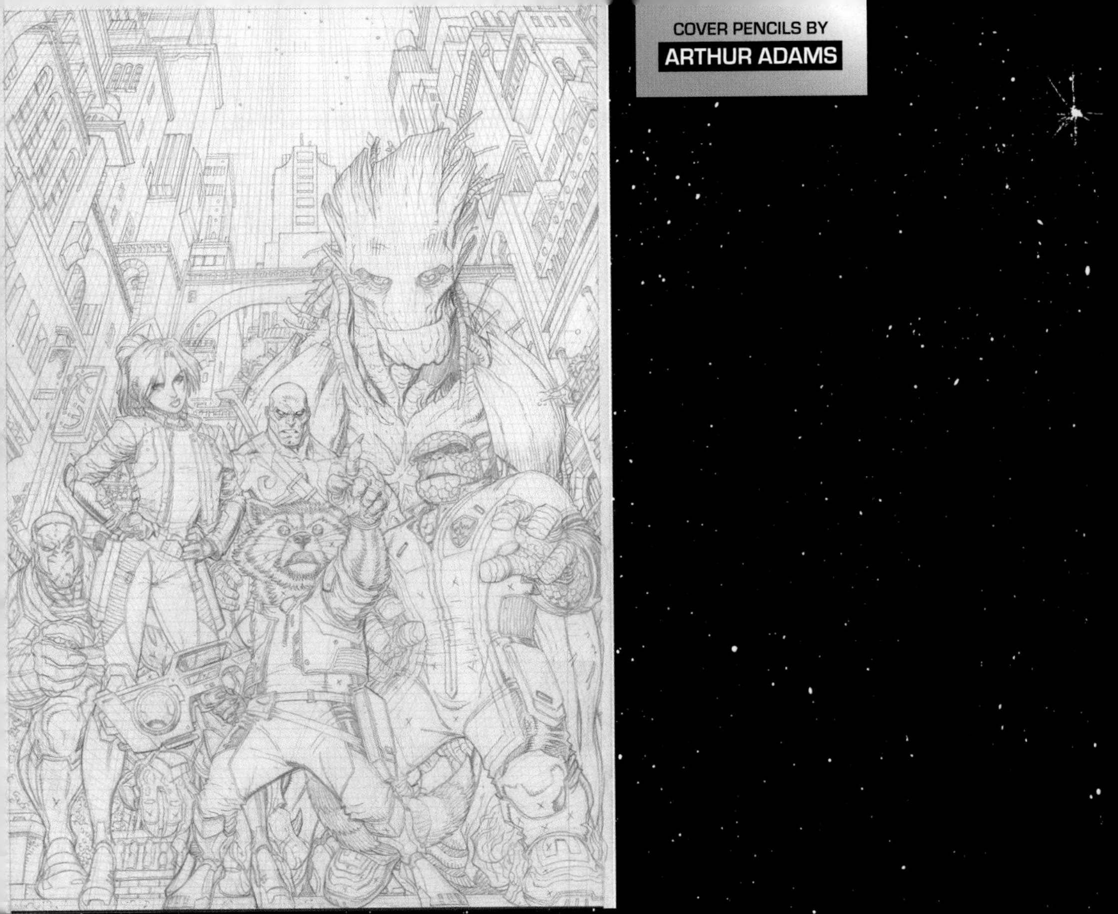

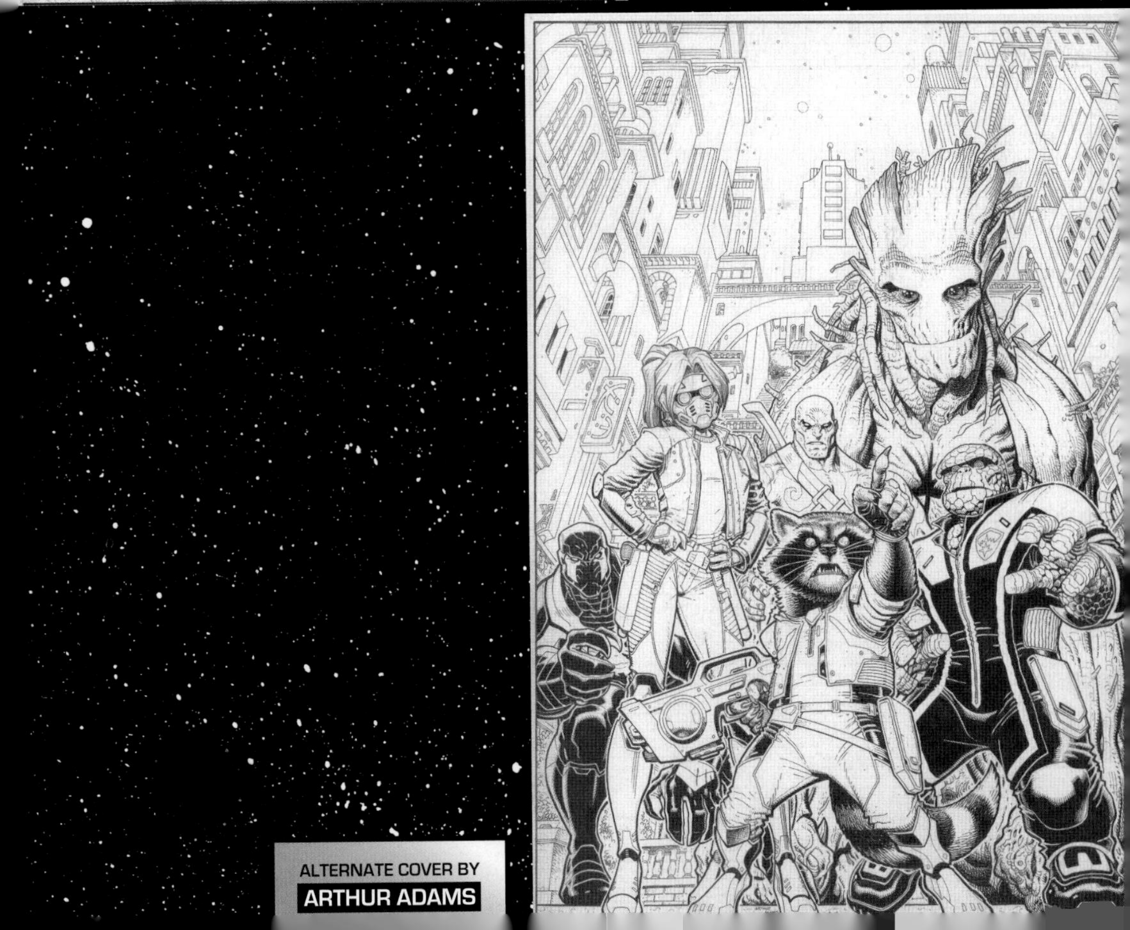

ALTERNATE COVER BY
ARTHUR ADAMS

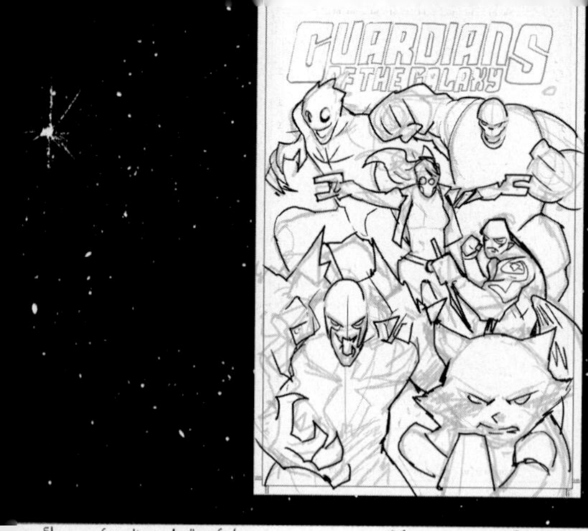
GUARDIANS
OF THE GALAXY

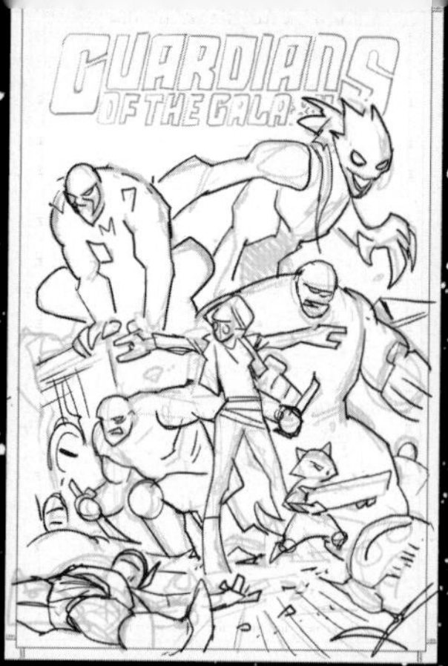
GUARDIANS
OF THE GALAXY

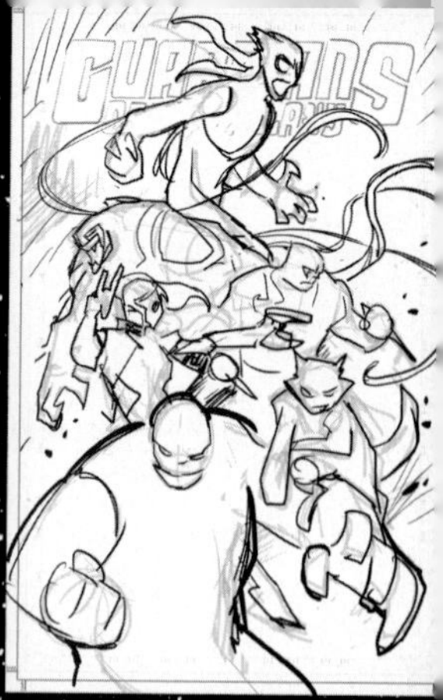

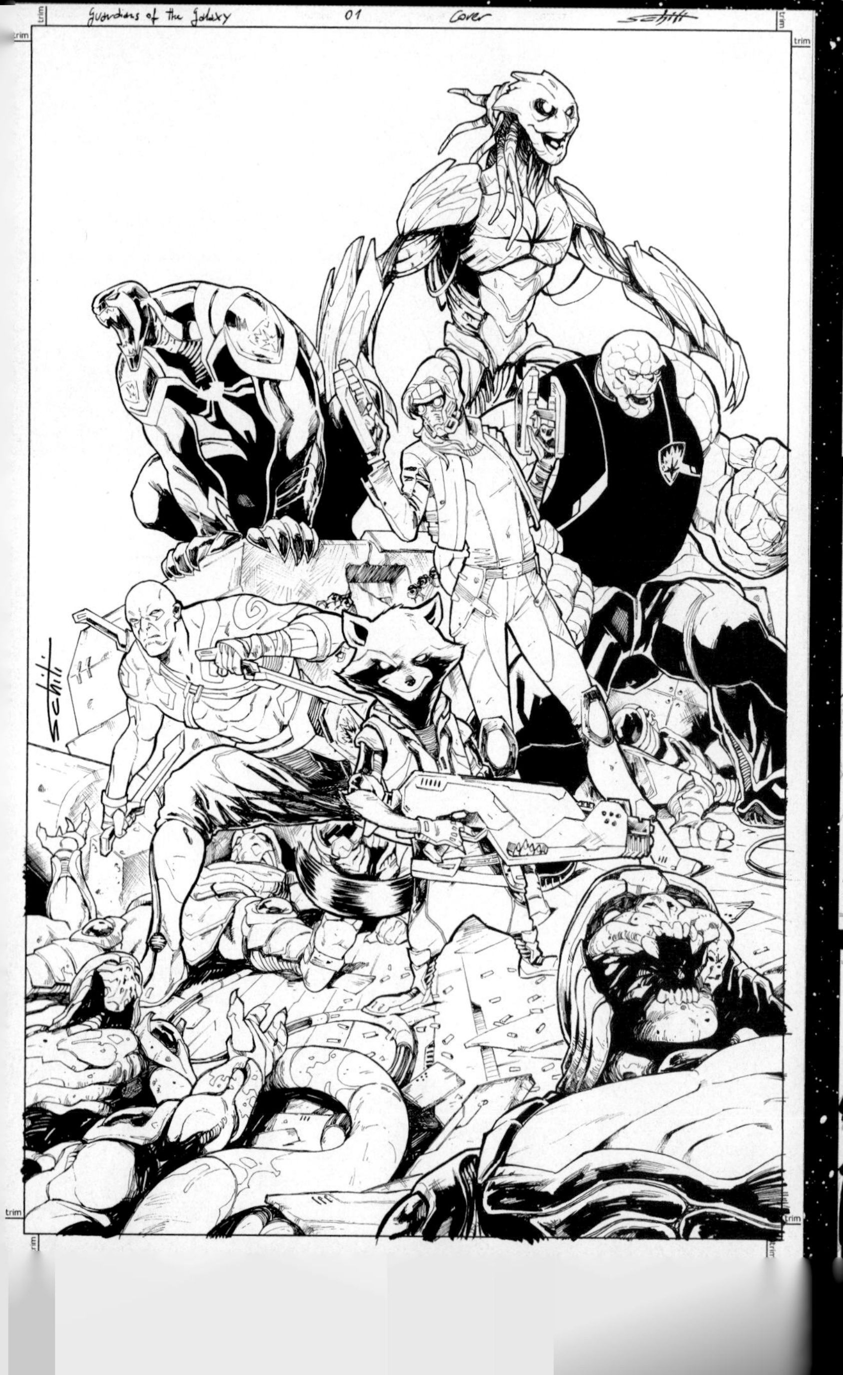
Guardians of the Galaxy
01
Cover
trim
trim
trim
trim

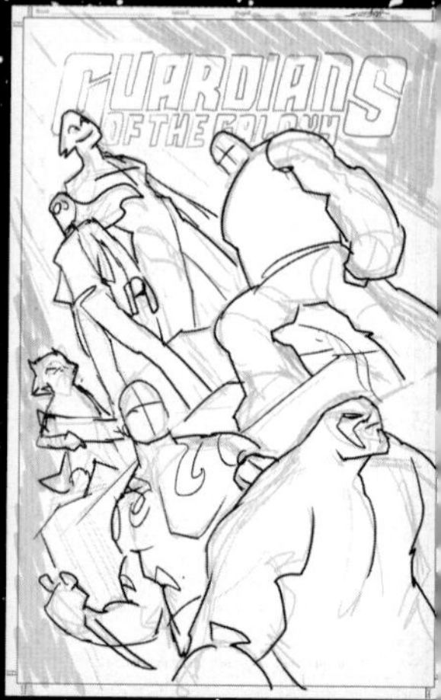
GUARDIANS
OF THE GALAXY

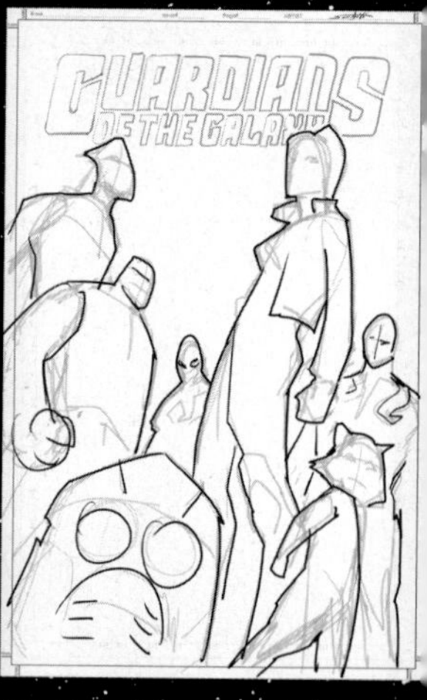
GUARDIANS

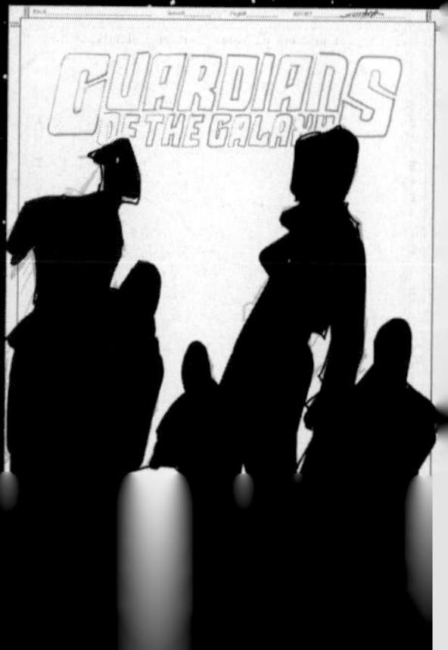
GUARDIANS

#2 COVER PROCESS BY

ARTHUR ADAMS

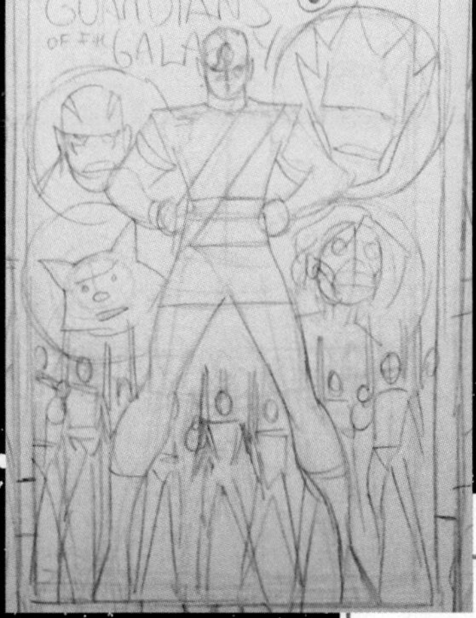

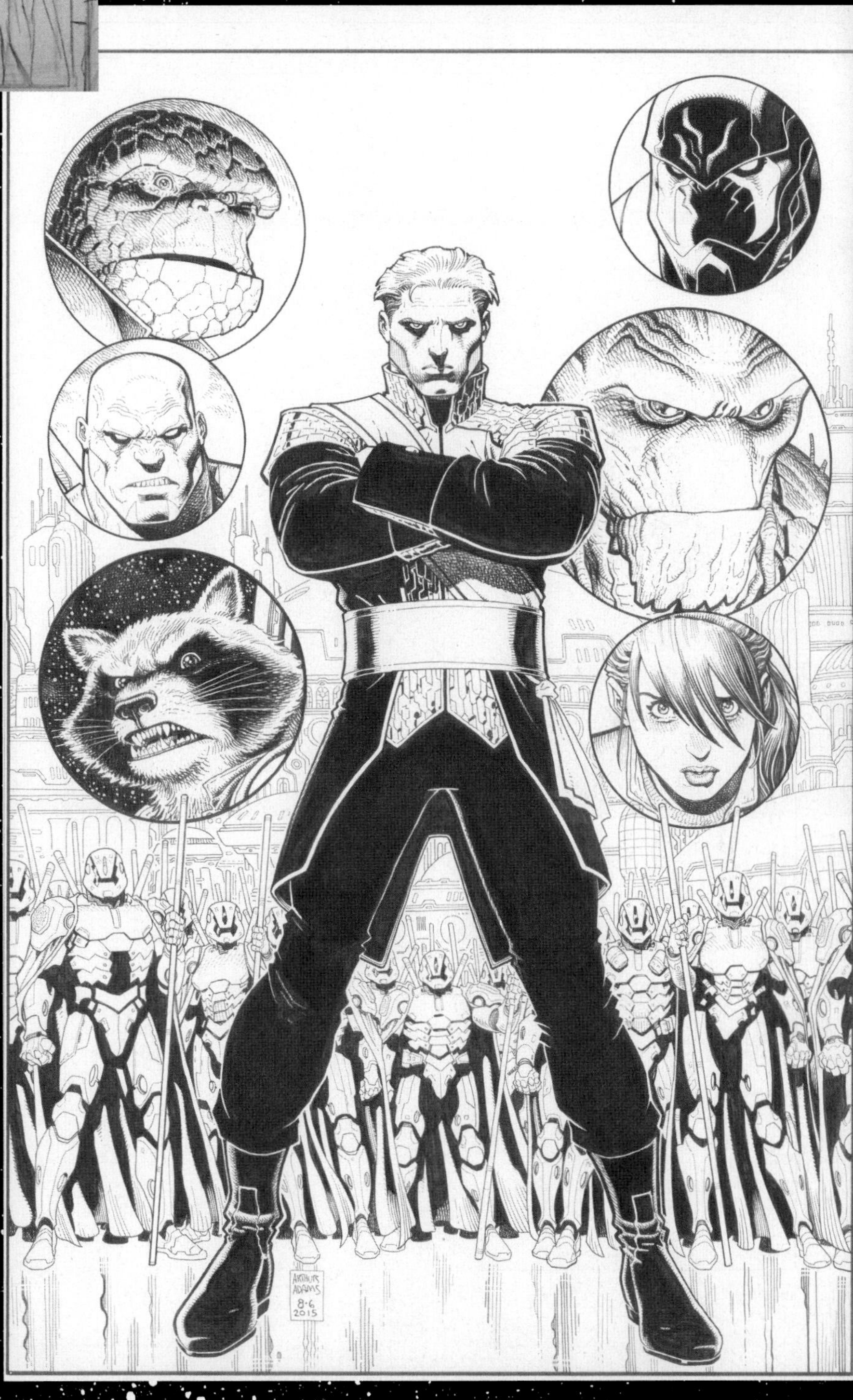
ARTHUR ADAMS 8·6 2015

3

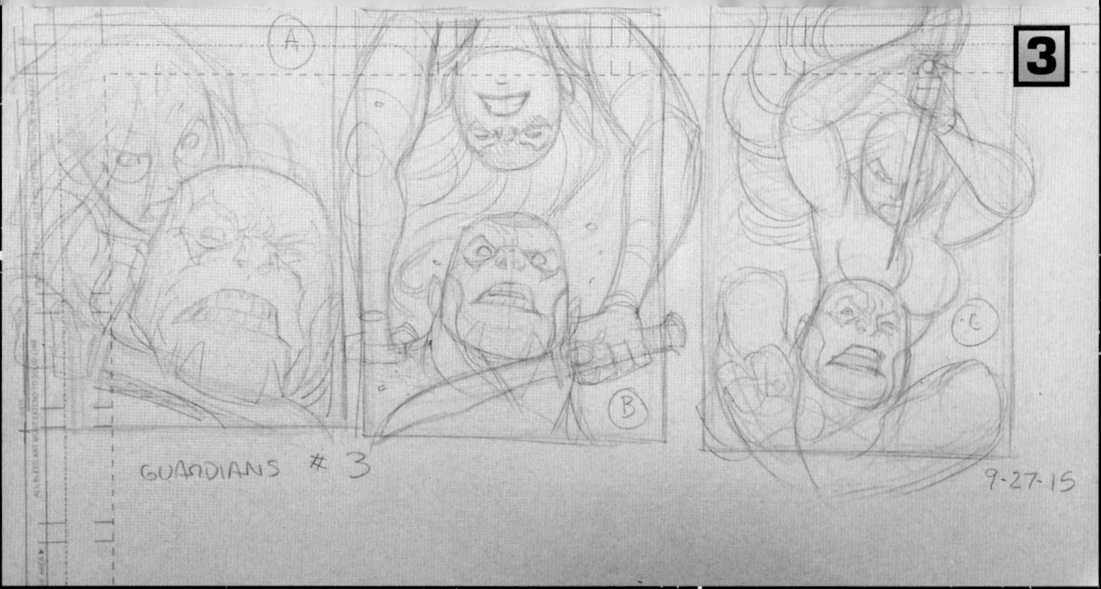

A
B
C
GUARDIANS #3
9-27-15

4

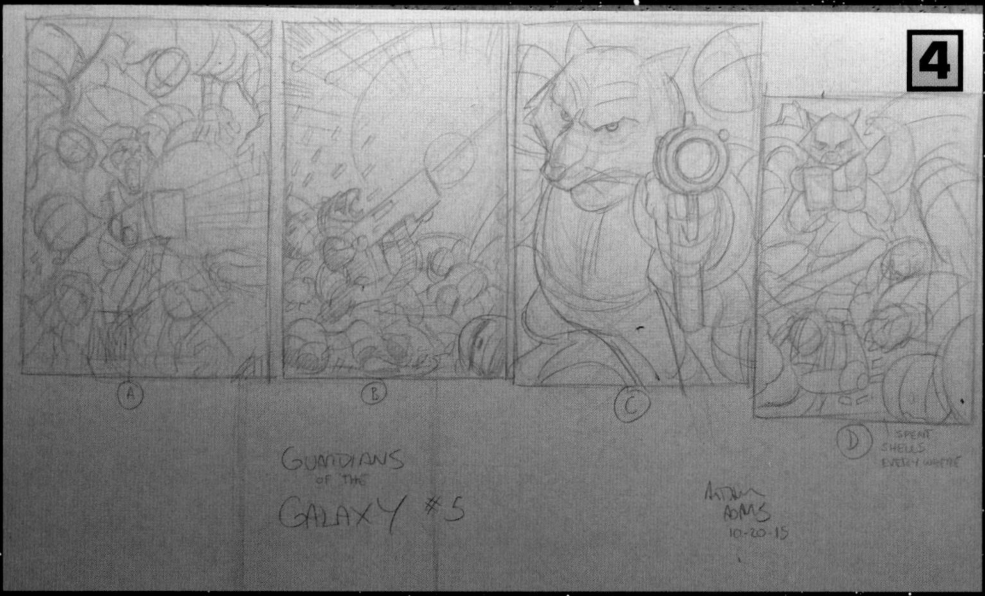

A
B
C
D
SPENT SHELLS EVERYWHERE
GUARDIANS OF THE GALAXY #5
10-20-15

5

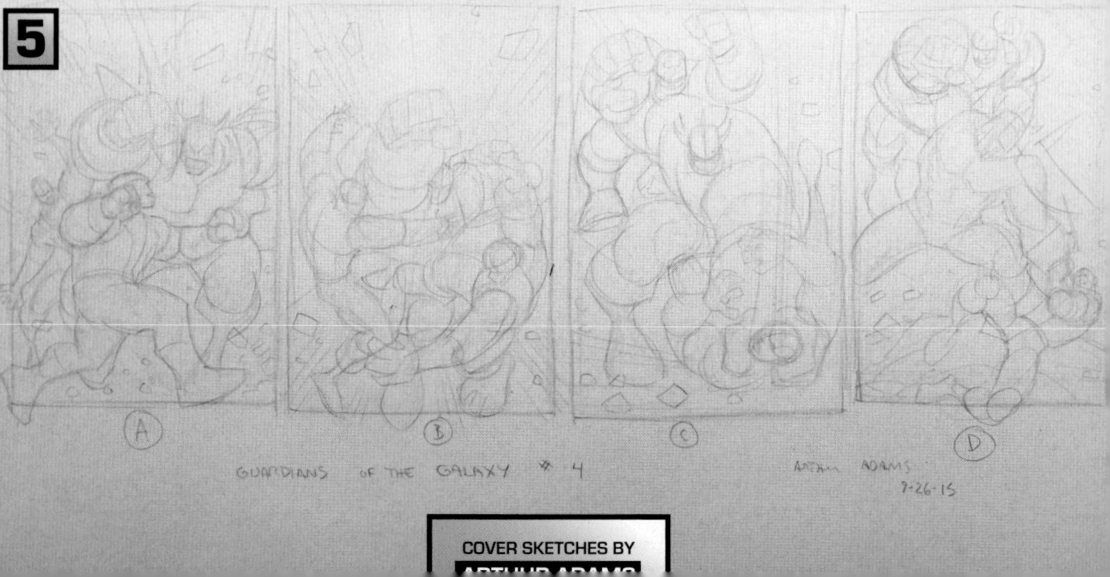

A
B
C
D
GUARDIANS OF THE GALAXY #4
9-26-15

COVER SKETCHES BY
ARTHUR ADAMS

4

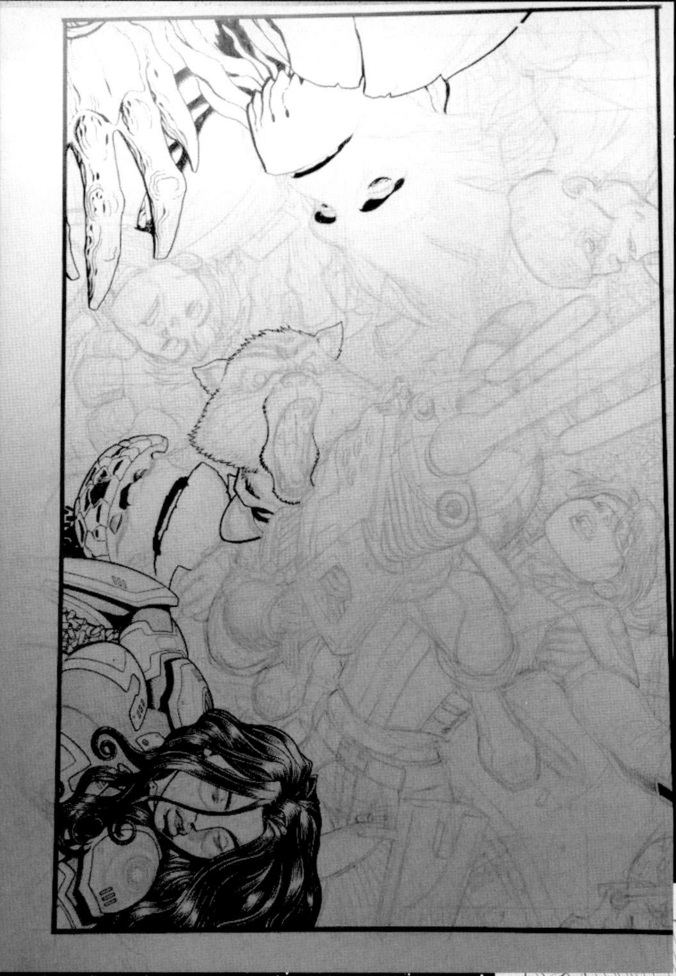

5

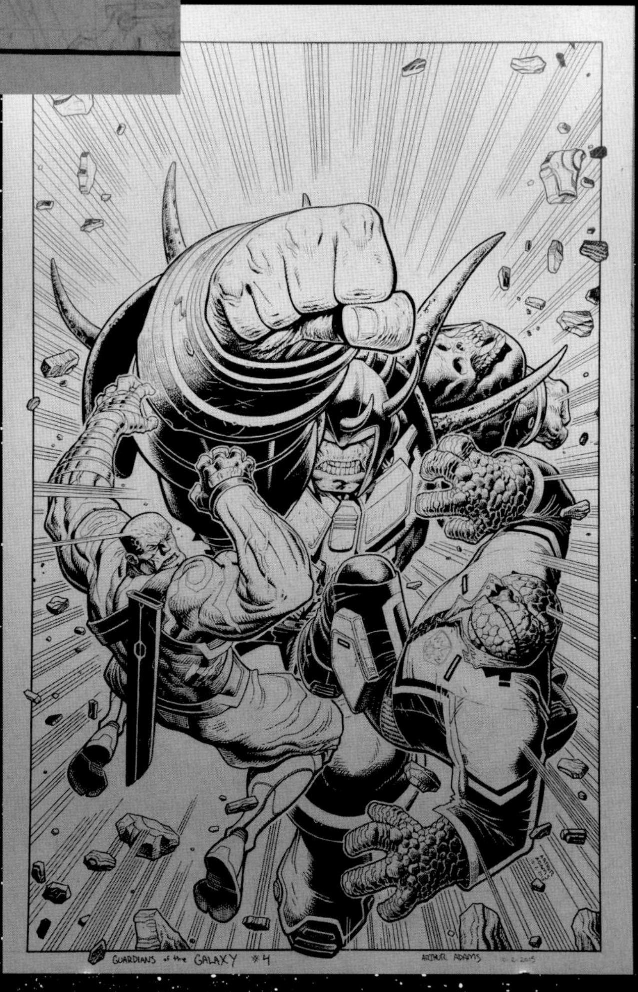
GUARDIANS of the GALAXY #4
ARTHUR ADAMS

COVER INKS BY
ARTHUR ADAMS

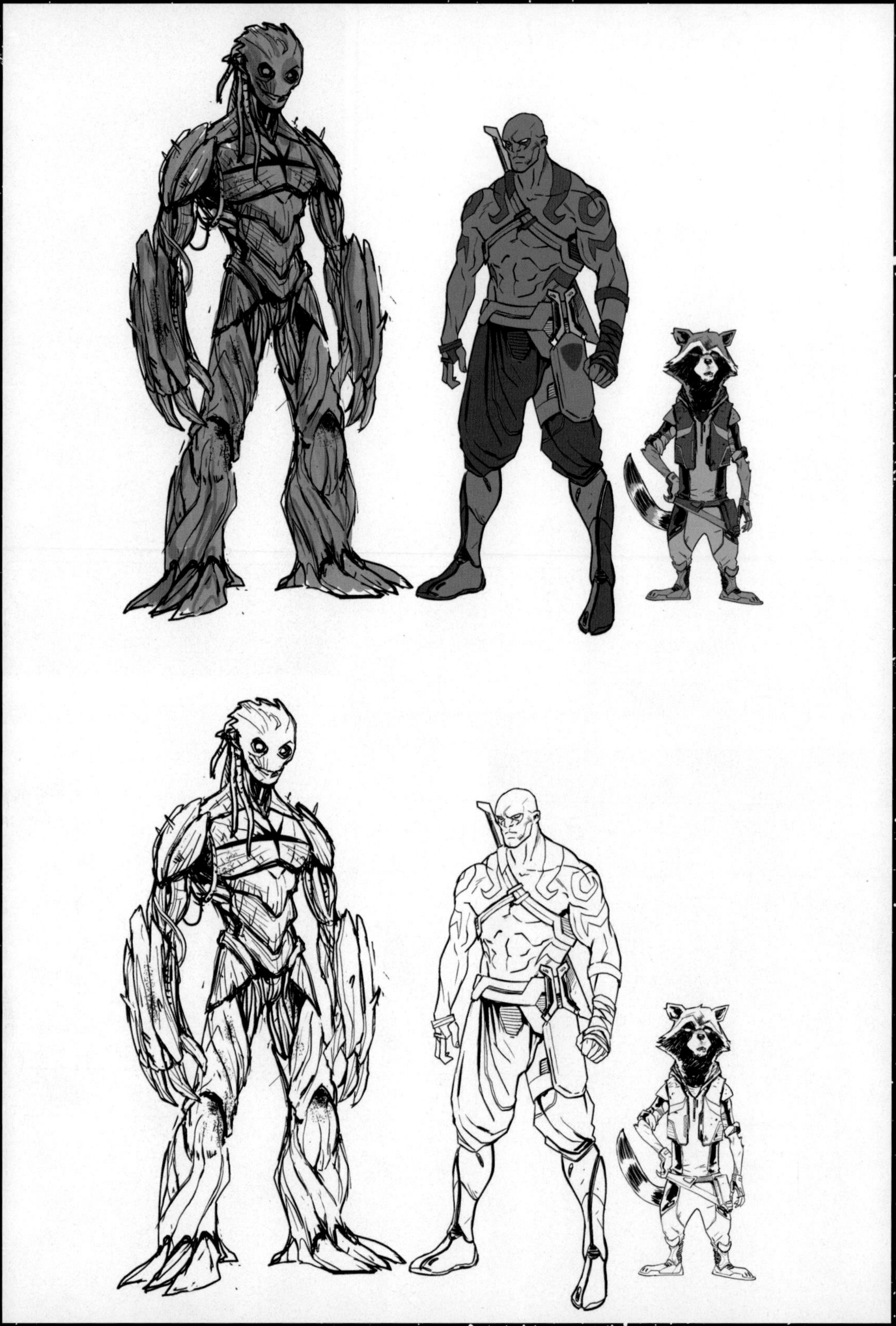

CHARCTER DESIGNS BY
VALERIO SCHITI

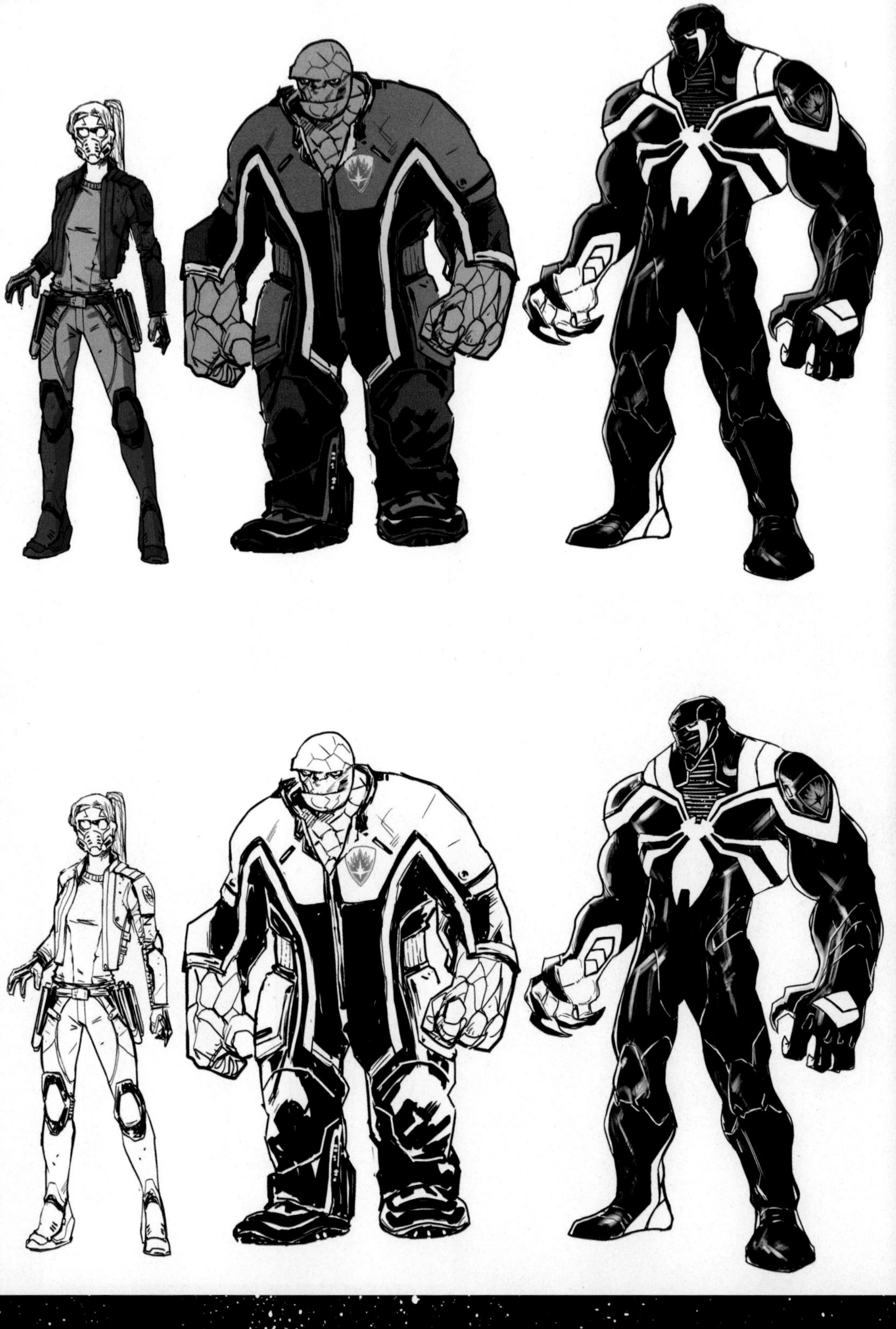

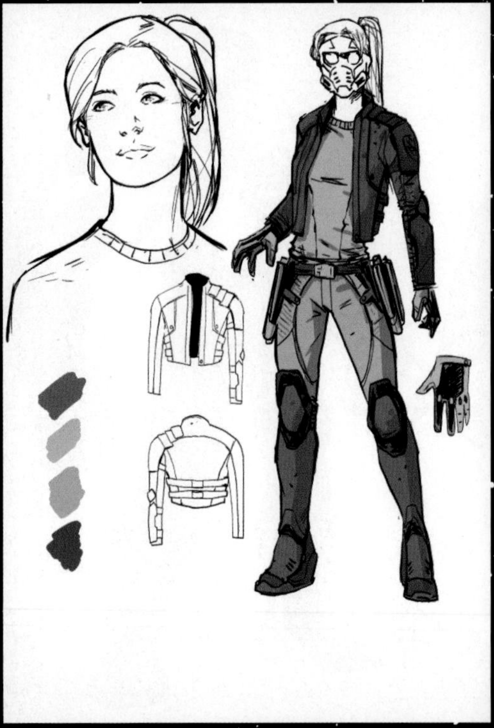

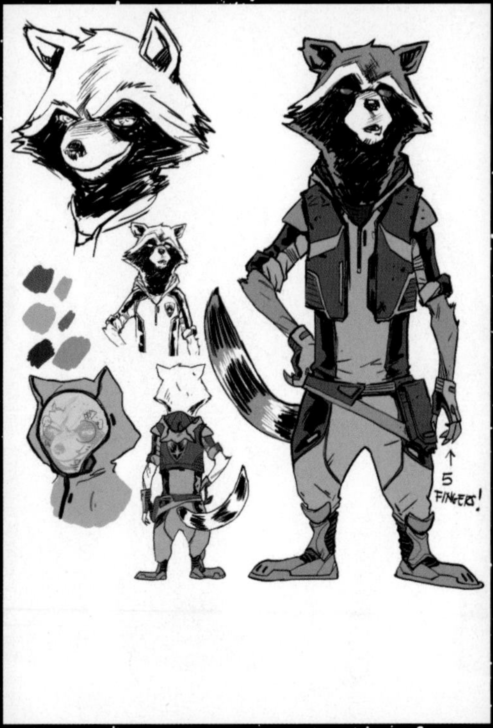
5 FINGERS!

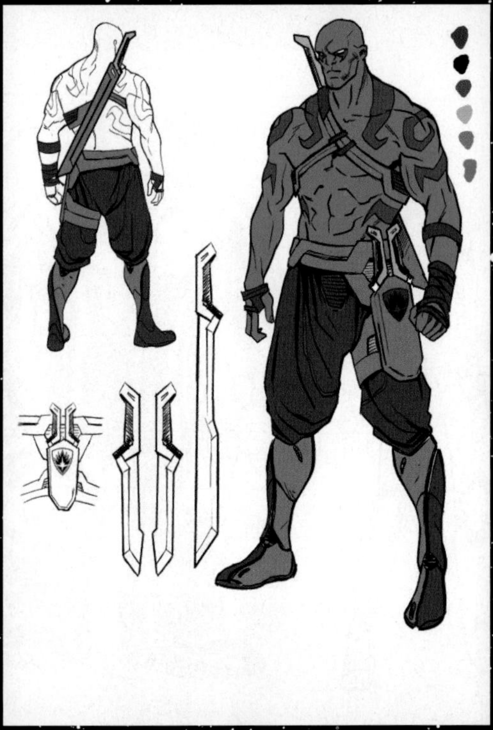

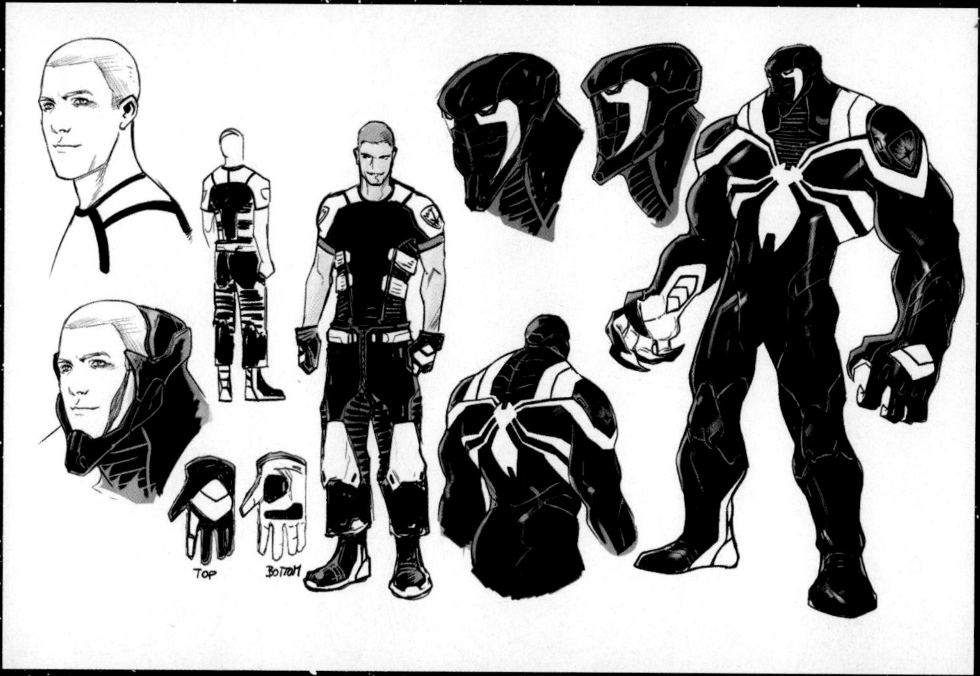
TOP
BOTTOM

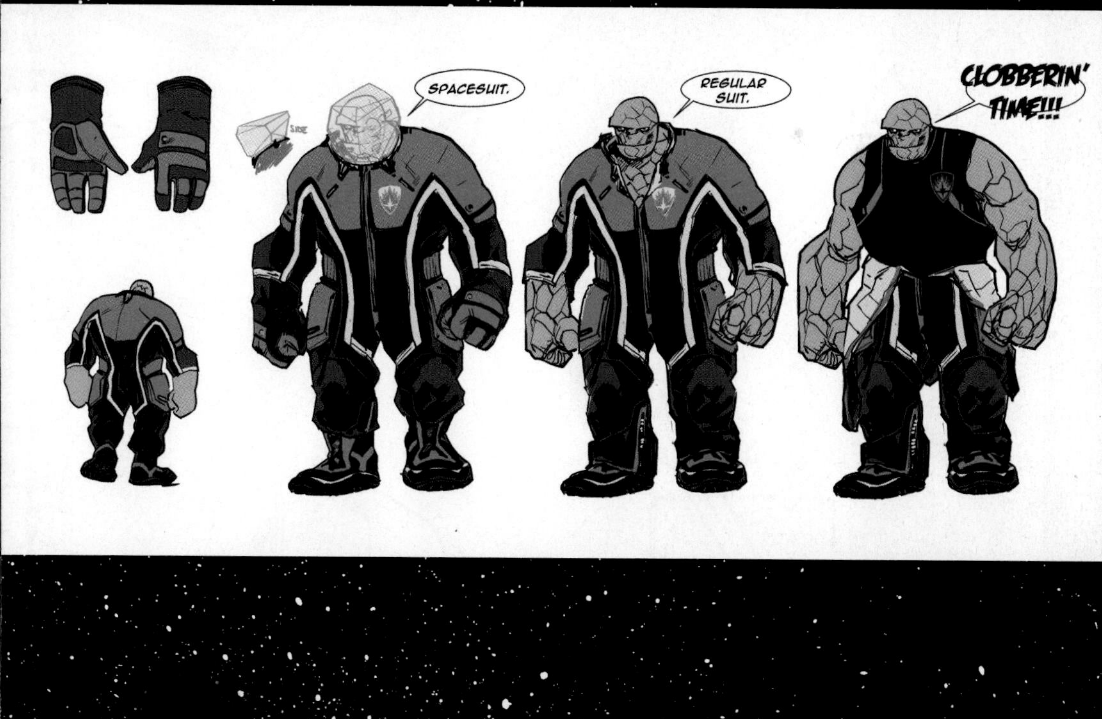
SIDE
SPACESUIT.
REGULAR SUIT.
CLOBBERIN' TIME!!!

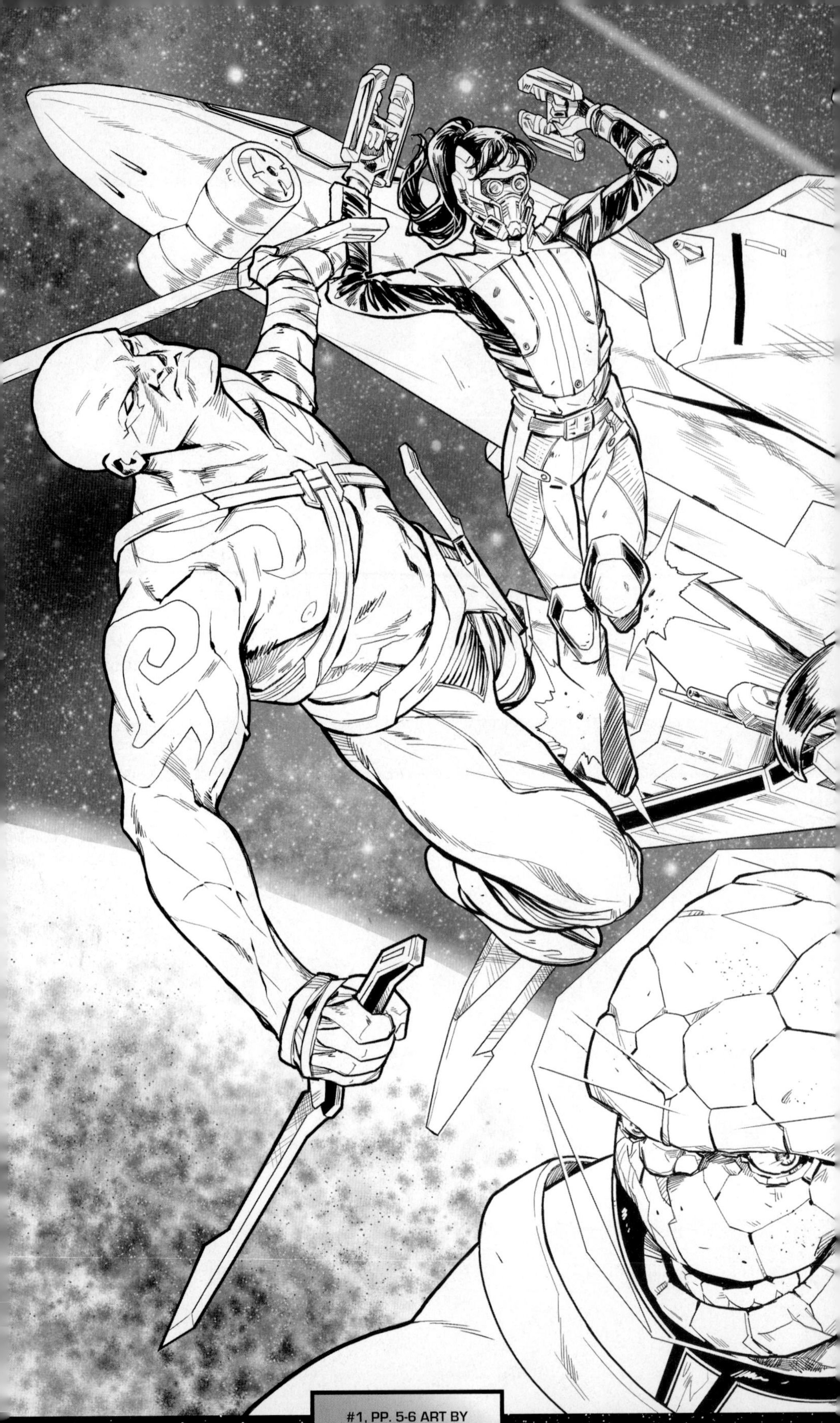

#1, PP. 5-6 ART BY

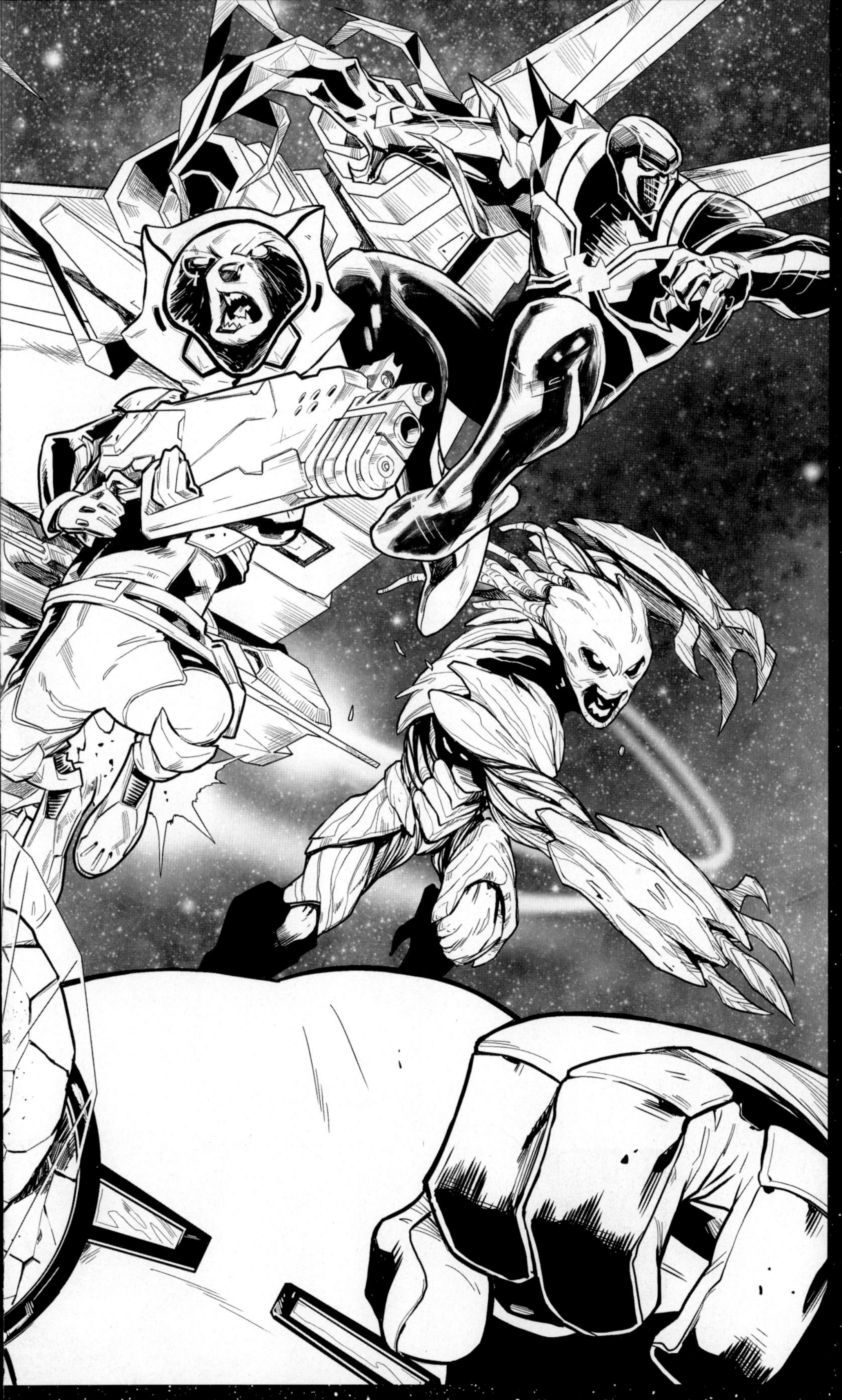

FREE
DIGITAL COPY

TO REDEEM YOUR CODE FOR A FREE DIGITAL COPY:

1. GO TO MARVEL.COM/REDEEM. OFFER EXPIRES ON 4/13/18.

2. FOLLOW THE ON-SCREEN INSTRUCTIONS TO REDEEM YOUR DIGITAL COPY.

3. LAUNCH THE MARVEL COMICS APP TO READ YOUR COMIC NOW.

4. YOUR DIGITAL COPY WILL BE FOUND UNDER THE 'MY COMICS' TAB.

5. READ AND ENJOY.

YOUR FREE DIGITAL COPY WILL BE AVAILABLE ON:
MARVEL COMICS APP FOR APPLE IOS® DEVICES
MARVEL COMICS APP FOR ANDROID™ DEVICES

TMA9IN4HMWGV